DAVID HUME

Laurence L. Bongie

DAVID HUME

PROPHET OF THE
COUNTER-REVOLUTION

LAURENCE L. BONGIE

With a Foreword by Donald W. Livingston

SECOND EDITION

LIBERTY FUND

INDIANAPOLIS

This book is published by Liberty Fund, Inc., a foundation established to encourage study of the ideal of a society of free and responsible individuals.

𒈬𒀀𒄄 𒂗𒈨

The cuneiform inscription that serves as our logo and as the design motif for our endpapers is the earliest-known written appearance of the word "freedom" (*amagi*), or "liberty." It is taken from a clay document written about 2300 B.C. in the Sumerian city-state of Lagash.

First published in 1965 by Oxford University Press

Printed in the United States of America

04 03 02 01 00 C 5 4 3 2 1

04 03 02 01 00 P 5 4 3 2 1

LIBRARY OF CONGRESS CATALOGING-IN-PUBLICATION DATA

Bongie, Laurence L.
    David Hume: prophet of the counter-revolution/Laurence L. Bongie; with a foreword by Donald W. Livingston.
        p.   cm.
    Includes bibliographical references and index.
        ISBN 0-86597-208-7 (hardcover: alk. paper).—ISBN 0-86597-209-5 (pbk.: alk. paper)
        1. Hume, David, 1711–1776. History of England.   2. Great Britain—History—Puritan Revolution, 1642–1660—Historiography.   3. Great Britain—History—Early Stuarts, 1603–1649—Historiography.   4. France—History—Revolution, 1789–1799.   5. Conservatism—History—18th century.
6. Counter-revolutionaries.   I. Title.
DA30.H93B66   2000
942—dc21   99-25723

Liberty Fund, Inc.
8335 Allison Pointe Trail, Suite 300
Indianapolis, Indiana 46250-1684

Contents

FOREWORD
vii

PREFACE TO THE LIBERTY FUND EDITION
xi

INTRODUCTION
xiii

I. *Before 1789*

1. ROYAL PANEGYRICS 1
2. THE SCIENCE AND ART OF ENGLISH HISTORY 2
3. JEHOVAH AMONG THE HEBREWS 10
4. PAPIST OR PYRRHONIAN? 15
5. THE SCOTTISH BOSSUET 35
6. DEBATE WITH TURGOT 54
7. EARLY HOSTILITY: MIRABEAU, MABLY, AND BRISSOT 60
8. DEFENCE AND DEFIANCE 65
9. ANTICIPATING THE STORM 75

II. *The Revolution and the Rôle of History*

1. HISTORY AS A WEAPON OF COUNTER-REVOLUTION 79
2. HISTORY AS THE SUPERSTITION OF SLAVES 93

CONTENTS

III. *From 1789 to the Trial of Louis XVI*

1. PROPHETIC PARALLELS AND THE COUNTER-REVOLUTIONARY LESSONS OF HUME 103
2. THE LONG PARLIAMENT: BRISSOT VERSUS CLERMONT-TONNERRE 123
3. A REPUBLICAN ANTIDOTE: CATHERINE MACAULAY-GRAHAM 132

IV. *The Trial of "Le Stuart Français"*

1. LOUIS XVI AND CHARLES I: A CONDEMNED KING'S MEDITATIONS 141
2. DAVID HUME AND STUART HISTORY FOR THE DEFENCE 149
3. CROMWELL IN THE CONVENTION: THE JUDGEMENT OF POSTERITY 156
4. THE PARALLEL REJECTED: BRUTUS TO THE RESCUE 165
5. PRINCIPLES VERSUS PRECEDENTS 171

V. *The Aftermath*

1. REPUBLICAN QUALMS 177
2. WAITING FOR GENERAL MONK 186
3. CONCLUSION 196

INDEX OF NAMES AND TITLES
203

FOREWORD

Philosophers rarely write history, and David Hume (1711–76) is unique in being recognized as one who made canonical contributions to both philosophy and history. Many think of Hume as a philosopher but in his own time he was known as an essayist and author of the six-volume *History of England* (1754–62). The *History* was a classic in his lifetime and went through at least 167 posthumous editions. It was the standard work on the subject for nearly a century, until Thomas Babington Macaulay's *History of England* began to challenge it in 1849. Even so, Hume's work was published—if finally only in an abridged form—continually into the twentieth century. Some editions issued in printings of 100,000. The young Winston Churchill learned English history from one of these abridgements known as "the student's Hume."

The most substantial part of the *History* is Hume's account of the reign of the Stuarts, which included the English Civil War, the trial and execution of Charles I, and the establishment of a Puritan republic under Oliver Cromwell. The claim that the people had the legal authority to put to trial and to execute their sovereign shocked seventeenth-century Europe and cast a shadow far into the eighteenth century. Hume's account of these events quickly became the most forceful and memorable.

But the influence of the *History* was not confined to the English-speaking world. Laurence Bongie demonstrates that during the events leading up to the French Revolution and for a considerable time thereafter, Hume's account of the English Civil War was used by the French to make sense of the terrible events through which they were living. Hume had interpreted the revolution in England that led to the execution of Charles I and a Puritan republic under the military government of Cromwell as an intellectual and spiritual pathology mingled with ambition. What the Puritans eventually sought was not reform but a total transformation of the social and political order in accord with a religious ideology. Hume's narrative seemed isomorphic to what was happening in France. The goal of the French Revolution was not reform but a root and branch transformation of society. The Jacobins stood for the Puritans, and the Jacobins' self-evident truths of the rights of man stood for the self-certifying enthusiasms and revelations of the Puritans; Louis XVI was Charles I, and Napoleon was Cromwell.

Edmund Burke's *Reflections on the Revolution in France* is commonly viewed as the origin of the modern conservative intellectual tradition, because he deemed the French Revolution to be an event unique to modern times: not at all an effort at reform but the hubristic attempt to transform the whole of society in accord with an ideology. But Hume before Burke had attached essentially this interpretation to the Puritan revolution in England. Additionally, if the intellectual core of conservatism is a critique of ideology in politics, then Hume's *History*—not Burke's *Reflections*—would appear to be the primal source of modern conservatism. Laurence Bongie, in *David Hume: Prophet of the Counter-revolution,* gives us good reason to think this was true of French conservative thought. Therefore, one might well wonder whether much of what Burke perceived in the French Revolution as a spiritual disorder was what Hume's account of the Puritan revolution had prepared him to see.

Thomas Jefferson considered Hume's *History* such a formidable force that he banned it from the University of Virginia. Of the work he wrote to William Duane on August 12, 1810, that it "has spread universal toryism over the land." Six years later, on November 25, 1816, Jefferson wrote of Hume's work to John Adams that, "This single book has done more to sap the free principles of the English Constitution than the largest standing army. . . ." Jefferson preferred John Baxter's *A New and Impartial History of England* (1796), which was a reworking of Hume's *History* from the Whig perspective and which Jefferson called "Hume's history republicanized." What Jefferson did not know (because he had not read the letters of the last decade of Hume's life) was that Hume supported complete independence for the American colonies as early as 1768 and—to the astonishment of his friends—held to that position until his death on August 25, 1776, five days after the complete text of the Declaration of Independence was published in Edinburgh's *Caledonian Mercury.* On October 27, 1775, Hume declared to his old friend Baron Mure, "I am an American in my principles, and wish we would let them alone to govern or misgovern themselves as they think proper." The man who dared "to shed a generous tear for the fate of Charles I" also resisted using violence to coerce the colonies back into a union from which they wished to secede.

Hume's political philosophy is dialectical and subtle and has given rise to contrary interpretations. But it is not Bongie's task to interpret it nor to judge whether Hume's *History* was correctly understood by those who read it during the revolutionary period in France. Rather, his task is to record the extraordinary influence that Hume's work exercised during this period. Drawing from a vast deposit of archival materials, Bongie has chipped away to reveal an unexpected glimpse through the wall of time that separates us from the French Revolution. A scene unfolds, rich in detail, in which the participants are allowed to speak for themselves through their words, their mute gestures, and above all their context. As with Bongie's other archival work—on Diderot, Prince Charles Edward Stuart, Condillac, and De Sade—one is left with an image in the memory more powerful than what a theoretical interpretation could provide. And, one comes away viewing Hume's *History* not simply as a narrative of events but as a force in the creation of modern political life.

Donald W. Livingston

April 1998

PREFACE TO
THE LIBERTY FUND EDITION

Much has changed in Hume studies since this book was first published in 1965. For example, the introduction to the first edition noted that Hume's *History* was "neither widely read nor readily available." The complete work had then been out of print since the end of the nineteenth century. Today, Hume's *History* is handily available in the Liberty Fund edition (1983–85, 6 vols.), and dozens of books along with scores of articles have focussed attention in recent years on Hume the historian. Perhaps most important of all, long-overdue recognition of the integral linkage between Hume's historical and philosophical writings has opened up one of the most rewarding avenues of inquiry in current Hume studies.

History being one of the more ephemeral arts, most studies like this one, after an interval of several decades, have necessarily forfeited some degree of relevance. If this work is still able in some measure to make a contribution, it is no doubt because—in an area wherein the violent battles of the past are constantly being reformulated and refought by the factions of the present—it chooses to focus exclusively on interrogation of the primary texts, texts that are invited to speak as much as possible for themselves. *David Hume, Prophet of the Counter-revolution* does not set out to decree what "really" happened during the Great Rebellion in England or what was "really" going on during France's even greater Revolution when, in an ongoing conflation of day-to-day history and counter-revolutionary historiography, the lessons and parallels drawn from Hume's *History of the Stuarts* were regularly weighed and scrutinized. Rather, my study focusses on the interplay of conflicting perceptions, privileged as the only "facts" that are relevant to the investigation. Whether such facts can exist independently of their interpretative perceptions and whether they can be stripped bare and objectively recovered in uncorrupted form by the "scientific" historian are very large questions that I do not pursue here.

As much the courageous contrarian, sceptical exploder of myths, and lucid revisionist in history as he was in philosophy, David Hume prided himself on having written the first impartial account of the English Revolution. England's Whig establishment hotly disputed Hume's claim, but on the other side of the Channel the French reading public's admiration and praise for the "godlike" fairness of the "English Tacitus" knew no bounds. With the coming of the French Revolution, Hume's much lauded impartiality, the tear he shed for the fate of Charles I, became an important element in counter-revolutionary ideology. The ghost of our philosopher-historian who wrote his *History* for fame almost as much as for truth was probably not displeased by the flattering attention accorded the "lessons" of his *History* at every stage of France's bloody upheaval. Now, two centuries later, delighted by the explosion of renewed interest in his great work, David Hume's ghost is undoubtedly still smiling benevolently and taking well-deserved curtain calls.

NOTE: In this Liberty Fund edition, all of the French documentation, representing over one-third of the original Oxford University Press text, has been translated into English. All of the translations are my own.

L. L. B.

April 1998

INTRODUCTION

I

David Hume was undoubtedly the eighteenth-century British writer whose works were most widely known and acclaimed on the continent during the later Enlightenment period. Ample proof of the great reputation he acquired in France as an historian and philosopher at this time is readily available. Contrary to various expectations, however, evidence of a profound influence as opposed to the mere reputation of his purely philosophical writings has proved to be disappointingly meagre. Occasionally even, Hume's most telling impact in this respect appears, not in the works of his brother *philosophes*, who largely misunderstood or wilfully ignored his highly original epistemological doctrine, but—usually through the device of retortion—in the writings of their greatest enemies, the religious traditionalists.[1]

Less surprising, perhaps, is the fact that these same traditionalists in formulating their political principles found it possible to profit to an even greater extent from Hume's historical writings. His unrivalled history of the Stuarts had not only enjoyed spectacular success in eighteenth-century France; it had related as well what many viewed as the most significant, or at least the most horrifying, series of political events in the annals of modern Europe, namely the seventeenth-century English revolution. The particular manner in which Hume had narrated the hapless career of Charles I and had presented the short-lived English republican experiment was to seem to many French conservatives, both before and after 1789, of great practical applicability in their defence of the *ancien régime*. It will be seen, I think, that Hume's impact here was of undeniable importance, greater even for a time than the related influence of Burke, although it represents a contribution to French counter-

---

1. See my "Hume and skepticism in late eighteenth-century France," in J. van der Zande and R. H. Popkin, eds., *The Skeptical Tradition Around 1800: Skepticism in Philosophy, Science, and Society* (Dordrecht: Kluwer, 1998), pp. 15–29.

revolutionary thought which, unlike that of Burke, has been almost totally ignored by historians to this day.

It is perhaps necessary to indicate at this point certain limitations which I have felt it wise to impose on this study. I have attempted—admittedly not always with complete success—to disregard the question of Hume's "true" intentions or the real nature of his political thought. Such considerations, however important they may be in themselves, seem largely irrelevant to an investigation of the kind I have undertaken. Similarly, I have not tried to make any general assessment of the merits of David Hume as an historian.[2] Whether Hume interpreted well or badly the events of Stuart history, whether he was more of a Tory than Burke was a Whig, is of little consequence to my purpose. My chief concern has not been with what really happened in England between 1603 and 1660 nor even primarily with what Hume really said about the Great Rebellion although, with regard to this last point, I have provided in the second part of my introduction a brief survey of his general views concerning the activities of that period.

What has been my major concern in the present study is rather the manner in which the French, from the *ancien régime* to the counter-revolutionary period, interpreted Hume's very popular history of those crucial English events. That the French *misinterpreted* the Scottish historian in many instances is, of course, entirely possible, but I have not insisted on this point. Influence thrives on illusion as easily as on truth. It is the image—whether faithful or distorted—that transmits influence. It will be seen that Hume's version of English history projected at first against the background of pre-revolutionary politics a number of blurred and even contradictory images. Later, however, the continental focus of interpretation sharpened acutely as the urgency of contemporary events compelled the Scottish historian's various French readers to unify more militantly their political views.

II

When, in his *History of the Stuarts,* Hume came to consider the scholarly merits of his predecessor Clarendon, he gave expression to a sentiment

---

2. In general, I have throughout this work relinquished the use of secondary source materials, since it would seem especially important in a study of image and influence to allow the original documents to speak as much as possible for themselves. Spelling in the quotations has been standardized.

which he might easily have allowed, I think, to be quite properly applied to himself. The "entertaining" Clarendon in his most "candid" history of the Great Rebellion is, Hume tells us, "more partial in appearance than in reality"; for though he seems perpetually anxious to apologize for the King, his apologies "are often well grounded."[3]

In the seventeen-fifties when Hume composed his *History of the Stuarts* it was clearly neither fashionable nor profitable to apologize for King Charles. The Whig party, Hume tells us, had, for a course of nearly seventy years, enjoyed the whole authority of government. In some particulars the state had not suffered as a result. But history, certainly, had suffered and truth had suffered. The biased writings of such apologists as Rapin-Thoyras, Locke, and Sidney were praised and propagated as if they equalled the most celebrated compositions of antiquity. "And forgetting," Hume complains, "that a regard to liberty, though a laudable passion, ought commonly to be subordinate to a reverence for established government, the prevailing faction has celebrated only the partisans of the former, who pursued as their object the perfection of civil society, and has extolled them at the expense of their antagonists, who maintained those maxims that are essential to its very existence" (IX. 524). Liberty is a good and noble principle but it has its dangers and if one has to choose, it is surely much better for human society "to be deprived of liberty than to be destitute of government" (VII. 125–26). Hume also observes that extremes of all kinds in these matters are to be avoided; truth and certainty are most likely to be met with on middle ground. There is little doubt that Hume hoped his own history would be seen as brilliantly impartial. In fact, he may even have believed that he would, by some miracle, please all factions with his "moderate opinions."

As he set about his attack on the fortress of Whig dogma, Hume made persistent and unwavering use of one favourite weapon: his contrary—and, many thought, perverse—view of what the English constitution was like before the accession of the Stuart kings. The partisans of liberty were in the habit of affirming that the English constitution, long before the settlement of 1688, was "a regular plan of liberty." They heaped abuse on James I and Charles I as usurpers and innovators in the hated arts of despotism. But what a paradox in human affairs it is, Hume objected, that Henry VIII should have been almost adored in his lifetime

---

3. David Hume, *The History of England*, London, 1808–10, VIII. 414. Further references in this section to *The History of England* will be placed within parentheses in the text itself.

and his memory be respected, "while Charles I should, by the same people, at no greater distance than a century, have been led to a public and ignominious execution, and his name be ever after pursued by falsehood and by obloquy!" (X. 205, note F to vol. VIII.) Hume found a similar paradox in Whig estimates of Elizabeth's reign. However different it may have been in other particulars, the government of England under Elizabeth bore, with respect to the question of liberty, a distinct resemblance to that of the eighteenth-century Turks (VI. 414). Under Elizabeth the legislative power of Parliament was a mere illusion, the liberty of the subject nonexistent. And yet, Hume adds, the Whigs have long indulged their prejudices against the Stuarts "by bestowing unbounded panegyrics" on the virtue and wisdom of that Queen. They have even been so extremely ignorant of her reign as to praise her for a quality "which, of all others, she was the least possessed of; a tender regard for the constitution, and a concern for the liberties and privileges of her people" (VI. 403).

The popular party, on the other hand, exclaimed constantly against the arbitrary principles of Charles I. This was yet another paradox, to be sure, for "one may venture to assert," Hume tells us, "that the greatest enemies of this Prince will not find, in the long line of his predecessors, from the conquest to his time, any one king, except perhaps his father, whose administration was not more arbitrary and less legal, or whose conduct could have been recommended to him by the popular party themselves, as a model, in this particular, for his government" (X. 205, note F to vol. VIII).

We are not to believe, however, that Hume looked back with fond regret to the days of the Tudors or Stuarts. This would be missing the entire point he attempted to make. No, the eighteenth-century English had no reason, following the example of their ancestors, to be in love with the picture of absolute monarchy "or to prefer the unlimited authority of the prince and his unbounded prerogatives to that noble liberty, that sweet equality, and that happy security, by which they are at present distinguished above all nations in the universe" (VI. 429–30). But the eighteenth-century English did have one obligation at least as they looked back on their own political history: this was the duty to approach past events with a proper sense of perspective. The activities of the Stuart kings, though they might appear arbitrary and illegal to Englishmen in the seventeen-fifties, could, if judged according to the principles and practices of the times in which they were carried out, "admit of some apology." After all, most of the modern liberties were, in the days of the Stuarts, and to an even greater extent during the Tudor period, totally unknown and deemed everywhere to be incompatible with all good government. "It seems unreasonable," Hume maintained, "to judge of the measures embraced during one period, by the maxims which prevail in another" (VII. 204).

Hume clearly felt that he had achieved this just sense of perspective and the result is that he made every effort while dealing with the civil-war period to understand and forgive the policies of James I and Charles I. Whether he also understood and forgave with equal sympathy and justice the policies of their opponents has remained, however, a matter of much heated debate ever since the first volume of his *Stuarts* appeared in 1754.

For Hume the moral issues of the case are not simplified, moreover, by the fact that what were traditionally described as the major vices of these early Stuarts could equally well be viewed as ill-timed but honest virtues. These were not the grander virtues, to be sure, but the every-day virtues of sincerity, integrity, and conviction. These kings were not "great" men but they were "good" men. In all history, for example, it would be difficult to find a reign "less illustrious, yet more unspotted and unblemished, than that of James" (VI. 662). Perhaps James erred occasionally in forgetting to ask himself the question *What is best?* This is because he believed in all piety that the question *What is established?* was more important. Hume has no doubts about what was established when James came to the English throne. Everyone accepted in those times the doctrine of blind and unlimited passive obedience to the prince. Under no pretence had it ever been seen as lawful for subjects to depart from or infringe that doctrine. So completely had these principles prevailed that, during the reigns of Elizabeth and her predecessors, opposition to them was regarded as the most flagrant sedition not only by the monarch but by the people as well. James I had thus inherited an absolute throne. His predecessor was, for example, allowed to have a *divine* right; was not James I's title quite plainly the same as that of his predecessor? Was it not natural for him to take the government as he found it and to pursue the long-applauded measures of the popular Elizabeth? Perhaps, Hume adds, but it is something of an afterthought, James should have realized that his character and his circumstances could not support so extensive an authority. In fact his major difficulties arose chiefly from these circumstances which had suffered during his reign a radical transformation. Partly as a result of the changing economic situation, partly as a result of the increase in knowledge, a new spirit of liberty was born at this time and spread rapidly under the shelter of "puritanical absurdities"—that theological plague which had so suddenly and inexplicably infested the people. The results were disastrous to all hopes for stable government, since the religious spirit, when it mingles with faction, contains in it, our sceptical historian believed, "something supernatural and unaccountable" (VI. 569). Ordinary human prudence, the usual trust in cause and effect is baffled by it and the operation of every motive which normally influences human society fails (VII. 171).

Now this spirit of religion or rather of *enthusiasm*, uncontrolled, obstinate, and dangerous, violently inclined the Puritans to adopt republican principles and to form a strong attachment to civil liberty. The two principles are "nearly allied" (VI. 473), and by this prevalence of fanaticism a gloomy and sullenly independent disposition established itself among the people who became animated with a contempt for authority and a hatred for all other religions and especially for Catholicism. James, of course, helped matters not at all when, for essentially worthy reasons, he attempted to civilize the barbaric austerity of the sects by infusing a small tincture of ceremony and cheerfulness into this "dark spirit of devotion." Nor, alas, was Charles subsequently more fortunate in the consequences of his efforts to abate the people's extreme rage against popery. And yet, it must be confessed, Laud's innovations deserve our praise, for pious ceremonies, however ridiculous they may seem to a philosophical mind, can be very advantageous to the rude multitude and tend to mollify that fierce and gloomy spirit of devotion to which the rude multitude is subject. Even the English Church "may justly be thought too naked and unadorned, and still to approach too near the abstract and spiritual religion of the Puritans" (VII. 589). Laud and his associates by reviving a few primitive institutions of this nature had corrected the error of the first reformers. It is true that Laud had attempted to introduce the fine arts into religion "not with the enlarged sentiments and cool reflection of a legislator, but with the intemperate zeal of a sectary" (VII. 590). The net result of his action was to inflame that religious fury which he meant to repress. It is, however, "sufficient for his vindication to observe, that his errors were the most excusable of all those which prevailed during that zealous period" (loc. cit.). Indeed, whereas the crude political advantages derived by the parliamentary party from the judicial murder of the "magnanimous" Strafford, "one of the most eminent personages that has appeared in England" (VII. 330, 356), could perhaps in some degree palliate the iniquity of the sentence pronounced against him, the execution of England's old infirm prelate, on the other hand, "can be ascribed to nothing but vengeance and bigotry in those severe religionists, by whom the Parliament was entirely governed" (VII. 587).

Mainly as a result of his worldly distaste for "enthusiasm," Hume, we see, held a rather low opinion of the various parliamentary heroes. Was not Parliament after all the aggressor during this unhappy period of civil discord? The Stuart kings had fought only a defensive campaign forced on them by the fact that Parliament had unilaterally seen fit to change the rules of the game and had innovated violently in constitutional matters. All things considered, Hume readily admitted that many constitutions in the history of human affairs and "none more than the British" have in fact been improved by such violent innovations. He felt compelled to insist, nevertheless, that "the praise bestowed on those patriots to whom the nation has been indebted for its privileges, ought to be given with some reserve, and surely without the least rancour against those who adhered to the ancient constitution" (VI. 404). The motivation of these patriots is suspect. Hume notes, for example, that the untimely end of Hampden leaves doubtful and uncertain whether his conduct was founded in a love of power or a zeal for liberty. With Cromwell, of course, there is no such doubt and uncertainty. Hume sees him as a fanatical, ambitious hypocrite; an artful and audacious conspirator who from the beginning engaged in his crimes "from the prospect of sovereign power," a temptation, Hume adds, which is, in general, "irresistible to human nature" (VII. 572). Hume admits, however, that Cromwell, by making some good use of the authority he had attained by fraud and violence, "has lessened, if not overpowered, our detestation of his enormities, by our admiration of his success and of his genius" (loc. cit.).

More repelled than amused by the "cant," "mystical jargon," "hypocrisy," "fury," and "fanaticism" of the Parliamentarians, Hume found himself unable to take too seriously patriotic attempts to dignify the Civil War with causes more considerable or noble than bigotry and theological zeal. Of course the Royalists too were zealots "but as they were at the same time maintaining the established constitution, in state as well as church, they had an object which was natural, and which might produce the greatest passion, even without any considerable mixture of theological fervour" (X. 183, note DD to vol. VII). The opponents of Charles did not fight for liberty; they fought for ignorant and fanatical trivialities. "The generality of the nation," Hume writes, "could never have flown out into such fury in order to obtain new privileges and acquire greater liberty than they and their ancestors had ever been acquainted with. Their fathers had been entirely satisfied with the government of Elizabeth: why should they have been thrown into such extreme rage against Charles, who, from the beginning of his reign, wished only to maintain such a government? And why not, at least, compound matters with him, when by all his laws, it appeared that he had agreed to depart from it? Especially, as he had put it entirely out of his power to retract that resolution" (loc. cit.).

Perhaps the revolution, up to a certain point and despite its trivial origins, did achieve some positive good. During the first period of the Long Parliament's operations, if we except the cruel iniquity of Strafford's attainder, the merits of its transactions may be judged to outweigh its mistakes and even entitle those measures which remedied abuses and redressed grievances to the praise of "all lovers of liberty" (VII. 36I). Hume even confesses a willingness at one point to admit that a few old eggs had to be broken to make the new omelette. Such is the price of progress, and if the means used to obtain these salutary results savour often of artifice and violence "it is to be considered, that revolutions of government cannot be effected by the mere force of argument and reasoning; and that factions, being once excited, men can neither so firmly regulate the tempers of others, nor their own, as to ensure themselves against all exorbitances" (VII. 362). But, while exalting their own authority and diminishing the king's, the patriots went too far and totally subverted the constitution. They forgot that authority as well as liberty is requisite to government and is even requisite to the support of liberty itself, by maintaining the laws which can alone regulate and protect it (VII. 406). Soon, not a limitation but a total abolition of monarchical authority appeared as the true aim of these "sanctified hypocrites." Their violence disgraced the cause of liberty and was injurious to the nation: "It is seldom," Hume concluded, "that the people gain any thing by revolutions in government; because the new settlement, jealous and insecure, must commonly be supported with more expense and severity than the old: but on no occasion was the truth of this maxim more sensibly felt, than in the present situation of England. Complaints against the oppression of ship-money, against the tyranny of the Star Chamber, had roused the people to arms: and having gained a complete victory over the crown, they found themselves loaded with a multiplicity of taxes, formerly unknown; and scarcely an appearance of law and liberty remained in the administration" (VIII. 102).

So great were the alterations imposed forcibly on the constitution in this later period that Hume feels Charles I was essentially right in saying, "that he had been more an enemy to his people by these concessions, could he have prevented them, than by any other action of his life" (VIII. 110). Having violently pulled the government to pieces, the patriots of course thought up schemes for establishing a perfect republic in its place, parts of which, Hume observes, were plausible but other parts were "too perfect for human nature" (VIII. 122, 412). Such schemes when held by men in power are dangerous. Dangerous also was the current doctrine of popular sovereignty. That the people are the origin of all just power is a principle which, Hume asserts, "is noble in itself, and seems specious, but is belied by all history and experience" (VIII. 124).

Finally, "the height of all iniquity and fanatical extravagance" (VIII. 123), the public trial and execution of England's legal sovereign, remained to be added to the list of parliamentary crimes. It is clear from the *History* that the King's behaviour during the last scenes of his life commanded Hume's greatest admiration. Our historian notes that Charles in all appearances before his judges never forgot his part "either as a prince or as a man" (VIII. 131). The people too, "though under the rod of lawless unlimited power, could not forbear, with the most ardent prayers, pouring forth their wishes for his preservation" (VIII. 132). How they regretted the blind fury with which they had earlier rejected their king! The enormity of the trial "was exclaimed against by the general voice of reason and humanity; and all men, under whatever form of government they were born, rejected this example, as the utmost effort of undisguised usurpation, and the most heinous insult on law and justice" (VIII. 133).

I shall not dwell further on Hume's account of the grief, indignation, and astonishment which struck the whole nation as soon as the news of Charles I's execution, or rather his "murder," reached the nation. Hume's version of these events will be encountered with perhaps more than sufficient frequency in the various French counter-revolutionary writings dealt with later in this study.

The English soon realized that they had murdered an honourable and honest king, who was, moreover, innocent of the crimes with which he was charged. "And though," Hume adds, "some violations of the Petition of Right may perhaps be imputed to him; these are more to be ascribed to the necessity of his situation, and to the lofty ideas of royal prerogative, which, from former established precedents, he had imbibed, than to any failure in the integrity of his principles" (VIII. 142). Nor is it even possible to say that with a little more tact here, a little more imagination there, Charles could have perhaps avoided this fatal clash with Parliament. Even long after the event, when it is commonly a simple matter to sort out the errors of bygone quarrels, one is at a loss to determine what course Charles, in his circumstances, could have followed to maintain the authority of the Crown and preserve the peace of the nation. Had Charles been born an absolute prince, "his humanity and good sense" would have rendered his reign happy and his memory precious. If the English constitution and the extent of prerogative had been in his day quite fixed and certain, his integrity would have made him regard as sacred the boundaries of that constitution. "Unhappily," Hume concludes, "his fate threw him into a period when the precedents of many former reigns savoured strongly of arbitrary power, and the genius of the people ran violently towards liberty" (VIII. 141).

Hume drew—or at least seemed to draw—various lessons from the great events of this period, and these too we shall leave until they are pointed out again by the French traditionalists who opposed, almost a century and a half later, what they considered to be extraordinarily similar tendencies and events in their own country. One of these lessons which was to strike with especially great force a good many disillusioned Frenchmen not long after 1789 nevertheless deserves mention here. It is, in effect, that the English revolution had been a pernicious act of folly, a wasted venture, and that perhaps all similar revolutions are condemned to a like fate. The King once out of the way, the English revolutionary factions set about eliminating one another in an endless striving for greater and greater "sanctity." In the end, from the too eager pursuit of liberty, the nation fell into the most abject servitude. To emphasize the point, Hume concluded his chapter immediately preceding that which is devoted to Cromwell with the following warning: "By recent, as well as all ancient, example, it was become evident that illegal violence, with whatever pretences it may be covered, and whatever object it may pursue, must inevitably end at last in the arbitrary and despotic government of a single person" (VIII. 240).

DAVID HUME

I

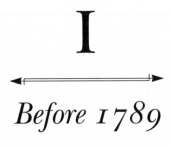

Before 1789

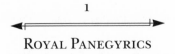

Royal Panegyrics

In 1763 David Hume arrived in Paris to take up duties with Lord Hertford, Britain's first peacetime ambassador to France since the outbreak of the Seven Years' War. Author of a famous *History of the Stuarts,* David Hume, frequently hailed as the "English Tacitus," was given an official and personal welcome such as few foreign authors have ever received in the French capital.

The story of France's adulation is too well known to need retelling here,[1] although one example of it is particularly relevant to our purpose. Let us read Hume's own account of his presentation at Versailles in 1763 to the children of the Dauphin, three future kings of France:

> The scene which passed today really pleased me without embarrassing me. I attended Lord Hertford to Versailles in order to be presented to the Dauphiness and the young Princes, the only part of the royal family whom we had not yet seen. When I was presented to the Duc de Berry, a child of ten years of age, he said to me, "Monsieur, you are much admired in this country; your name is very well-known; and it is with great pleasure that I welcome you." Immediately upon which his brother the Comte de Provence, who is two

---

1. See E. C. Mossner, *The Life of David Hume* (Nelson), 1954, pp. 441–506.

---

years younger, advanced to me and said with great presence of mind, "Monsieur, you have been long and impatiently expected in this country: I count on having much enjoyment when I am able to read your fine history." But what is more remarkable, when we were carried to make our bows to the Comte d'Artois, who is about five years of age, and to a young Madame of between two and three, the infant prince likewise advanced to me in order to make me his harangue, in which, though it was not very distinct, I heard him mumble the word *Histoire,* and some other terms of panegyric. With him ended the civilities of the royal family of France towards me; and I may say it did not end till their power of speech failed them: for the Princess was too young to be able to articulate a compliment.[2]

David Hume, we see, was merely flattered. At the time, he could not have known the extent to which events described so skilfully in his *History* would one day assume a new and urgent meaning in the political life of the French nation. Nor could he have known that, not quite thirty years later, the eldest of these charming children, condemned to die by the will of that same nation, would once more take up the famous Monsieur Hume's great work as part of his last searching meditations.

2

THE SCIENCE AND ART OF ENGLISH HISTORY

The quite unusual popularity of Hume's *History of England* in eighteenth-century France requires perhaps some preliminary general explanation. His *Political Discourses* and *Philosophical Essays* introduced on the continent several years earlier had won him little more than the unflatteringly mild contempt of the devout and the intense but largely uncomprehending praise of a number of *philosophes* and *salonnières.* Originality in epistemological writings has rarely given any philosopher a great popular audience. The

---

2. David Hume to Alexander Wedderburn, from Paris, 23 November 1763, in *The Letters of David Hume,* ed. J. Y. T. Greig, Oxford, 1932, I. 414–15.

story is complicated too by the fact that the *philosophes* did not wish originality in a field which they believed had been definitively treated by Locke.

But history was a very different matter. As a genre it represented to the eighteenth-century reading public the most digestible form of narrative and was contrasted frequently with the novel which, though equally appealing to the mass of readers, was rarely considered to be a serious or worthy vehicle of truth. Such was the reputed superiority of history as a vantage point from which to view the human passions that many good and bad novels of the day conventionally attempted to pass themselves off as personal histories, memoirs, or collections of letters.[3]

Voltaire, Hume, and Gibbon, the three greatest historians of the century, were in agreement that history represented the most popular species of writing. History was an art the models of which were best found in antiquity. To be called, as Hume often was, the Tacitus of the English was to receive, even in that "modern" period, the highest possible tribute. Seen not only as an art, history was viewed too as perhaps the most valuable of the human sciences —a unique storehouse of empirical facts without which no generalizations about man's nature, his motivations and passions, were possible. Speculation on almost any subject other than the physical sciences was considered worthless unless Clio had first been heard. Grimm, pointing out in 1767 that not a single "line of history" was cited in a work by the economist Le Mercier de La Rivière, concluded: "That in itself proves what we must think of his work."[4] Similarly, Louis de Bonald singled out Rousseau's *Contrat social* for attack "because the author... constantly sacrifices... his-

---

3. Note on this point the common eighteenth-century antithesis of the words *novel* and *history,* as in Voltaire's *Lettres philosophiques* (13th Letter), where we find the terms contrasted in a parallel of Locke (who wrote "the history of the soul") and Descartes ("the novel of the soul"). For a defence of the truth of the novel, see Choderlos de Laclos's review of Fanny Burney's novel, *Cecilia,* in the *Mercure de France,* 17 April 1784, pp. 103ff. See also Pierre Choderlos de Laclos, *Oeuvres complètes* (Pléiade), Paris, 1943, pp. 523–25.

4. *Correspondance littéraire, philosophique et critique,* ed. Tourneux, Paris, 1877–82, 15 October 1767, VII. 449.

tory to his opinions."[5] De Bonald adds that "general or *abstract* propositions relating to society, that is to man, apply only through history, or the actions of man in society."[6]

Joseph de Maistre, Louis de Bonald's spiritual ally in the counter-revolution, agreed: "History is applied politics, its only valid form; and as in physics, a hundred volumes of speculative theory can be reduced to nothing by a single experiment, similarly, in political science, no system can be accepted if it is not the probable corollary, more or less, of well-attested facts."[7]

The *idéologue* Volney speaks of history as "the physiological science of governments" and as a "series of experiments that the human race conducts on itself," the purpose of which is to find "a genealogical order of cause and effect, from which to deduce a theory of rules and principles appropriate for the guidance of both individuals and nations toward goals of survival or advancement."[8]

History at its best was thus a pleasantly disguised form of social science long before Cambacérès triumphantly proclaimed to the Institut National on 25 February 1798 the advent of that new saviour: "Legislators, philosophers, jurisconsults, the age of social science has arrived, and, we might add, that of true philosophy."[9] I shall have occasion to come back to this view as well as to an important body of eighteenth-century thought which violently disagreed with it. For the moment it might be worthwhile to quote Hume's own similar view of history's purpose as expressed in the *Enquiry concerning Human Understanding* (1748):

> Its chief use is only to discover the constant and universal principles of human nature, by showing men in all varieties of circumstances and situations, and furnishing us with materials, from which

5. *Théorie du pouvoir politique et religieux dans la société civile, démontrée par le raisonnement et par l'histoire* (1796); in *Oeuvres de M. de Bonald,* Paris, 1843, XIII. 14.

6. Ibid., XIII. 17.

7. *Etude sur la souveraineté* (1794–96); in *Oeuvres complètes de J. de Maistre,* Lyon, 1884, I. 426.

8. *Séances des écoles normales,* Paris, 1800, I. 78; II. 219, 441.

9. "Discours sur la science sociale," in *Mémoires de l'Institut National des Sciences et Arts,* III. 13.

we may form our observations, and become acquainted with the regular springs of human action and behaviour. These records of wars, intrigues, factions, and revolutions, are so many collections of experiments, by which the politician or moral philosopher fixes the principles of his science; in the same manner as the physician or natural philosopher becomes acquainted with the nature of plants, minerals, and other external objects, by the experiments, which he forms concerning them. Nor are the earth, water, and other elements, examined by Aristotle, and Hippocrates, more like to those, which at present lie under our observation, than the men, described by Polybius and Tacitus, are to those, who now govern the world.[10]

It should also be noted that Hume's earlier writings in philosophy and economics could only add to his potential success and stature as an historian in the eyes of the eighteenth-century reader. History, as we know, had to be "philosophical"—*l'histoire raisonnée* as opposed to *l'histoire simple.* Only the profound thinker was judged worthy of attempting it and such non-professionals as Smollett did little more than anger the French with their amateurish and pretentious imitations. "How could Mr. Smollett take it into his head," indignantly writes Chastellux in 1766, "to write his History at the same time as Mr. Hume is writing his! The match is not equal...."[11] That history ought to be written only by men "profoundly versed in the science of politics" is the corresponding sentiment expressed in the fashionable *Mercure de France* of 1763.[12]

To recapitulate, then, history in the eighteenth century was a very popular literary genre, vested also with an almost sacred function; and Hume was judged to be of a sufficiently reflective turn of mind to put a soul into its otherwise dead bones.

Another explanation of Hume's great success in this field lies undoubtedly in the fact that he had chosen to write a history of the English nation at a time when a strange anglomania was at its height on the continent. French interest in all things English from

10. *Essays Moral, Political and Literary, by David Hume,* ed. T. H. Green and T. H. Grose, London, 1875, II. 68.

11. *Gazette littéraire de l'Europe,* February 1766, p. 382.

12. June issue, p. 54.

jurys to jockeys, from fist-fights to glorious naval battles, despite the frequently inane sacrifice of national pride involved, hardly subsided, even during the Seven Years' War. Gibbon tells of his welcome in Paris in 1763 and speaks of how English opinions, fashions, even games were adopted in France at this time and of how every Englishman was viewed as a born patriot and philosopher.[13] Garat gives an account of the phenomenon that conveys perhaps a special meaning to readers of our own space age:

> After Voltaire published his *Letters* on the English and Montesquieu his two chapters of the *Esprit des Lois,* a strange appetite developed in France for knowing everything that happened or might happen, or might be thought, spoken or dreamed of in England. If a telescope like Herschel's and a listening device with similar range had existed at the time, these would have been pointed at England more often than at the moon and the other heavenly bodies. This enthusiasm was as much a matter of deeply reasoned admiration, as it was a kind of craze.[14]

British national history naturally reaped the benefits of the current mania and Hume is but the first in rank of many authors on the subject who were read widely in France at this time. In 1765 the *Bibliothèque des Sciences et des Beaux-Arts,* seeking an appropriate metaphor to describe the great number of recent publications in the field of English history, felt compelled to exclaim: "Histories of England are pouring down on us!"[15]

Anglomania, however, is not a sufficient explanation of this torrent. One must also bear in mind the fact that English history, *per se,* was judged to be peculiarly superior to all other modern national histories, both as an artistic theme-source and as a scientific repository. Hume himself had written to the Abbé Le Blanc in

13. Edward Gibbon, *Autobiography,* Everyman's Library, p. 114.

14. D.-J. Garat, *Mémoires historiques sur le 18e siècle et sur M. Suard,* Paris, 1821, I. 72.

15. January–March 1765, p. 232.

1754 that he esteemed the Stuart period "both for signal events and extraordinary characters to be the most interesting in modern history."[16] Voltaire, who frequently complained of the "insipidness" of French history and wondered even if it were worth writing,[17] agreed that the superiority of English events gave Hume an advantage in the field. Writing in 1769 to Gabriel-Henri Gaillard, he expressed the following bitter sentiments on the subject:

> I can see nothing, in short, from the time of Saint Louis to Henri IV. That is why the compilations of French history bore everyone to death, myself included. David Hume has a great advantage over the abbé Velly and his ilk, because he has written the history of the English, and in France no one has ever written the history of the French. Every husbandman of means in England is entirely familiar with that nation's constitution and keeps a copy of Magna Carta in his home. As for our history, it is made up of petty court squabbles, great battles lost, small battles won, and *lettres de cachet*. Were it not for five or six famous assassinations, and especially the Saint Bartholomew's Day massacre, nothing could surpass us in insipidity. Note too that we have never invented anything; and, finally, truth to tell, we exist in the eyes of Europe only in the century of Louis XIV. I'm sorry, but that is how it is.[18]

Later on in the century, Soulavie, commenting on a similar view of the dullness of French history—this time expressed by Rousseau—showed to what extent the question of whether their subject truly "existed" or not had become a matter of serious concern to French historians. His conclusions were, however, rather hopeful: "Our circumstances... have been sufficiently varied, and human passions have exercised their power in our midst with enough energy and effect to provide interest and instruction for every age and every nation. However, even if we have so many lit-

16. Greig, op. cit., I. 193.

17. See, for example, his letter to the Marquise Du Deffand, 20 June 1764, in *Voltaire's Correspondence,* ed. Besterman, D11939.

18. Ibid., 28 April 1769; Best.D15614.

erary masterpieces in every genre, we are still lacking a history that will do honour to France."[19]

We see that a nation's history, to be interesting and significant, had to present the greatest possible variety of human social situations; first, because such variety was aesthetically necessary in a literary composition and, second, because the greater the number of events permutated and combined, the greater the resulting information about man's moral nature. English history best fulfilled both of these requirements according to an anonymous counter-revolutionary work of 1793: "The history of nations, and particularly that of Great Britain, instructs and interests by the variety of its tableaux and events; it is in that faithful mirror that one sees reflected the interplay of every passion that stirs the human heart."[20] The *Journal Encyclopédique* thirty years earlier had made the same point: "... no nation offers more varied scenes, characters more diverse or illustrious; no history provides a richer or more sweeping background of instruction, amazement and pleasure than the history of Great Britain....; what other European people has witnessed more frequent alteration in its manners, laws and government?"[21]

Perhaps the only serious competitor to English history was, as could well be expected in this neo-classical age, that of the ancients. Sénac de Meilhan in 1787 expressed his opinion on the problem in the following manner: "Few modern historians can be placed side-by-side with Thucydides, Xenophon, Sallust, Livy, and, especially, Tacitus: Hume and Robertson appear to have followed most closely in their footsteps; perhaps they would have even caught up with them had they written in their language and been provided with equally interesting scenes to depict."[22] Mme de Staël, writing some years later, agreed and also explained the superiority of the ancients in history by the superiority of their subject matter:

19. Jean-Louis Giraud Soulavie, *Traité de la composition et de l'étude de l'histoire*, 1792, p. 64.

20. *L'Angleterre instruisant la France*, Londres, 1793, p. 70.

21. August 1764, V. 8–10. See also ibid., June 1760, IV. 3–4.

22. *Considérations sur l'esprit et les moeurs*, Londres, 1787, pp. 364–65.

"The historians of antiquity remain unsurpassed because no other period in history has witnessed superior men play such influential rôles in the affairs of their country." English historians, however, were next in rank: "It is the nation in England that possesses greatness, more so even than any particular individual; that is why historians there are less dramatic but more philosophical than the ancients."[23]

Other opinions expressed during the first decades of the nineteenth century suggest that this view of English national history still widely prevailed. We read the following observation, for example, in *La Quotidienne* of 1826: "Of all modern national histories, the most fascinating is unquestionably the history of England: as in a drama, suspense constantly increases, calamities and sudden shifts of fortune are at every moment renewed."[24]

We see how important this largely eighteenth-century concept of the *art* of history still was in 1826—not just the art of the individual historian, but the dramatic art, as it were, of a nation's own past in its unfolding. The great variety of events in English history and the order in which these had occurred seemed to permit a perfect fusion of both artistic and scientific elements in one literary genre. The modern world had, quite plainly, no greater or more significant story to tell. This view was to change only after a somewhat delayed realization came to Europe that the events of the French revolution had suddenly presented historians with an even greater story.

We shall in the course of this study see that there are many additional reasons which explain why David Hume succeeded so well in eighteenth-century France as an historian. These are of a more particular nature and more complex to analyse. Generally, and perhaps truistically speaking, however, we might initially conclude that his great success was to a large extent founded on the fact that he could have chosen no other topic more suited to satisfy at the same time both the political curiosity and the artistic interests of most French readers of his day.

23. *De l'Allemagne;* in *Oeuvres complètes de Mme La Baronne de Staël,* publiées par son fils, Paris, 1820–21, XI. 113.

24. *La Quotidienne,* No. 39, 8 February 1826.

3

JEHOVAH AMONG THE HEBREWS

Already in 1754, even before the English publication of his *Stuarts,* Hume had intimated to the Abbé Le Blanc, translator of his moderately successful *Political Discourses,* that the *History* would succeed well in France.[25] Hume proposed at this same time that Le Blanc should also translate the *History* and Le Blanc accepted, although he later found it necessary to give up the translation, which was continued by the Abbé Prévost and published in 1760.[26] There is a good deal of evidence to show that, even before the long-delayed appearance of Prévost's translation, impatient readers in France had turned to the original English version. Morellet tells us how, imprisoned in the Bastille in 1760, he had asked Malesherbes to bring him a copy of Tacitus and Hume's *History* in English.[27] Chastellux the social historian declared to friends that he had learned English only to read Hume;[28] and Turgot at this time felt the *Stuarts* important enough to justify a personal translation.[29] Several hundred pages of excerpts from the *Stuarts* also appeared in various French journals before 1760. Additional proof of such pre-translation success is provided by the results of a survey which I carried out some years ago in the "Delta" series at the Bibliothèque Nationale in Paris. Out of 240 private library sale catalogues from the pre-revolutionary period chosen completely at random, 109 listed Hume's historical writings. Of these 109, 12 included versions of the *Stuarts* in English as well as in French. This work, in fact, was already well enough known in France by 1759 for Hume

25. Greig, op. cit., I. 193.

26. For further details on Hume's French translations, see my "David Hume and the Official Censorship of the Ancien Régime," *French Studies,* 1958, XII. 234–46.

27. *Mémoires de l'Abbé Morellet,* Paris, 1821, I. 92.

28. Greig, op. cit., II. 348.

29. See *Oeuvres de Turgot et documents le concernant,* ed. G. Schelle, Paris, 1913, I. 27. Turgot's translation was not published.

to convey to his fellow-historian Robertson in March of that year the facetious warning that the latter would find it more difficult to thrust him out of his place in Paris than he had in London.[30]

Once Prévost's translation was published in 1760, page after page of acclamatory notices appeared in the leading French journals. Similar editorial attention was generously accorded in 1763 and 1765 to Mme Belot's translations of the *Tudors* and the *Plantagenets*. During this time too Hume received in his correspondence a great many tributes from distinguished continental readers. A letter in 1761 from the Comtesse de Boufflers is extreme in its praise but quite sincere; parts of it are worth quoting here as fairly typical of the reactions to Hume's *Stuarts* among the fashionable Parisian nobility:

> I cannot find the words to convey to you what I feel as I read this work. I am moved, carried away, and the emotion it causes in me is so sustained that it becomes in a sense painful. My soul is uplifted, my heart is filled with sentiments of humanity and beneficence....
>
> You are, Monsieur, a masterly painter. Your portrayals have a gracefulness, a genuineness and an energy that surpass what even the imagination can attain.
>
> But what expressions shall I employ to tell you how your divine impartiality affects me? I would have need of your own eloquence to express my thoughts fully on this subject. In truth, it is as though I have before my eyes the work of a celestial being, freed of all passions, who for the benefit of mankind has deigned to write an account of recent events.... [31]

Similar references to David Hume as the "angel of truth," the "voice of pure reason," the "voice of posterity," are not uncommon at this time. Rousseau, who was soon to write of Hume in a different tone, made equally laudatory statements in a letter of February 1763 to the Scottish philosopher: "Your grand perspectives, your astonishing impartiality, your genius, would raise you too much above ordinary mortals, did not the kindness of your heart bring

---

30. Greig, op. cit., I. 302–3.
31. Greig, op. cit., II. 366–67.

you once more near to them...."[32] Helvétius too wrote in 1763, bursting with enthusiasm for Hume's "impartial philosophical spirit,"[33] and a year later the Président de Brosses, who judged that Hume had surpassed even Tacitus, repeated the same sentiment: "You have painted with unparalleled impartiality a true picture of your country, its manners, its characters, its government."[34] In another letter Chastellux told Hume that his name had become "as estimable in the republic of letters as was that of Jehovah among the Hebrews."[35]

The words *impartial* and *impartiality* seem to occur also in nearly every press review of Hume's *History* at this time, whether of traditionalist or *philosophe* inspiration. Fréron, one of Voltaire's greatest enemies, after making the usual comparison with Tacitus, affirmed that Hume was the first "English" author ever to have "done justice to our nation and to the ministers of our religion when he thought that the truth was *favourable* to them."[36] The *Journal Encyclopédique* pointed out that no historian of the Stuart period had been impartial before Hume. Most Englishmen had, like Burnet, written as paid propagandists of the usurper William of Orange. Foreign historians of the English revolution had not succeeded either. Some, like the Huguenot Rapin-Thoyras, were blinded by the prejudices of their religion and had interpreted events only in the light of an apology for Protestantism. Others, like le Père d'Orléans, though not unfavourable to the Catholic side, had shown an inadequate knowledge of the English system of government. "It has been said," the journal goes on, "and experience has confirmed the maxim only too often, that *nations would be supremely happy were they governed by philosopher kings*. Let us add that history will never be well written except by philosopher

32. Ibid., II. 382.

33. *Letters of Eminent Persons addressed to David Hume*, ed. J. H. Burton, Edinburgh, 1849, p. 13.

34. Ibid., p. 275.

35. Greig, "Some Unpublished Letters to David Hume," *Revue de littérature comparée*, 1932, XII. 830.

36. *Année littéraire*, 1763, III. 39–40; see also ibid., 1760, IV. 313.

historians; that is to say by men who, without regard to any country, any faction, any sect, have as their only ambition to write the truth. Our author comes very close to that model...."[37]

Voltaire, the most important historian of the day, praised Hume on much the same grounds in a long review published in 1764:

> One can add nothing to the fame of this History, perhaps the best ever written in any language....
> Never has the public so clearly sensed that only philosophers should write history....
> The philosopher belongs to no country, to no faction. One would like to see the history of the wars between Rome and Carthage written by a man who was neither a Roman nor a Carthaginian....
> ...Mr. Hume, in his History, seems neither a parliamentarian, nor a royalist, nor an Anglican, nor a Presbyterian; we find in him only the fair-minded man....
> The fury of parties has for a long time deprived England of both a good history and a good government. What a Tory wrote was denied by the Whigs, themselves given the lie in turn by the Tories. Only Rapin-Thoyras, a foreigner, seemed to have written an impartial history; but the stain of prejudice is yet visible even in the truths that Thoyras recounts; whereas in the new historian we find a mind that rises above his matter, one who speaks of failings, errors and barbarities in the same manner that a physician speaks of epidemic disease.[38]

The apparent total agreement of such unlike men as Voltaire, Fréron, and Rousseau on the subject of Hume's impartiality should be enough to indicate in this respect the unanimity of opinion in France. Since, however, many of my later conclusions concerning the influence of the Hume image must stand or fall on the basis of a careful evaluation of that image, and since it is important to show that this view of Hume's history persists in France[39] with a few no-

37. June 1760, IV. 3–6.

38. *Gazette littéraire de l'Europe*, 2 May 1764, I. 193–200; see also *Oeuvres complètes de Voltaire*, ed. Moland, XXV. 169–73.

39. Hume's great reputation in history was, of course, by no means restricted to France. In Italy, for example, such men as Beccaria, Algarotti, and Genovesi were no less flattering in their praise.

table exceptions right up to the time of the Revolution, I may be permitted to labour this point a little longer.

Dom Louis-Mayeul Chaudon in a work of 1772 again reviewed the three most widely read authors of English history: Hume, Rapin-Thoyras, and le Père d'Orléans. Rapin, as was usual in French Catholic estimates at this time, is accused of Huguenot prejudices: "He can be deservedly reproached for showing bias against the land of his birth, made hateful to Protestants by the harshness of Louis XIV, and for favouring the Puritans, those dangerous enthusiasts whose religious views are fit only to make men grimly ferocious and whose system of political independence is calculated only to manufacture malcontents and rebels." As for le Père d'Orléans, Abbé Chaudon shows surprising frankness in judging his fellow-ecclesiastic: "He is too obviously biased in his treatment of the Stuart period. Most of this French Jesuit's determinations are designed to fit either the interests of the papacy in Rome or the principles of the French monarchy." Hume's fairness is seen, on the other hand, as unique, quite without precedent: "Never before has any author raised himself so much above the sectarian bias and party prejudices that divide the kingdom; ever impartial, he seems to be the spokesman of posterity...."[40]

Also defending Hume's impartiality, the Reverend Samuel Formey, secretary of the Berlin Academy and formerly hostile editor of the French translation of Hume's *Philosophical Essays* (1758), contrasted in 1777 the anticlericalism of the *philosophes* with Hume's fairness toward the representatives of the church:

> There is nothing quite so curious as the relentless enmity directed against them by persons who, far from having any cause for complaint against them, owe them a genuine debt of gratitude, since it is they who in the majority of countries preserved learning and a foundation of humanity, beneficence, and charity throughout the centuries of barbarism; were it not for them, the lawlessness of those unhappy times would have been carried to a far greater degree of excess. Hume, whose testimony will not be challenged, formally ac-

---

40. *Bibliothèque d'un homme de goût,* Avignon, 1772, II. 178–80. See also similar opinions of Court de Gébelin and de Tressan, in *Le guide de l'histoire,* ed. Jean-François Née de la Rochelle, Paris, 1803, I. 161–62, 280.

knowledges the fact with regard to England and this admission does honour to his impartiality. In contrast, we are roused to indignation when we encounter on every page of the writings of Helvétius those bitter ironies, those derisive and almost always furious sorties against a clergy that certainly deserved his consideration and who became the target of his displeasure only because they attempted to protect France from the venom of his doctrine.[41]

The section *Histoire* of the *Encyclopédie Méthodique* in 1788 gave perhaps the ultimate in praise to the impartiality of Hume's *History of England:* "One of the finest pieces of history and philosophy that exists in any language, and perhaps the most impartial and most reasonable work that has come from the hand of man."[42] It is obviously impossible to say more!

4

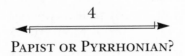

PAPIST OR PYRRHONIAN?

It is well known that the English at this time did not agree with the French about Hume's impartiality. The strange combination of two reputations which Hume enjoyed in England, one as a foolish atheist, the other as a perverse Jacobite, was scarcely of a nature to please any large group in that country.

In *My Own Life* Hume speaks of his disappointment at the domestic reception given the *Stuarts:*

> I was, I own, sanguine in my expectations of the success of this work. I thought that I was the only historian that had at once neglected present power, interest, and authority, and the cry of popular prejudices; and as the subject was suited to every capacity, I expected proportional applause. But miserable was my disappointment: I was assailed by one cry of reproach, disapprobation, and even detesta-

41. "Examen de la question si toutes les vérités sont bonnes à dire?" in *Nouveaux Mémoires de l'Académie Royale des Sciences et Belles-Lettres*, Berlin, 1777, XXXIII. 336.

42. *Encyclopédie Méthodique: Histoire* (1788), III. 111.

tion; English, Scotch, and Irish; Whig and Tory; churchman and
sectary, freethinker and religionist; patriot and courtier, united in
their rage against the man who had presumed to shed a generous
tear for the fate of Charles I and the Earl of Strafford; and after the
first ebullitions of this fury were over, what was still more mortifying,
the book seemed to sink into oblivion. Mr. Millar told me, that in a
twelvemonth he sold only forty-five copies of it. I scarcely, indeed,
heard of one man in the three Kingdoms, considerable for rank or
letters, that could endure the book. I must only except the Primate
of England, Dr. Herring, and the Primate of Ireland, Dr. Stone;
which seem two odd exceptions. These dignified prelates separately
sent me messages not to be discouraged.

Hume was, nevertheless, discouraged and he tells us in this
same brief autobiographical sketch that, had not the war at that
time been breaking out between France and England, he would
have retired forever from England to some provincial French
town. Horace Walpole clearly reflects the typical attitude to the
History in England in a letter to Montague from Paris in 1765.
Parisians, he affirmed, were totally lacking in literary taste:
"...could one believe that when they read our authors, Richardson
and Mr. Hume should be their favourites? The latter is treated
here with perfect veneration. His History, so falsified in many
points, so partial in as many, so very unequal in its parts, is thought
the standard of writing...."[43]

The French were fully aware of the discrepancy between their
own estimates of Hume's worth and those of the English. We read,
for example, in the *Journal Etranger* of 1760 the following statement on that subject:

Mr. Hume has been accused by his compatriots of striving too eagerly after singular opinions; it is not our function to debate this reproach. We will note only that, although Mr. Hume is English, a
republican, and a Protestant, he has always spoken of the French
with esteem, and of kings and Catholics with moderation; and it is
possible that this singularity has offended a nation that is too much
in the habit of seeing in monarchies only a herd of slaves and in *pa-*

43. W. S. Lewis and R. S. Brown, *Horace Walpole's Correspondence with George
Montague,* New Haven, 1941, II. 176, letter of 22 September 1765.

pists only a band of fanatics; a nation, in short, that is too prone to denying the existence of liberty, virtue, and philosophy in any government but its own.[44]

To show how wrong they feel the English are with respect to Hume, the editors of this very orthodox *ancien-régime* journal do not hesitate to call his work "the only good history written in English, and undoubtedly one of the best to be found in any language." Hume is also commended for being "the first English writer who has dared to state that monarchies are about as favourable to progress in the arts, in philosophy and in commerce as republics."[45]

In a work intended for the instruction of Marie-Antoinette, the future *Historiographe de France,* Jacob-Nicolas Moreau, implied that Hume had probably carried impartiality to an undesirable extreme: "...he ought only to be impartial but he prides himself on the most exaggerated indifference. The English, who possess the Roman virtue of partiality for their country, have themselves blamed him for this fault and they think a good deal less of this author than we ourselves do."[46]

It must be noted, however, that Moreau's attempt to understand and forgive England's hostility to Hume the historian is a French attitude rarely encountered at this time. Much more common is the indignant reaction of the former Jesuit and future speech writer for Mirabeau, Joseph-Antoine-Joachim Cerutti, who wrote in 1783: "Mr. Hume's History could be given the title: The History of English Passions, as written by human reason. The English have reproached him for causing tears to be shed over the fate of Marie Stuart and of Charles I. They have called him 'old woman Hume' for it. This simple good heartedness makes his impartiality more noble and his philosophy more touching."[47]

44. See May issue, 1760, pp. 169–70.

45. Ibid., p. 171.

46. *Bibliothèque de Madame la Dauphine:* No. 1, *Histoire,* Paris, 1770, p. 125.

47. "L'Aigle et le Hibou," in *Oeuvres diverses de M. Cerutti ou recueil de pièces composées avant et depuis la Révolution,* Paris, 1792, II. 47. Hume in fact shed few tears for Mary Stuart: see my article "The Eighteenth-Century Marian Controversy and an Unpublished Letter by David Hume," *Studies in Scottish Literature,* April 1964, pp. 236–52.

More angry still was the response of one of Hume's French anthologists, Damiens de Gomicourt, who pointed out that the ungrateful English seemed to make more fuss over their racehorses than they did over a Hume. De Gomicourt makes astute conjectures as to the reasons for this neglect: "This dispassionate way of writing about his country and its enemies . . . is precisely what harms him most in the eyes of his fellow-countrymen; if they were as philosophical as M. de Voltaire says they are *when he calls England the island of philosophers,* they would not allow themselves to be carried away so frequently by their ruling anti-French passions; the good that Mr. Hume has to say about the French nation when he thinks praise is deserved, the moderation with which he speaks of the church of Rome, or of the unfortunate Stuarts, would not be a reason for them to accuse this author of *popery,* of *Jacobitism,* and of *Francomania,* and his works would be as famous in London as they are in Paris."[48]

Popery, Jacobitism, and *Francomania*—three qualities well calculated to enhance an English historian's reputation in France; their effect would, of course, be just the opposite in England. That Hume himself felt his history would hold a special appeal for Catholic, monarchical France is made clear in his original letter to Abbé Le Blanc in 1754 proposing a French translation of the *Stuarts.* "Considering," Hume wrote, "some late transactions in France, your Ministry may think themselves obliged to a man, who, by the example of English history, discovers the consequences of puritanical and republican pretensions. You would have remarked in my writings, that my principles are, all along, tolerably monarchical, and that I abhor that low practice, so prevalent in England, of speaking with malignity of France."[49] One month later, Hume came back to this point, advising Le Blanc to make any necessary attenuations in his translation of the *Stuarts:* "If there be some strokes of the *L'esprit fort* too strong for your climate, you may soften them at your discretion. That I am a lover of liberty will be ex-

---

48. *L'Observateur Français à Londres,* Londres, 1769, I. 349–50; IV. 109.
49. Greig, op. cit., I. 193–94, letter of 12 September 1754.

pected from my country, though I hope that I carry not that passion to any ridiculous extreme."[50]

For an example of current French reactions to British historians who did indulge in "that low practice" of speaking with malignity of France, we have only to see what the French thought of Smollett's *History*. A fairly typical review of it can be found in the *Journal Encyclopédique* of 1764:

> Mr. Smollett believes himself to be entirely above all national prejudice and jealousies; he sees himself as perfectly free of those unjust partisan sentiments that dishonour the works of several English historians; he assures the reader that no religious controversy, no political faction commands his ardent allegiance.... This manner of declaration appears to us all the more astonishing in that we can scarcely think of any historian who surpasses Mr. Smollett in partiality, whether in the various parallels he has drawn between the monarchs of France and the kings of Great Britain, or in the exaggerated praises he is forever heaping on his fellow-countrymen. More circumspect at times, but also more satirical and more caustic than Rapin de Thoyras, he rails against Catholicism, he dredges up everything that indecency and irreligion have expounded against the venerable bishops who brought renown to England; he sees their zeal as blind fanaticism, their candour as hypocrisy, their attachment to the Roman church as criminal, outrageously independent, an unpardonable felony.[51]

To find a French-language equivalent of English hostility to Hume's history during this early period, it is necessary to look through the pages of the erudite "Dutch" journals, edited by Huguenot refugees. Here the similarity of views seems almost automatic. Maty, in the *Journal Britannique*, speaking of the first volume of Hume's *Stuarts*, declared: "So little does the work I have before me seem a model to imitate that, quite to the contrary, I find in it the various defects that an author whom Mr. Hume would

---

50. Ibid., I. 198, letter of 15 October 1754.

51. August 1764, V. 6–7. The probable author of the above is J.-L. Castilhon, who repeated his charges six years later in *Le Diogène moderne ou le désapprobateur*, Bouillon, 1770, II. 228. See also E. Joliat, *Smollett et la France*, Paris, 1935.

not disown as his master regards as incompatible with the duties of an historian." Maty then cites Voltaire's *Défense du Siècle de Louis XIV* on the necessity for the historian to stick to the truth.[52]

The *Bibliothèque des Sciences et des Beaux-Arts,* published at The Hague, spoke unfavourably of the same work in 1756: "We have said nothing of this *History* because nothing in it seems to us to be worthy of praise except the style, and we have no desire to be constantly at loggerheads with this author.... We have never before seen a history so dominated by the dangerous art that makes the most evil characters seem bearable by hiding certain traits and by softening what remains through the use of clever shading and nuances. But that is not all. Mr. Hume has here taken it upon himself to identify *fanaticism* as the Reformation's distinctive characteristic...."[53]

The year following, the same journal reviewed the second volume of the *Stuarts* and warned its readers again about Hume's dangerous portraits: "...one must be always on one's guard with his portraits! His taste for paradox and his partiality are often only too glaringly apparent in his character portrayals of several important personages.... The portrait of James II is so lacking in features resembling the original that one must needs have seen attached to it the name of this monarch to believe that it is he whom Mr. Hume has sought to depict as a prince who was *steady* in his counsels, *diligent* in his schemes, *brave* in his enterprises, *faithful, sincere,* and *honourable* in his dealings with all men." Obviously, no continental "Whig" could accept such a picture of the monster who had been driven out by the Glorious Revolution of 1688. Quite to the contrary, the Huguenot editor asserts, James II had been, in fact, *cruel, vindictive, cowardly and treacherous.*[54]

A fairly similar tone predominates in this same journal's review of the *Tudors* in 1759, although, for obvious reasons, now that the Jacobite question was left behind, the editors found, as had

---

52. *Journal Britannique,* May–June 1755, p. 133.

53. April–June 1756, p. 498.

54. January–March 1757, pp. 245–46.

contemporary English readers, that Hume's *History* was somewhat improved in quality:

> The partisan spirit that encumbered the author in his treatment of the Stuart period and caused him, in combination with his affectation of impartiality, to fall into so many revolting contradictions, hinders him less as he moves away from modern times. . . . But on the other hand, one would like to find these same improvements in what he has to say of the origins and progress of the Reformation and of the spirit that inspired the Reformers. There are passages where one is tempted to think that Mr. Hume is a *papist*, did we not already know him for a *pyrrhonian*.[55]

Hume points out in *My Own Life* that the English accorded at last "tolerable" success to the *Plantagenets*, the third and last part of the *History*. The *Bibliothèque des Sciences et des Beaux-Arts*, reviewing that work in 1761, naïvely confessed to a similar change of heart: "This history improves as the author moves away from our own times. A proper sense of historical writing that sets aside or touches only lightly the unessential, that selects and arranges interesting events judiciously and presents them clearly, can be detected everywhere in these two new volumes."[56] It is perhaps unnecessary to point out that any attacks Hume made against religious fanaticism in this part of the *History* which deals with the Middle Ages would not normally be interpreted as immoderately hostile by the Protestant editors.

If we now compare these "Dutch" accounts with opinions expressed in the Catholic French journals, we find that the progression of ideas on the subject of Hume's *History of England* is neatly reversed. The pious *Mémoires de Trévoux* enthusiastically devoted many pages to reviewing Hume's *Stuarts* and commended Hume as an author who had written "without bias."[57] The manner in which Hume had dealt with the civil war period seemed especially appealing:

55. January–March 1759, pp. 211–12.
56. October–December 1761, p. 460.
57. *Mémoires de Trévoux*, February 1759, p. 468.

The horrendous consequences of it are only too well known: all of Europe was horror-struck and roused to indignation: these just feelings are renewed in their entirety as we peruse this history. Possessing all the virtues of the good king, Charles I reappears here, hunted down, arrested, held a prisoner in captivity. This monarch, charged by unlawful procedure, judged without legitimate authority, condemned for no crime, here moves to tears all readers who will find him even greater on the scaffold, even more steadfast, generous, and virtuous than he had appeared during the triumphs and reversals that were the glory, as they were the misfortune, of his reign.[58]

Every passage in which Hume rehabilitates the names of English Catholics is underlined by the Jesuit editors. Concerning the London fire, attributed by certain historians to the malevolence of Catholics, they are especially pleased to note that Hume "accuses neither the Catholics nor the Presbyterians of it: he agrees that this imputation was nothing more than a calumny given countenance by popular prejudice."[59] As for the Popish plot, Hume "acknowledges its patent imposture without denying the unfortunate effect the gross absurdities of such an ill-constructed fable had on the English...."[60] On one occasion only do the Jesuit editors find Hume biased—when he is seen as "equally hostile to the enthusiasm of the Puritans as he is prejudiced against the Catholics."[61]

More significant still were the "lessons" the *Mémoires de Trévoux* editors derived from their reading of Hume's *Stuarts*. These lessons are quite explicit and, in part, anticipate some of the more eccentric and extreme interpretations of the work by counter-revolutionary thinkers after 1789:

One has only to compare this history of the reign of Charles I with others that have also been written in accordance with Protestant prejudice, to sense Mr. Hume's superior genius, style, accuracy, and impartiality. Without including in this comparison any Catholic

58. Ibid., p. 471.
59. Ibid., March 1759, p. 184.
60. Ibid., p. 188.
61. Ibid., January 1759, p. 217.

writer, we can draw the following conclusions: 1. That since their separation from the Roman Church, Protestants, left to their own thinking, can have only an irresolute and uncertain doctrine which leaves them exposed to the most frightful aberrations, with no solid means to regulate their belief and bring it to true uniformity. 2. That the influence of their doctrine has given rise to the most horrible disruptions in England, and the most abominable crimes against sovereigns. 3. That under the cover of disputes over dogma among the Protestant sects, fanaticism, at first insidiously, and afterward with great clamour, put the finishing touches on the nation's disorders. 4. That this heretical fanaticism not only spreads with great rapidity, it also provides a rich and inexhaustible breeding ground for dangerous monsters; since the *Independents,* had their leader Cromwell not forestalled the danger, were on the point of being subjugated by the *Agitators,* or the *Levellers,* a sect whose enthusiasm, grafted onto the fanaticism of these same *Independents,* aimed to introduce perfect equality among the citizens, and, consequently, the most monstrous confusion and anarchy in the government. 5. That debate, *as Mr. Hume insinuates,* even of a speculative nature, on the extent and limits of the royal prerogative, must never be brought before the people's tribunal; that in such matters the strictest silence must be imposed, even among philosophical *reasoners;* and that in general it is safer to keep the people ignorant of the limits of their obedience, than it is to instruct them on the limits that sovereigns ought to observe.[62]

As I have already pointed out, the question of whether Hume really implies all this, whether the Jesuits made a correct or distorted interpretation of his intentions, is somewhat irrelevant to my purpose. The essential fact is that such interpretations *were made* and made frequently by an astonishing variety of readers in eighteenth-century France. Of course, the *Mémoires de Trévoux* editors are forced to dodge about rather awkwardly when they encounter passages inspired by Hume's more frankly irreligious moods. Still, this aspect of the *History* was not seen as an insuperable problem. The *Stuarts* was after all by a "Protestant" and even a Hume must be expected to wander from the truth from time to time. The Protestant *Bibliothèque des Sciences et des Beaux-Arts,* we re-

62. Ibid., February 1759, pp. 475–76.

---

member, had found Hume's portrait of James II totally false. The *Mémoires de Trévoux,* on the other hand, did not find it sufficiently "false," that is to say, sufficiently "true": "We must not expect Mr. Hume to be strictly impartial in his treatment of this reign: he is too biased against the person, the court, and the religion of James II, as well as against France, Louis XIV, and all forms of zeal, to prevent his pen from leaving traces of his prejudices in this history."[63] Hume's occasional lapses were seen as faults only in some absolute sense; on this question the journal concluded: "In any case, among Protestant historians who have dealt with English history of the last century, Mr. Hume is still the least biased against the Roman Church, and the least prejudiced in favour of the Protestant sects; for this he deserves due credit."[64]

The same aspects of the *Stuarts* pleased Voltaire's enemy Fréron in the *Année littéraire.* He points out first of all that Hume displays none of the "odious prejudices common to English authors, which even French historians show at times."[65] He notes with particular approval Hume's treatment of Charles I's trial and execution: "I would have to copy out several entire pages to present to your humanity and sense of outrage the horrifying scene in which this king was judged, condemned, and executed by his own subjects."[66] All the horrors surrounding the monster republican Cromwell, the regicide fanaticism of the hated Puritans, are evoked in this *ancien-régime* Frenchman's review. Later, while examining the *Tudors,* Fréron shows the same highly favourable attitude to the Scottish historian's impartiality. He underlines the fact that Hume, for example, "stoutly defends Cardinal Wolsey... against the attacks of Protestant writers who have sullied his memory."[67] On the question of Henry VIII's divorce he is happy to point out also that Hume "pertinently justifies the Pope's inflexible resistance to the

63. Ibid., March 1759, p. 197.
64. Ibid., p. 198.
65. *Année littéraire,* 1760, IV. 313.
66. Ibid., IV. 323.
67. Ibid., 1763, II. 297.

English king's imperious and threatening solicitations."[68] Along the same lines, Hume's impartiality is contrasted with Burnet's bias on the question of the suppression of monasteries:

Doctor Burnet complacently relates all the infamies the monks were accused of in the reports prepared by the commissioners Henry VIII sent to all the religious houses to make inquiries regarding the conduct and morals of the nuns and friars. Mr. Hume, wiser and more circumspect in his judgements, does not rely much on the accuracy of these reports; ever on guard against the partisan spirit that dictated them, he acknowledges that in times of faction, especially of the religious variety, little truth is to be expected from even the most ostensibly authentic testimony.... He refuses as well to impute to the Catholic religion abuses that the Church in fact condemns, such as exposing false relics, and the pious impostures employed in some places by the monks *to increase the devotion and consequently the contributions of the people. Such fooleries,* he writes, *as they are to be found in all ages and nations, and even took place during the most refined periods of antiquity, form no particular or violent reproach to the Catholic religion.* It must be admitted, Monsieur, that nothing resembles less the ordinary rantings of Protestant writers than does such language.[69]

Fréron too admits that Hume experienced difficulty occasionally in stripping himself entirely of "English" ideas when speaking about religion; he states, however, that it would be ridiculous and unjust to judge the Scot "according to the principles received among us."[70] Hume is occasionally wrong, but he is wrong with sincerity: "It can be seen that he seeks the truth in a sincere manner and if he sometimes drifts from it, it is less the result of a premeditated intention to disguise or corrupt it, than it is a consequence of the fact that the human mind is not always capable of finding it."[71]

It would be difficult to find any other subject on which Voltaire and Fréron seem to have been in such complete agree-

68. Ibid., II. 301.
69. Ibid., II. 302–3.
70. Ibid., 1760, IV. 313.
71. Ibid., 1763, III. 35.

ment. But even here we must make a distinction. Fréron's praise so far has been for the *Stuarts* and the *Tudors*. Voltaire, when he extolled Hume's virtues in the long review of 1764 already referred to, was judging the English edition of the *History* in its completed form—after, that is to say, the publication of the *Plantagenets*. It was especially this last section which permitted the French historian to praise the work as a more geographically restricted version of his own *Essai sur les Moeurs*. Conversely, when Fréron considered the *Plantagenets* in 1766, his admiration suddenly became considerably less warm: "Half of the first volume is only remotely connected to what is supposed to be its subject. If you remove from the remainder the author's frequent attacks on the Church and its clergy... his harangues against the old Catholic religion, you will discover that this History of all the Plantagenet princes is very succinct."[72] There is no doubt that Fréron was genuinely surprised to find what appeared to be a wealth of insulting epithets and vulgar abuse directed against religion in this work. Hume no longer seemed to be the divinely impartial historian, that rare angel of truth. He is now accused of having failed in the first duty of an historian, and Fréron notes that it was not with works like the *Plantagenets* that Hume had built up his great reputation in the literary world.[73]

Just as many traditionalists in France had been disappointed in 1758 to see the free-thinking *Philosophical Essays* appear only a few years after the fairly orthodox *Political Discourses* of 1754, a number of conservative French admirers of the *Stuarts* and *Tudors* withdrew their support for the historian after the appearance of the *Plantagenets*. As in the case of the *Philosophical Essays*, however, a much smaller group, the *philosophes*, greeted Hume's apparent return to sanity with a sigh of relief.

To say that the *philosophes* liked the last part of Hume's *History* with its *à la Voltaire* treatment of the Middle Ages, and disliked the *Stuarts* and the *Tudors*, would be to propose a rather neatly symmetrical but not entirely true simplification. One can note, however, among members of this group, a distinct preference for

72. Ibid., 1766, II. 4.
73. Ibid., II. 28.

the more "philosophical" Hume who had angered the Frérons with his essay "Of Miracles," his *Natural History of Religion,* and his *Plantagenets.* The *philosophes* too spoke admiringly of impartiality but felt, certainly, that it should never be allowed to develop to the point where it might become a source of comfort to the enemy. Lockian in their political outlook—one is very tempted to see in them a close French equivalent of the English Whigs—they were chary of the Tory flavour of Hume's *Stuarts.* Grimm, perhaps the most critically astute and alertly orthodox of the "brother-hood," accused Hume as early as 1754, while reviewing the *Political Discourses,* of having slightly unsound political views: "I have only one grievance against Mr. Hume, it is that he is rather too fond of paradox, a failing that sometimes leads his reasoning astray; he is also a Jacobite."[74] In the same year he expressed certain doubts concerning Hume's over-all ability as an enlightened thinker and added: "Either I am mistaken, or his fellow-countrymen must reproach him his great fondness for the French, and the French should not feel too flattered by it since he does not really see them from their most estimable side. . . . "[75] This same author was one of the first to express dissatisfaction several years later with those essays in the *Understanding* which did not attack miracles or Providence. Why, Grimm complained, did Hume feel it necessary to add to the confusion of the philosophic battle by discussing rather sceptically—and, yes, with an appalling lack of originality—the epistemological doctrines Locke had settled once and for all?[76]

Similarly, in the very year that Voltaire praised Hume's *History,* the defender of Jean Calas confided to the Marquise Du Deffand: "I like, even much more than his historical writings, Mr. Hume's philosophy. The best part of all this is that Helvétius, who in his book *De l'esprit* has not said one-twentieth of the wise, useful, and

---

74. *Correspondance littéraire,* 15 August 1754, II. 393.

75. Ibid., 1 October 1754, II. 415.

76. See the *Correspondance littéraire,* 15 January 1759, IV. 70, and my article "Hume, 'Philosophe' and Philosopher in Eighteenth-Century France," *French Studies,* 1961, XV. 216.

bold things for which we are grateful to Mr. Hume and twenty other Englishmen, has been persecuted in the land of the *Welches* [the French] and his book has been burned there. All of which goes to prove that the English are men and the French are children."[77]

Hume in his *History* perhaps flattered those naughty children too much. The more unified story of how English liberty had emerged from despotism as told in the *Lettres philosophiques* was a much better way to improve *les Welches* than shedding sympathetic tears for a beheaded king or making statements that the *Mémoires de Trévoux* could interpret as great lessons. There is more than a hint of the back-handed compliment in at least one of Voltaire's recorded comments made during the guided tour he sometimes gave visitors through his vast library at Ferney. After pointing to the volumes of Shakespeare, Milton, Congreve, Rochester, Shaftesbury, Bolingbroke, Robertson, and Hume, Voltaire once turned to his guests and added for the last-mentioned author that David Hume had written his history "to be praised" and that he had attained his goal.[78]

The fact remains that the *philosophes* did identify or did their best to identify the historical efforts of Hume and Voltaire. They, as well as Dr. Samuel Johnson and Horace Walpole—though not with the same cranky and contemptuous hostility these two Englishmen affected—saw Hume as Voltaire's pupil: an accusation which Hume, who held a fairly low opinion of Voltaire's merit as an historian, frequently denied. There is no doubt that it was the occasional Voltairian tone of the *History* which appealed most to the *encyclopédiste* party. Helvétius, for example, writing to Hume on Prévost's forthcoming translation of the *Stuarts,* characteristically expressed the fear that the Abbé would not dare "tell all."[79] In doing so he probably betrayed unwittingly an interpretation of Hume's intentions which scarcely corresponds to the very complacent advice Hume had given Le Blanc to attenuate at will all

---

77. See Best.D11939, letter of 20 June 1764.

78. See *Lettres de Madame de Graffigny,* Paris, 1879, p. 431.

79. *Correspondance générale d'Helvétius,* ed. A. Dainard, J. Orsoni, D. Smith, and P. Allan, II. 258, letter of 12 July 1759.

strokes of *esprit fort* too strong for the French climate. Helvétius speaks of the *boldness* of the *Stuarts* but makes no particular mention, on the other hand, of the manner in which Hume had shed a tear for Charles I. Similarly, the *Plantagenets* aroused his greatest admiration, and in a letter to Hume of 1763 he especially commended that work for its "philosophical and impartial spirit."[80] Moreover, in his own bold composition, *De l'homme,* Helvétius made good use of the anti-clerical arsenal he was able to find in this part of the *History.*

Perhaps no better evidence exists of this *philosophe* view of Hume as yet another soldier in the Voltairian war of propaganda against *l'infâme* than the numerous, almost urgent, appeals he received from his closest friends among the *encyclopédistes* to write an ecclesiastical history. In the same letter written to congratulate him on his "esprit philosophique" in the *Plantagenets,* Helvétius also begged the Scottish historian to continue his efforts with "the finest project in the world"—a history of the Church: "Only think," he writes, "how worthy the subject is of you, and how you are worthy of the subject. It is therefore in the name of England, France, Germany, Italy, and in the name of posterity, that I entreat you to write this history. Remember that you alone are in a position to write it; that many centuries will pass before another Monsieur Hume is born, and that it is a benefit you owe to the universe, both present and future."[81]

Grimm in 1766 formulated the same wish: "During his stay in France, we often begged M. Hume to write an ecclesiastical history. It would be, at this juncture, one of the finest of literary enterprises, and one of the greatest services rendered to philosophy and to humanity. . . . M. de Voltaire no longer has the sustained mental vigour required to undertake such a task; he would turn his subject too much in the direction of jesting and ridicule. . . . "[82]

Diderot, congratulating Hume for having finally retired from his public functions, added in a letter of 1768 the advice that it

80. Ibid., III. 73, letter of 2 June 1763.

81. Loc. cit.

82. *Correspondance littéraire,* 1 April 1766, VII. 13.

was now high time to get on with more serious matters: "Return, return quickly, my dear philosopher, to your books, to your pursuits. I much prefer seeing you whip in hand, dealing out justice to all those celebrated ruffians who have disturbed the peace of your country. . . ."[83]

After the *Plantagenets,* Hume abandoned English history. Although he had at one time thought of continuing the work, the plan was never realized. D'Alembert, writing to Hume in 1766, urged him on in this project and showed in his letter that he too saw Hume's chief historical merit as a wielder of the philosophic scourge: "If you choose to, you will have some very pertinent truths to tell about all the stupidities committed by France and her enemies during the War of Succession, and about the causes of those stupidities. But no matter how interesting that subject might be in your hands, I would nevertheless have preferred to see you undertake an ecclesiastical history. It is a greater curiosity, it seems to me, to see men cutting each other's throats for theological irrelevancies, than for provinces and kingdoms which are somewhat more deserving of the effort."[84]

What the *philosophes* wanted from an ecclesiastical history is not a matter of doubt. D'Alembert himself had given only a year before an example of the best clichés of the genre in his anonymously published work, *Sur la destruction des Jésuites en France* (1765). Ecclesiastical history would show all manner of usurpation of the spiritual powers over the temporal, the hideous crimes and bloody wars caused by religious fanaticism, the persecutions and murders committed in the name of Christ—such were the gifts of Christianity to mankind that would be recorded in a good "philosophically" inspired ecclesiastical history. In a letter of 1773, d'Alembert once again solicited Hume on the subject and commiserated at the same time on the fate of that "poor lady" who is called *Philosophy:* ". . . those who would like to write on her behalf dare not—those like you who could, prefer to sleep and digest,

83. *Oeuvres complètes,* ed. Lewinter, VII. 653, letter of 22 February 1768.
84. *Letters of Eminent Persons,* p. 183, letter of 28 February 1766.

and perhaps they have made the best choice. Still, I shall never get over being denied the ecclesiastical history I requested of you so many times, which you alone perhaps in Europe are capable of writing, which would be quite as interesting as Greek and Roman history, were you willing to give yourself the trouble of painting our holy mother the Church *au naturel*."[85]

It is perhaps not strange that the practical implications of the *Stuarts* as interpreted by the *Mémoires de Trévoux* were largely ignored by the *philosophes* rather than overtly attacked or even commented on. Clearly it was the medieval section of the *History* which proved most useful to them. In the work, *De la félicité publique,* which Voltaire perversely judged as at least equal in merit to Montesquieu's *Esprit des Lois,* the *philosophe* Chastellux showed how valuable the *Plantagenets* could be if properly used—used, that is, as a work to supplement Voltaire's more famous catalogue of medieval barbarities. A disciple of progress, Chastellux had no patience with those who rhapsodized (as Burke was to do twenty years later) on the glories of the age of chivalry, the former splendour of the nobility, the stability of feudal law, the exalted courage of the crusaders, &c. Those who superstitiously lamented the departure of those good old days could be cured by reading two authors espe-

---

85. Ibid., p. 218, letter of 1 May 1773. Hume's sceptical lack of anti-clerical or anti-religious militancy was also a source of considerable disappointment to the atheist Naigeon. Writing in 1792 he tells us how, try as he might, and after two careful readings of Hume's posthumously published *Dialogues concerning Natural Religion,* he was unable to find in the work any clear-cut statement that God did not exist. Why, he asks, should a man be timid about the truth once he is dead? "One may be forgiven for compromising with error and vulgar prejudice when, by overtly trampling them underfoot, one might fear the reprisals of fanatics and persecutors; but when one is supposed to be addressing men from the depths of the tomb, one must tell them the truth, plainly and bluntly...." (See the *Encyclopédie Méthodique: Philosophie ancienne et moderne,* par M. Naigeon, Paris, 1792, II. 748.) It would have been better, Naigeon added, had Hume remained entirely silent on the matter of religion, since his last word on the subject "basically offers only the same difficulties, the same doubts, that he had proposed forty years earlier in his essays on human understanding. Whence we may conclude that Hume, with respect to the most fundamental of all *theological truths,* never advanced beyond scepticism...." Diderot, Naigeon concluded, had handled the whole question of God rather more skilfully. (Ibid., II. 750–51.)

---

cially: "Let them consult," Chastellux advises, *"l'Essai sur l'histoire générale,* the model of historico-philosophical writings; let them consult Mr. Hume, illustrious in the same career. . . ."[86]

Delisle de Sales, another of Voltaire's understudies but fond too of calling Hume "the Tacitus of England,"[87] found materials for the good cause not only in the *Plantagenets* but in the *Tudors* and *Stuarts* as well. Particularly useful to his purposes was Hume's account of the religious massacres in Ireland, seen by the French author as having been unequalled even by that of Saint Bartholomew's Day, the event, we remember, which made French history almost worth writing about in the opinion of Voltaire. Delisle de Sales ignored, curiously enough, Hume's own estimate of the number of victims, established in the *History* at the sufficiently horrifying figure of 40,000, and chose instead the more polemically useful figure of 200,000.[88]

As an illustration of how the same passage from Hume's *History* could at times inspire both the *philosophes* and their enemies to reach completely antithetical conclusions, it is amusing to note that the Abbé Bergier, a Roman Catholic apologist to whom we shall refer again, discussed in 1767 this same massacre; and he was delighted to point out that religion was not the only, nor even the principal, cause of it: "Mr. Hume, a witness whose testimony will not be seen as suspect, admits in good faith that the inveterate animosity of the Irish toward the English, their attachment to freedom, property, and their ancient customs, their envy of the English recently transplanted to Ireland and fear that even worse mistreatment from them would follow, in short, dissatisfaction with

86. *De la félicité publique* (1772), nouvelle édition, augmentée de notes inédites de Voltaire, Paris, 1822, II. 48–49; see also II. 10, 13, 24, 31, 43, 91.

87. *De la philosophie de la nature ou Traité de morale pour l'espèce humaine tiré de la philosophie et fondé sur la nature,* troisième édition, Londres, 1777, II. 274; VI. 412.

88. Ibid., VI. 317–18. Hume's text is as follows: "By some computations, those who perished by all these cruelties are supposed to be a hundred and fifty, or two hundred thousand: by the most moderate, and probably the most reasonable account, they are made to amount to forty thousand; if this estimation itself be not, as is usual in such cases, somewhat exaggerated." (*The History of England,* VII. 388.)

the English government, these were the true causes of this civil war. Those who estimate the number of dead to be sixty or eighty thousand, exaggerate by half."[89]

Quite obviously there were possibilities for distortion, in this and in other instances, by all sides, including Hume's no doubt. The major conclusion that emerges from an examination of the evidence is, however, that the *History*, valuable as it may have seemed to the *philosophes*, proved to be infinitely more exploitable by the traditionalists. It is, in fact, quite possible that, as a group, the *philosophes* seriously misjudged Hume's capacity to further their cause. An anonymous eighteenth-century commentator of the Hume-Rousseau quarrel obliquely suggested that this was the case:

> You are aware no doubt that our philosophers had fallen into great disrepute, at the time they concluded that David Hume would make a suitable recruit for their sect and would help to raise it up. He was a foreigner, imperturbably stolid, bold in his speculations, and sufficiently well behaved in his actions. He had written the History of his country for England, and four volumes of philosophy for France. His History, which had little success in London, succeeded very well in Paris, among our philosophers and their disciples, because of the four volumes of philosophy that buttressed their principles. They spoke of it with great enthusiasm: it was purchased, scarcely read, and praised to the skies.[90]

That Hume was more routinely praised than carefully read by the *philosophe* party is entirely possible. With the exception of the Turgot-Hume correspondence which we shall examine later and in which are clearly apparent the genuine differences that separated the Scottish philosopher's rather pessimistic, perhaps complacent, acceptance of the *status quo* and the young Intendant's eagerly optimistic hopes for change, the many letters Hume received from his *philosophe* friends seem strangely misdirected. Helvétius flatters himself, at the beginning of a letter to Hume in

89. *Oeuvres complètes de Bergier*, publiées par M. l'Abbé Migne, Paris, 1855, VIII. 228.

90. *Réflexions posthumes sur le grand procès de Jean-Jacques avec David* (1767), p. 12.

1759, that he is in almost total agreement with his correspondent concerning ethical motivation. A few lines farther along in his letter, however, he shows that nothing could be more distant from the truth and displays an almost wilful tendency to ignore the fact that Hume's *Enquiry* specifically combats such simplistic "self-interest" theories as his own. D'Holbach, in a letter of August 1763, calls Hume one of the greatest philosophers of any age. There is evidence to show too that he had read, or at least that he owned, all of Hume's works and yet, again on the question of ethics, he maintained in several of his own compositions that only ignorant theologians deny self-interest as the basis of morality.[91]

We have perhaps another example of this basic lack of comprehension, I think, in Helvétius's rather earnest reaction to Hume's fairly ironically titled essay on the "perfect" commonwealth. Hume warns in his preliminary remarks that all plans of government that pre-suppose a great change in man's nature are "imaginary." He seems to intend, as he does so often in his epistemological inquiries, little more than a good intellectual exercise; but it is a game which we suspect Helvétius takes perhaps too seriously when he solemnly speculates in *De l'homme* on the practical applicability of the means Hume proposes.[92] D'Alembert, though perhaps Hume's closest friend in Paris, seems to labour under a somewhat similar misconception in a letter to the Scot introducing his neighbour and friend, the latitudinarian Abbé de Vauxcelles: "He is going to England," d'Alembert writes without any excessive

91. G.-J. Holland, in the most valuable of the many contemporary refutations of d'Holbach's *Système de la Nature,* pointed out on this question that Hume —who did defend ethical motivation as involving more than self-interest—could hardly be classed as an ignorant theologian. See *Réflexions philosophiques sur le Système de la Nature,* Paris, 1773, p. 129. Also in this work, in an analysis quite unusual before Kant, Holland uses Hume's causality doctrine to combat d'Holbach's determinism. (See ibid., pp. 5–6, 16–17.)

92. See *Oeuvres complettes de M. Helvétius,* Londres, 1781, IV. 268. This same essay was commented on at great length in the revolutionary period by Joseph-Michel-Antoine Servan, *Correspondance entre quelques hommes honnêtes,* Lausanne, 1795, III. 136–78. See also Joseph de Maistre, *Considérations sur la France* (1796) in *Oeuvres complètes,* I. 72–73.

appearance of irony, "in order to have the pleasure of shouting along with you 'Wilkes and Liberty!'...."[93] David Hume, it need hardly be said, never waved a *mouchoir à la Wilkes!*

5

THE SCOTTISH BOSSUET

Ideally for the *philosophes,* Hume's presentation of England in the *History* should have confirmed most of the polemical doctrine of Voltaire's famous *Lettres philosophiques,* holding up the English to the French as an enlightened, tolerant, politically and religiously emancipated nation. There is very little in the pages of Voltaire's *Letters* which was calculated to give comfort to the French except perhaps the general message that Corneille and Racine wrote better tragedies than Shakespeare.

But, quite to the contrary, there is much evidence to suggest that Hume's *History* was often used to show how wrong Voltaire actually was and to illustrate to the French how lucky they were not to be English. Gallic self-esteem, in the thirty years following the first appearance of the *Lettres philosophiques,* had taken some very hard knocks from France's intellectual leaders. Reaction was inevitable.

An example of how Hume's *History* was used by traditionalists to combat the *philosophes'* exploitation of England as a propaganda symbol can be found in the *Dictionnaire social et patriotique* of the French lawyer Claude-Rigobert Lefebvre de Beauvray. Published in 1770, his work, bearing the epigraph "Be English in London and French in Paris," was intended as a remedy for the disease of *philosophisme anglais,* seen thirty years later by some extreme commentators of the Right as one of the chief causes of the Revolution.

93. *Letters of Eminent Persons,* p. 214.

Voltaire had spoken of the English as tolerant in religion, moderate and free in politics and, most important of all, profound in their philosophical thinking. If only, Voltaire seemed to be saying, France took England for its model, then all would be well.

Lefebvre de Beauvray disagreed vehemently. Quoting as evidence Hume's sentiments on England's lack of an equivalent of the French Academy, he stated that the city of Paris by itself had more to offer the intellectual than the whole of Great Britain.[94]

As for England's hideous "republican" liberty, so often praised by the *encyclopédistes,* de Beauvray proposed the following counterarguments in his article "Frondeurs":

> We are harangued every day on how little liberty is afforded under monarchical government....
>
> To silence these critics, I shall ask them only to weigh the following considerations, set out in good faith by Mr. Hume himself, in his *Histoire de la Maison de Stuart,* volume III, page 429 [VIII. 143–44]: "Government is instituted in order to restrain the fury and injustice of the people; and being always founded on opinion, not on force, it is dangerous to weaken, by these speculations, the reverence which the multitude owe to authority.... Or should it be found impossible to restrain the license of human disquisitions, it must be acknowledged that the doctrine of obedience ought alone to be *inculcated* and that the exceptions, which are rare, ought seldom or never to be mentioned in popular reasonings and discourses. Nor is there any danger that mankind, by this prudent reserve, should universally degenerate into a state of abject servitude."[95]

The bloody revolutions of England's history strongly suggest to de Beauvray that liberty is not a worthwhile political goal. Hume's paraphrased opinion of the British parliamentary leaders during the Civil War is seen as sufficient proof of this point:

> "If one cannot deny that the first group (the extreme supporters of English liberty) had more noble aims and held views more advan-

94. *Dictionnaire social et patriotique ou précis raisonné des connaissances relatives à l'économie morale, civile et politique,* Par M.C.R.L.F.D.B.A.A.P.D.P., Amsterdam, 1770, p. 141.

95. Ibid., pp. 176–78.

tageous to mankind, it must also be admitted that their methods are more difficult to justify. . . . Obliged to curry favour with the Populace, they saw themselves obliged to applaud its folly, or to fall in with its rage. . . ." (*Hist. de la Maison de Stuart,* t. 1 & 6.)[96]

Hume is especially commended as a "judicious writer" for having analysed with great truth and force the character of the usurper Cromwell. Cromwell was not just the worst of these parliamentary leaders; no man since Mohammed, de Beauvray affirms, had exhibited to the same degree such a harmful mixture of genius and low cunning.[97]

Voltaire had painted a very rosy picture of religious toleration in England; each Englishman, we remember, is seen as going to heaven by the road of his choice. Hume, in his descriptions of the Civil War period, gives us a rather different version of things and, still according to Lefebvre de Beauvray, his picture is one which deprives the British people of any right to accuse other nations of religious persecution:

> Never was there an Inquisition like that instigated by the Puritans of England and the Covenanters of Scotland. The supposedly religious confederation known as the Covenant brought fire and sword to all parts of the Three Kingdoms. It was, in a sense, this league that prepared the horrific tragedy whose outcome was so fatal to the royal family and still causes sons to lament the crime of their fathers.
>
> Never, perhaps, has any writer preached humanity in harsher tones, or liberty in more despotic terms, than the author of the *Émile.* Similarly, those who make a great show of tolerance often reveal a most intolerant character. Without themselves deigning to tolerate anyone, they want everyone to tolerate them.
>
> We are confirmed in this opinion by the singular admission of an English historian: "It must be acknowledged, to the disgrace of that age and of the British Isles, that the disorders in Scotland entirely, and those in England mostly, proceeded from so mean and contemptible an origin, such as aversion to the surplice, the rails placed about the altar, the liturgy, embroidered copes, the use of

96. Ibid., pp. 179–80.
97. Ibid., pp. 225–26.

the ring in marriage and of the cross in baptism." (See *l'Histoire de la Maison de Stuart sur le trône d'Angleterre*, t. 2, p. 327.)[98]

De Beauvray also cites Hume on the advantages of the monarchical form of government as compared with the English "republican" system.[99] In support of such anti-liberal views, the article "Liberté" of the *Dictionnaire* reproduces a long quotation from Hume which de Beauvray interprets as a lesson to the French on the worthlessness of England's much-vaunted Magna Carta.[100]

Intellectually backward, intolerant in religion and bloody in politics, the English are seen by de Beauvray as perversely wrong even in the way that they treat their only good historian, the judicious David Hume: "It is far from being the case that Mr. Hume's work has received an equally favourable welcome from all Englishmen. Some reproach him his Scottish birth and his predilection for the Court party. As a consequence they deny him the acclaim his writings and research deserve. If they persist in the assertion that Mr. Hume is not a good historian, then England does not yet have a national history and can never have one."[101] Not only is Hume a great historian, he is, "among all the political philosophers, the one who is most familiar with the interests and resources of his country."[102]

We see that it was only too easy, albeit with a certain measure of misrepresentation, for *anti-philosophes* like de Beauvray to interpret much of Hume as supporting the cause of the *ancien régime* against the lessons of Voltaire's *Lettres philosophiques*. Voltaire had

98. Ibid., pp. 257–58.

99. Ibid., pp. 356, 365, 469, 514–15.

100. Ibid., pp. 275–78.

101. Ibid., p. 284.

102. Ibid., p. 446. Readers of de Beauvray's *Dictionnaire* may be somewhat surprised after such praise to discover that in a parallel of English and French thinkers matching Hobbes and Gassendi, Shaftesbury and Montaigne, and in which no English equivalent of Montesquieu can be found, Hume is labelled the English equivalent of Buffier. (Ibid., p. 26.) The mystery is solved, however, when we encounter, buried away in another part of the *Dictionnaire,* proof that de Beauvray considered Buffier to be "the most judicious, and perhaps the most profound, of all our philosophers" (p. 329).

also praised the English for their civic virtues. He had especially applauded the English nobility for its modern commercial spirit and contrasted its efforts at honest capitalism with the nonexistent contributions of the foppishly ornamental French *petits-maîtres* who refused to engage in trade and commerce because of feudal prejudices. To show his feelings in this respect, Voltaire had even set a precedent in French theatre by dedicating his tragedy *Zaïre* to an English businessman.

But was England really such a model island of patriots and philosophers? Another French lawyer, Basset de la Marelle, asked the question in a speech delivered in 1762 to the Académie de Lyon. His answer, given while the Seven Years' War was still in progress, was, of course, vehemently negative. What is significant for us is that he too found proofs for his arguments in the impartial Mr. Hume. Hume frankly admitted, for example, that the English at the time of the Norman Conquest showed very little of that patriotism which they liked to boast of as almost hereditary in their nation.[103] Moreover, there was little to admire in Britain's modern commercial conquests. The British attitude to trade formed the basis of a vicious imperialism and was a constant cause of England's unjust wars. The British Cabinet had always known that its unruly subjects had either to be amused or to be feared:

> To avoid being reduced to this last extremity, it seeks to keep its restless population occupied. If the people fall into a state of calm, it is always a sign of danger ahead, of stormy times or revolution; it seeks therefore to engage them on the continent in matters foreign to their interests, matters it represents to them as their own; it holds up the dominion of the seas as an Englishman's natural right, to the exclusion of all other nations; it tempts the greed of its citizens with projects to capture, to the detriment of all other nations, through commercial enterprise in both the New World and the Old, the wealth of the entire universe.... And if such enterprises turn out to be ruinous for the nation, it lulls the people with celebrations of these glorious triumphs that in fact exhaust it. That is why one of the most astute political thinkers of England (Mr. Hume, *Of the Balance*

---

103. *La différence du patriotisme national chez les François et chez les Anglois,* Lyon, 1762, pp. 16–17. The author was executed during the Terror.

of Power) states that above half of England's wars with France, and all its public debts, are owing more to its own imprudent vehemence than to the ambition of its neighbours....[104]

Let us proceed now to examine the writings of a number of French traditionalists who exploited Hume's impartiality as they defended not only the *ancien régime*'s national self-esteem and its politics but its religion as well. Here too the *philosophes*' false brother, David Hume, was deemed to have made valuable contributions. Immediately after the French publication of his *Philosophical essays,* for example, he was recognized by yet another enemy of Voltaire, the Abbé Trublet, as a useful source of ideas against the current irreligion. Voltaire and the *philosophes* had made a great man of John Locke and had praised especially Locke's rejection of innate ideas. In the *Journal Chrétien* of 1758 Abbé Trublet applauded the "judicious" Hume for having shown at last that Locke's ideas on this subject, as well as on many other subjects, were totally confused.[105]

It is a strange irony that the *philosophes,* who at this time praised Hume so highly as a kindred spirit, had failed to recognize his originality in epistemology even as Christian apologists, however insincerely, were using Hume's theory of knowledge to attack the very basis of Enlightenment philosophy. Hume's scepticism, perhaps even charitably viewed as an unavoidable first step toward fideism, seemed particularly useful to Trublet against the dogmatic conclusions of rationalism. In the same way, the French abbé had earlier defended Berkeley against the charge made by some Catholic apologists that the Irish bishop's strange idealism was impious. British philosophers, it had to be admitted, could be rather eccentric but they were "unequally erroneous" and proper distinctions had to be made if one rejected them.[106] With such dis-

104. Ibid., pp. 60–62. French *anglophobes* of the Napoleonic era seized upon similar passages from Hume's writings. See, for example, the anonymous pamphlet, *Le peuple anglais bouffi d'orgueil, de bière et de thé, jugé au tribunal de la raison,* Paris, An IX–1803, pp. 67–87.

105. August 1758, IV. 59–63. The same debate is repeated in Abbé Chaudon's *Dictionnaire anti-philosophique,* Avignon, 1767, pp. 375–77.

106. See ibid., May 1759, III. 91–92; March 1760, II. 36–38.

tinctions in mind, Trublet and other eighteenth-century apologists occasionally attempted to revive the old technique of retortion, the rhetorical engine of war that had earlier been used with success against the Protestants and rationalists of the Renaissance.

David Hume's scepticism, with its dialectic based on the maximum multiplication of view-points, was particularly vulnerable to exploitation by this technique. The *philosophes* were not to be allowed the satisfaction of thinking that all of modern philosophy supported their cause. They prided themselves on having recourse to reason alone, but if a sceptic could show, as David Hume, for example, had shown, that many of their arguments were based on Lockian "acts of faith," then that sceptic, though not a religious man, could be useful in the defence of religion. Hume was not really an angel of truth, but he could be spirited away from his evil brothers and put to work against their incredulity. "Monsieur Trublet's purpose in most of the articles that appear throughout this journal," notes the Abbé Joannet, editor of the *Journal Chrétien*, "... has always been to remove from the rosters of impiety and irreligion the men of letters whom our so-called philosophers have had the vanity to list as supporters of materialism and incredulity."[107]

In 1768, although all of Hume's works were by then on the *Index,* the future cardinal, Hyacinthe-Sigismond Gerdil, showed that even some of the higher church officials were on occasion able to view David Hume in this same friendly light. In his *Discours sur la divinité de la religion chrétienne,* for example, Gerdil attacked the *philosophes* for their irreverent views on the lives of the Christian saints. Happily, there was a remedy for their blindness:

> More judicious authors have remedied this failing with more accurate studies, based on authentic documentation. If among those persons who have fallen away from religion because of unfortunate prejudices there can be found minds of rectitude and equity and hearts inclined to virtue, what better way for them to be cured of their prejudices and reconciled to Christianity than by reading the life of Jesus Christ and the lives of the saints who, imbued with the spirit of Jesus Christ, have exemplified in all of their conduct the

107. Ibid., September 1762, p. 5.

grandeur and simplicity of the Gospels? There they will find human nature ennobled by the most exalted virtues, practiced in full brilliance and without ostentation.[108]

Apparently a perusal of Hume could be added profitably to readings from the gospels. Gerdil continues: "The portrait that Mr. Hume has sketched of the celebrated Lord Chancellor Thomas More can serve to substantiate the idea we bring forward of Christian justice in all of life's stations and situations." Gerdil then quotes Hume's portrait of the English saint at length.[109]

In a much more significant work of 1769, the *Discours philosophiques sur l'homme considéré relativement à l'état de nature et à l'état social,* Gerdil once again returned to Hume for inspiration and anticipated in his use of the Scot's political ideas the almost identical lines of reasoning proposed later on by such counterrevolutionary ideologists as Maury, Ferrand, de Bonald, and de Maistre. Already author of an anti-*Emile* and an anti–*Contrat social,* Gerdil set out again to attack the artificiality of contract theory. Society, he asserted, is a moral and political fact of man's nature. Quoting Hume's own analysis of the subject, Gerdil agreed that man is not solely motivated by self-interest. Man is born for society; the contracts of Hobbes, Locke, and Rousseau are false, the concept of natural equality is a harmful myth; ultimately, the organization of man in society is a reflection of the government of God.[110]

One is not surprised to find this learned ecclesiastic defending theocracy as the true basis of government. What is mildly astonishing, however, is the way he transforms David Hume's social naturalism into a specific defence of the divine-right doctrine attacked by Hume in the same essay in which he assails contract theory. Little more than a clever transition is required to perform this textual miracle. Society, it is agreed, is not based on an arbitrary contract but on the natural fact of man's sociability. The origin of

108. *Oeuvres du Cardinal Gerdil de l'ordre des Barnabites,* publiées par M. l'Abbé Migne, Paris, 1863, p. 989.

109. Loc. cit.

110. Ibid., pp. 1326–30. Gerdil, incidentally, also quotes a fragment of Hume's *Natural History of Religion* as evidence against deism (p. 1393).

public authority does not rest, then, in the free consent of individuals who have given up for this purpose part of their natural rights. Public authority takes all its force from the right that nature implicitly gives every society to see to its well-being and survival:

> Sovereign power in society is thus established by nature's law, and since natural law is decreed by God, it follows that sovereign power is founded on the very order established by God for the preservation and well-being of mankind: *Qui potestati resistit, ordinationi Dei resistit* [Whosoever therefore resisteth the power, resisteth the ordinance of God]: thus spoke the Apostle.

> Mr. Hume pays homage to this truth in his twenty-fifth moral and political essay: Once we admit a general providence, he writes, "and allow that all events in the universe are conducted by an uniform plan, and directed to wise purposes," we cannot deny that the Deity is the ultimate author of all government. And "as it is impossible for the human race to subsist, at least in any comfortable or secure state, without the protection of government, this institution must certainly have been intended by that beneficent Being, who means the good of all his creatures: And as it has universally, in fact, taken place, in all countries, and all ages, we may conclude, with still greater certainty, that it was intended by that omniscient Being, who can never be deceived by any event or operation."[111]

Gerdil applauds this argument as entirely solid. Unfortunately, Hume spoils his line of reasoning somewhat by his subsequent conclusions. Gerdil then quotes the passage in Hume's essay "Of the Original Contract," which his friend, the Abbé Maury, another "Hume-inspired" future Cardinal of the Church, did not dare cite later while debating the concept of sovereignty with Mirabeau on the floor of the Assemblée Nationale.[112] If the nature of things and providential arrangement are equated, the authority exercised by a pirate or a common robber is, Hume archly contends, as inviolable as that of any lawful prince. Gerdil gives the obviously confused but no doubt well-intentioned Monsieur Hume a kindly correction on this point:

111. Ibid., pp. 1414–15.
112. See below, chapter III. pp. 107–8.

"God who means the good of all his creatures, also intends that they be governed": that is Mr. Hume's principle. The establishment of government conforms to the *intentions of the omniscient Being,* and the sovereign occupies a place in society that is designated expressly by Providence; but the abuse that a bandit makes of his physical power in order to rob the passerby is a crime against the laws of God, who, while allowing this evil, disapproves of it, condemns and punishes it. How then could Mr. Hume suggest that the authority of the most lawful prince is not more sacred, or more inviolable than that of a brigand?[113]

After thus disposing of this minor lapse in what is otherwise seen as a brilliant argument, Gerdil returns to base his conclusion on Hume's authority:

We must therefore look upon the establishment of government not only as the simple effect of *this secret influence that animates all of nature* but also as an institution that God desires, that conforms to the intentions of the all wise Being and to his supreme beneficence. This conformity that Mr. Hume acknowledges is revealed to us by right reason, informs us by clear and immediate logic that we cannot attack the sovereign authority of government without at the same time defying the intentions, the laws, and the will of the omniscient Being. This proves sufficiently that such authority is sacred and inviolable. What reason demonstrates on this subject is fully confirmed by the testimony of the Scriptures which reveal to us in a more distinct and authentic manner the will of the Supreme Being. To be entirely convinced on this point, one has only to read the third book of Bossuet's *Politique tirée de l'Ecriture Sainte.*[114]

It can be easily imagined how Hume's alleged testimony in favour of what is in fact a full-blown system of theocracy was seen as all the more valuable by religious conservatives precisely because it did not come from Bossuet but rather from the sceptical and therefore "impartial" Hume. Joseph de Maistre, who was later probably even more thoroughly "influenced" by Hume in this direction, expressed the belief that one could trust such a man to

113. Ibid., p. 1416.
114. Ibid., p. 1417.

speak the truth because, as he tells us, "Hume . . . believed in nothing and consequently held back nothing."[115]

On another matter, the Jesuit Claude-François Nonnotte, remembered today especially as an adversary of Voltaire's *Essai sur les Moeurs* and *Dictionnaire philosophique,* also occasionally invoked the testimony of David Hume. In the article "Christianisme" of his own antidotal *Dictionnaire philosophique de la religion,* Nonnotte set out to disprove the common *philosophes'* contention that Christ's kingdom has been the scene of mankind's bloodiest wars. Christianity, he maintained to the contrary, has been a civilizing and beneficial factor in good government throughout the ages:

> . . . Christianity has had a civilizing effect on customs, it has checked the spirit of sedition, it has uprooted and destroyed the seeds of civil war. It is therefore undeniable that it has been a force for good in the universe.
>
> These same frenzied tubthumpers who constantly proclaim Christianity to be a religion of disorder and discord, a disruptive force that overturns states, kingdoms, and empires, also seek to depict it as a bloodthirsty religion, the most dangerous to crowned heads.
>
> In that, they are not of the same opinion as one of the most celebrated learned men of this century who, though a Protestant, acknowledges that, of all religions, Catholicism is the most favourable to sovereigns. (Hume, *Hist. de la Maison de Stuart.*)[116]

Nonnotte also attacks Voltaire for what he considers to be the French historian's too favourable attitude to the hypocritical assassin Cromwell and to the entire Puritan rebellion.[117] Moreover, Voltaire lies in his teeth when he praises Elizabeth as tolerant and attacks Mary as a persecutor: that "wise author, Monsieur Hume"

---

115. *Du Pape* (1817); in *Oeuvres complètes,* II. 413.

116. *Dictionnaire philosophique de la religion, où l'on établit les points de la religion attaqués par les incrédules, et où l'on répond à toutes leurs objections.* Nouvelle édition, Besançon, 1774, I. 368–69.

117. An example of Voltaire's opinion of the Protector may be found in the article "Cromwell" of the *Dictionnaire philosophique,* in *Oeuvres complètes de Voltaire,* XVIII. 294–99; see also *Essai sur les Moeurs,* ibid., XIII. 74–82.

in his "excellent *Histoire*" easily proves how wrong the great infidel is in both cases.[118]

In an article attacking d'Alembert's eulogy of George Keith, Hereditary Earl Marischal of Scotland and Governor of Neuchâtel, the future counter-revolutionary journalist Abbé Royou also illustrated how it was possible to appeal to Hume for aid in protecting the ideological inertia of the *ancien régime*.[119]

D'Alembert in his *Eloge* had spoken disparagingly of the Stuart kings and had referred specifically to James II as Jesuit-inspired and intolerant. As we have already noted, eighteenth-century French Catholics seemed to find it particularly important to defend James II's memory: "...the Jesuitism of King James," Abbé Royou insists, "is one of those popular opinions that are spawned by hatred and adopted through gullible malevolence; it has, however, never been testified to by any credible witness. *Hume* does not speak of it...."[120] As for the alleged intolerance of James II, that too, Royou affirms, is a malicious lie. Quite to the contrary, James was forced to leave the English throne because he was excessively tolerant. "Had he favoured the atrocious and sanguinary laws of the Anglican sect, he and his family would still be enjoying the entire affection of his subjects, earned for him from the beginning by his virtues. But he wished *to grant complete freedom of conscience to all sects within his kingdom,* and to mitigate the harshness of the laws against Catholics, without, however, as he persisted in asserting to his last breath (Hume, t. 6, p. 536), intruding on the

118. Nonnotte, op. cit., I. 370; III. 328–29. See also his *Erreurs de Monsieur de Voltaire,* Paris, 1770, I. 273–77; II. 407–10.

119. Abbé Royou's publication appeared in the *Année littéraire,* June 1779, IV. 73–113, and was reprinted in S.-N.-H. Linguet's *Annales politiques, civiles et littéraires du dix-huitième siècle,* 1779, VI. 15–48. Linguet, himself an enemy of d'Alembert, also lauded Hume's impartiality and quoted his authority in 1774 to prove that so-called English liberty was nothing more than the muddle-headed delusion of those who wished to foment political disorder. (*Oeuvres de M. Linguet,* Londres, 1774, II. 139, 244.) It is well known that Linguet, following a two-year imprisonment in the Bastille, was destined to revise his opinion somewhat on this last point.

120. Linguet, *Annales,* VI. 21; *Année littéraire,* 1779, IV. 77.

privileges and prerogatives of the Protestants. That was the source of his misfortunes!"[121]

D'Alembert's radical view of Stuart intolerance inspired this brother-in-law of Fréron and future editor of the counter-revolutionary journal *l'Ami du Roi* to attack the *philosophes* generally for endlessly speaking of tolerance and, at the same time, for being highly intolerant toward Catholics. Coming back to d'Alembert's portrait of James II, he proposed to show what that monarch was really like: "Let us contrast this truly *odious* and *culpable* depiction of the conduct of King James with the portrait drawn by Mr. Hume: a Protestant in origin, an unbeliever by profession, a subject and partisan of the House of Hanover: his authority should not be suspect to our panegyrist. Here is how he ends his history of James II...."[122] Royou's attack concludes with a triumphant confrontation of the impartial Hume and his vanquished *philosophe* friend d'Alembert.

The last example we will consider with regard to the influence of Hume's conservative image in the pre-revolutionary period is much along the same lines. It cannot be ignored, however, because of the sheer quantity of references to Hume's works involved and because of the importance of the Abbé Nicolas-Sylvestre Bergier, the apologist in question.

Abbé Bergier saw himself as rather like a new Samson sent by God to destroy the Philistines of eighteenth-century French philosophy. Some idea of the stature of his attacks may be had, perhaps, from the fact that, for a time, he frequented the d'Holbach *côterie* and that rival apologists occasionally complained that he treated his *philosophe* opponents with more respect and temperance than he accorded the Jansenists.[123]

The extent of Hume's philosophical influence on Bergier,

---

121. Linguet, VI. 21–23; *Année littéraire,* IV. 79–80.

122. Linguet, VI. 23–24; *Année littéraire,* IV. 81.

123. See the correspondence of Bergier published by Léonce Pingaud in the proceedings of the *Académie des sciences, belles-lettres et arts de Besançon* (1891). Bergier, whose dates are 1718–90, spent his last days editing the massive three-volume *Théologie* section of the *Encyclopédie Méthodique* (Paris, 1788–90).

following in the tradition already established by Trublet, is a question that need not detain us here.[124] More important to our purpose is an examination of the religious, social, and political image of David Hume that emerges from the mass of references found in the Abbé's works published between 1765 and the Revolution.

Any statement made by Hume that could be construed or, to be quite frank, half-construed and even misconstrued as testifying in favour of religion or of the Catholic Church is laboriously noted down in Bergier's works. The Abbé records emphatically, for example, that Hume "has expressed himself in a most forceful manner on the beneficial effects of religion: 'Those who attempt to disabuse mankind of religious prejudices, may, for aught I know, be good reasoners, but I cannot allow them to be good citizens and politicians; since they free men from one restraint upon their passions and make the infringement of the laws of equity and of society, in this respect, more easy and secure.'"[125] Like Voltaire quoting the Bible, Bergier does not hesitate to repeat his favourite Hume passages and he used this particular one, wrenched from the essay "Of Providence," in at least four different works.

The *philosophes* maintain that religion is unnecessary in a well-run society. But, objects Bergier, "no nation since the beginning of the world has possessed good civil laws, sound polity and government, without religion. No legislator has set out to bring under the rule of law a people deprived of a belief in God and in a future life. It is sheer folly to consider feasible an enterprise that no sage has ever dared to attempt. 'Look out for a people, entirely destitute of religion,' states Mr. Hume; 'if you find them at all, be assured,

---

124. Bergier, unlike the *philosophes,* gives ample proof of having recognized the originality of Hume's contributions to epistemology. Like Holland (see *supra* p. 34, n. 91), he makes clever polemical use of Hume's analysis of causation against the determinism of such materialist philosophers as d'Holbach. See in *Oeuvres complètes de Bergier* the following references: I. 38–42, 61–72, 624–30, 691–93; II. 40–44, 713; III. 749–50; IV. 786–87; V. 385–87; VI. 340–42, 358, 561–62, 602–15, 696–97, 941–42, 1002–3, 1031–32, 1346–47; VII. 813; VIII. 412–13, 527. It is fairly evident, however, that Bergier merely exploits Hume's scepticism against the philosophical dogmatists. He makes it clear, at the same time, that he wholeheartedly disapproves of the Scottish philosopher's irreligion.

125. Ibid., VI. 137, 451; III. 1357; VIII. 195.

that they are but a few degrees removed from brutes.' (*Hist. nat. de la relig.*, p. 133)....From this undeniable fact we may conclude that religion is an integral part, so to speak, of man's constitution...."[126]

Hume is also cited against those who maintain that religion takes its origins in the duplicity of priests and the credulity of the masses: "It would be fruitless to reply to the noisy clamours of those who claim that religion was invented by priests out of self-interest. First of all, it is absurd to suppose that there were priests before there was religion. Mr. Hume, who is anything but biased in their favour, acknowledges in good faith that they are not the original authors of religion or of superstition; that at most they may have helped to foster it. (*Hist. nat. de la relig.*, [section] 14, p. 127.)"[127]

Bergier defends religious belief as a normal part of man's nature. Is it sensible, then, he asks, to spend one's lifetime questioning a duty which is born with us, which makes for the happiness of virtuous people and determines our eternal fate? Even Hume—for the moment a Hume *pascalisant*—was forced to admit that no good can come of religious scepticism: "David Hume, a zealous partisan of philosophical scepticism, after setting forth all the sophisms he could devise for its foundation, is forced to admit that no good can come of it, that it is ridiculous to attempt to destroy reason by argument and ratiocination; that nature, more powerful than philosophical pride, will always maintain its rights over all abstract speculations. We can conclude without hesitation that the same is true of religion, since it is grafted on nature...."[128]

Even a certain fanaticism in a nation is preferable to the total absence of religion: "Fanaticism occurs, moreover, only when the people are much agitated and religion appears to be in peril; it is a passing frenzy that grows weak from its own efforts, and its crises cannot be frequent. 'Its fury,' writes Mr. Hume, 'is like that of thunder and tempest, which exhaust themselves in a little time, and leave the air more calm and pure than before.' Atheism is a slow

126. Ibid., VI. 156–57, 1347.
127. Ibid., VI. 105.
128. Ibid., V. 385–87.

poison that destroys the principle of social being and its effects are incurable...."[129]

With Hume defending religious fanaticism in small doses and even proving to the Abbé's satisfaction that the ancients were very much in need of Christ's mission,[130] let us now turn to hear what he has to say, still according to Bergier, specifically in defence of Christianity and the Catholic Church.

Bergier quotes from Hume's *Tudors* to show the important rôle played by the Church during the Dark Ages: "The barbarian nations that ravaged Europe in the fifth century and afterwards would have smothered even the last vestige of human knowledge, had religion not opposed barriers to their fury.... If some traces of humanity, morals, order, and learning are to be found in the fifteenth century, it is undeniably to Christianity that we must be grateful."[131] We remember that the Protestant minister Formey had cited Hume to the same effect. The clergy, Hume is quoted as maintaining, also served during this time as a barrier against political despotism.[132]

Attacking the Reformation, Bergier finds himself able to quote profitably page after page of Hume's works. Not only did the clergy of the pre-Reformation Church stand as a barrier against despotism, but the union of the Western Churches under one sovereign pontiff facilitated commerce and was a highly desirable, politically unifying principle. The wealth and splendour of the Church had the effect of encouraging the arts. Though some corruption in the Church indeed existed, it was not the main cause of the Reformation, nor was the issue of religion the main cause of the massacres which took place in England, Scotland, and Ireland at that time.[133] After giving consecutively five "impartial" Hume quotations to support this view, Bergier adds: "Here, it seems to me, is confirmation of everything we have already said about the so-

129. Ibid., VI. 149.
130. Ibid., VI. 269, 289.
131. Ibid., II. 34–35.
132. Ibid., VIII. 571.
133. Ibid., V. 82; VII. 896, 902; VIII. 228.

called Reformation, and it is a Protestant who provides it for us."[134] Were the Protestants right, Bergier asks, to attack the Church for depriving the faithful of scripture in the vernacular? "David Hume tells us that in England, after the advent of the so-called Reformation, access to the English translation of the Bible had to be withdrawn from the people for fear of the consequences and the fanaticism fostered by such readings. (*Tudor*, II. p. 426.)"[135] Hume also states that the destruction of the monasteries at the time of the Reformation in England did no possible good to the country: "A fine lesson," Bergier adds, "for those who would seek to reform the wealth of the clergy!"[136] For his defence of the utility of convents and for his denial that the celibacy of priests has base political motives, Hume receives once again the French Abbé's benediction. The Scot had shown on these matters "more discernment than our *philosophes*."[137] Like Louis de Bonald later on, Bergier also cites Hume's authority to support his arguments against divorce.[138]

One last example of Bergier's use of Hume must suffice although it by no means exhausts the list of references scattered throughout the Abbé's voluminous works. After stating on the great historian's authority that the *philosophes* were wrong to attach intolerance exclusively to religious opinions, that, in fact, any opinions men hold dear, whether out of vanity or self-interest, can occasion intolerance and that, consequently, atheists can be found who are just as intolerant as believers,[139] Bergier approached the problem of toleration in seventeenth-century France:

> The question is to determine whether the Calvinists had a legitimate claim, whether the government was obligated, in terms of natural law, to satisfy it, and whether it could do so as a matter of sound

134. Ibid., VIII. 228.
135. Ibid., VII. 925–26.
136. Ibid., VIII. 584.
137. Ibid., VIII. 538–39.
138. Ibid., III. 237–38; IV. 571; VIII. 1302.
139. Ibid., I. 329.

policy. In this regard, we invite dispassionate consideration of the following:

... The character of the first Calvinist ministers is well known, as is the nature of their doctrine; they taught that the Catholic religion was an abomination and that its adherents were denied salvation ... that the Church of Rome was the whore of Babylon and the Pope the antichrist; that it was necessary to abjure, proscribe, and exterminate that religion by all possible means.... David Hume acknowledges that in Scotland, in the year 1542, a bare toleration of the new preachers would have been equivalent to a deliberate plan to destroy the national religion; he proves the point by his account of the fanatical conduct of these sectaries, *Histoire de la Maison de Tudor,* t. III, p. 9; t. IV, p. 59 and 104; t. V, p. 213, etc. In France the situation was no different. Where the Calvinists managed to gain control, no practice of the Catholic religion was allowed: by what right then could they claim that their own should be tolerated?[140]

We see how Hume's impartiality, far from supporting the *philosophes,* often served the cause of their enemies. Apologists like Bergier and Gerdil quote Hume as naturally, almost, as they quote Bossuet. In fact, they both sometimes quote Hume and Bossuet together on the same point. Moreover, since Bossuet's authority meant much less to the eighteenth-century *philosophes* than Hume's, there was all the more reason to prefer Hume. Here was a Protestant Bossuet, nay even an atheist Bossuet, saying all the right things apparently and yet he was a member of the enemy camp and highly praised by Voltaire and d'Holbach. Bergier's sincerity and fairness in many of these quotations can certainly be questioned, but it is equally evident that he felt, at least some of the time, that he and Hume were in genuine agreement. Even during the Hume-Rousseau quarrel his sympathies were not with the "religious" Rousseau, but totally with the unbeliever Hume.[141] It is significant too that the *philosophes* themselves finally found it impossible to ignore Bergier's tricks. After he had quoted Hume for

140. Ibid., IV. 286–87; VII. 890–96.

141. See Bergier's letter to the lawyer Jacquin, from Besançon, 28 April 1767 (ibid., VIII. 1490).

about the fourth time to the effect that those who disabuse the human race of its religious prejudices may be good reasoners but are certainly not good citizens or legislators,[142] the d'Holbach *côterie* decided to mount a protest in their anonymously published *Recueil Philosophique ou Mélange de Pièces sur la Religion & la Morale.*[143] The work attacks Bergier on this very point:

> Monsieur Bergier, as is customary with theologians, ends by indicting his adversaries as disturbers of the peace and as bad citizens; he bases his claim on the authority of a renowned philosopher (Mr. Hume) who acknowledges that those who attack the established religion of a country may be good reasoners, but are clearly bad citizens. We will answer Monsieur Bergier by pointing out that it is scarcely fitting for theologians and priests to accuse philosophers of causing disorder in the state. We will say to him that it is theology, with its shameful abuses of power, that has been in a position over nearly the last eighteen centuries to disturb the peace of nations;...We will say to him that...we are no longer in the twelfth century...and that humanity, weary of authority, seems willing, finally, to have recourse to common sense and reason.
>
> As for the opinion of Mr. Hume which seems to provide Monsieur Bergier with such a triumphant victory, we will respond by saying to him that the authority of a philosopher does not carry the same weight for other philosophers, as the authority of a Church Father or Council might for a theologian; we will say to him that Mr. Hume could have been mistaken in his judgement of those who oppose established opinion and that if he had taken careful note of the countless evils brought down on the world by Christianity, he would have been obliged to admit that those who forcefully attack prejudice and superstition are, on the contrary, very good citizens indeed. Mr. Hume himself has done so in a manner that has earned him, and rightly so, the great reputation he enjoys throughout Eu-

---

142. See *supra*, p. 48. The future counter-revolutionary theoretician Abbé Duvoisin also quotes the passage in 1780, adding that "the political usefulness of the dogma of an afterlife is so obvious that impiety itself has been obliged to acknowledge it" (*Essai polémique sur la religion naturelle*, in *Oeuvres complètes de Duvoisin, évêque de Nantes,* publiées par M. l'Abbé Migne, Montrouge, 1856, p. 146).

143. ...*par différents auteurs*, Londres, 1770; possibly edited by Naigeon and containing works by d'Holbach and others.

---

rope where his history and his philosophical writings are everywhere read and admired by all those who do not think like Monsieur l'Abbé Bergier.[144]

6

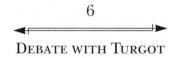

DEBATE WITH TURGOT

As their answer to Bergier indicates, the *philosophes* were fairly confident that Hume belonged, despite occasional appearances to the contrary, heart and soul to the camp of the d'Alemberts and d'Holbachs. Moreover, even though this first generation of *philosophes* saw the success of their cause as largely dependent on a victory over traditionalists in the religious controversy, they were probably quite willing to forgive not only David Hume's laziness or lack of militancy in not writing an ecclesiastical history but also the general ignorance of the harsher "religious" facts of life he at times displayed as when, for example, he confided naïvely to the astonished baron d'Holbach that he had never seen an atheist and that he did not believe such creatures existed.[145] Such errors were amusing or at least pardonable in a man who had already written so cleverly on miracles, divine providence, and the immortality of the soul. As for Hume's apparent lack of a liberally orientated political philosophy, the *philosophes* of this generation from about 1750 to 1770 could have no insurmountable objections on this point ei-

---

144. *Recueil philosophique*, II. 204–6. Bergier answered by pointing out that he was puzzled as to why Hume's testimony should not be used if he indeed had the great reputation his *philosophe* admirers attributed to him (Bergier, op. cit., VIII. 259). Ironically, the *Recueil philosophique* published at the same time, but anonymously, two of Hume's strongest dissertations, "Of the Immortality of the Soul" and "Of Suicide," both probably translated by d'Holbach. It also included in its pages some rather different comments by Hume on the clergy—chosen this time by the *philosophes* (*Recueil philosophique*, II. 237). All this was perhaps to show Bergier whose ally Hume really was. For the French Abbé's reactions to the two anonymous dissertations, see Bergier, op. cit., VIII. 262.

145. See Diderot's letter of 6 October 1765 to Sophie Volland; Lewinter, V. 946.

ther. Revolution, if not reform, was as far from their aims as it was from Hume's. Few *philosophes* showed any real objections to living under a political despot provided he, like Frederick the Great, for example, was witty and a good priest-hater as well.

As is well known, the intellectual mood in France was soon to change. A second generation of *philosophes* begins to emerge in the 1770s and 1780s, still anti-clerical—although this question was by now rather old hat—but more interested in investigating and pointing out the sins of kings than of priests. These last very definitely do not claim David Hume as an ally. There is even some apprehension on their part that he might be just what Trublet, Bergier, Nonnotte, Royou, Gerdil, Lefebvre de Beauvray, and others in their use of him had suggested he was—a treacherous enemy in disguise.

It is in the correspondence of Turgot and Hume exchanged between the years 1766 and 1768 that we catch perhaps our first real glimpse—and it is still only a glimpse—of what was to be a consciously acknowledged fundamental disagreement between Hume and the politically idealistic French intellectuals of this later period. Turgot was with d'Alembert one of Hume's closest friends on the continent. Unlike the other *philosophes,* however, he showed on the occasion of the Hume-Rousseau quarrel a certain unflattering if sincere reserve in judging the wrongs of the affair which left unsatisfied the wounded feelings of the Scottish historian. After receiving letters from Turgot in which Rousseau's ingratitude is called real but unpremeditated, more the result of madness than of villainy,[146] Hume could not help accusing the French physiocrat of "partiality" for the black-hearted *citoyen de Genève.*[147] This aspect of the correspondence will not concern us further here, but what is especially significant for us is the fact that it led finally to an open discussion between Hume and one of his liberal French admirers of their genuine political differences—differences which the earlier uncritical praise of Hume by the *philosophes* had all but totally obscured.

---

146. See *Letters of Eminent Persons,* pp. 139, 144–45, letters of 27 July and 7 September 1766.

147. Greig, op. cit., II. 91.

Hume opened the controversy by pointing out that Rousseau's writings, however eloquent, were extravagant and sophistical. Their tendency, moreover, was surely rather to do hurt than service to mankind.

In his reply the distinguished Intendant of Limoges, who was soon to attempt his great reforms and was already aware of the difficulties presented by ill-will and the routine immobility of privilege, defended Rousseau, and at the same time defended his own political involvement in the Enlightenment's hopes to improve the world. Speaking in the new political tones to be heard more and more frequently in France as 1789 approached, he warmly praised Rousseau's works:

> Unlike you, I am far from judging them to be harmful to the interests of mankind; on the contrary, I think that he is one of the authors who has contributed most to morals and the good of humanity. Far from reproaching him for having on this point set himself too much apart from common notions, I believe, on the contrary, that he has respected still too many prejudices. I think that he has not gone far enough along that road, but it is by following his road that we shall one day reach the goal of bringing mankind closer to equality, justice, and humanity.[148]

Turgot adds that of course Hume will not think he is defending Rousseau's early writings against the arts and sciences. These, he says, were the products of a beginning writer's vain desire to make his mark; Rousseau was consciously paradoxical here to avoid being trite. The *Contrat social,* however, is a different matter:

> In truth, this book sums up the precise distinction between the sovereign and the government; and that distinction offers a most luminous truth, one that settles for all time, no matter the form of government, our notions of the people's inalienable sovereignty. To my mind, *Emile* seems inspired by the purest morality ever taught in lesson form, although I think one could go even farther; but I shall be very careful not to tell you my ideas on that subject, for you would judge me to be even more mad than Rousseau.... [149]

148. *Letters of Eminent Persons,* pp. 150–51, letter of 25 March 1767.
149. Ibid., p. 152.

We have here, at last, the beginnings of an honest recognition of the vast distance between Hume's political views and those of the French reformers. Hume's *History* had been before the French reading public for several years already without eliciting anything approaching a similar response. Only the extreme right had taken grateful notice of his conservatism. Moreover, to the "lessons" of the *History* remarked upon by the *Journal de Trévoux*, Bergier, and others, had to be added the fairly explicit anti-liberal doctrine available in Hume's political essays. In these as well the French had been able to read Hume's opinion that the world was still too young and human experience too short to allow much in the way of scientifically valid political speculation. Hume had also declared that the contract theory and the corollary doctrine of the people's inalienable sovereignty were totally without foundation. Opinion, not contract, was at the basis of human government and most governments had, in fact, been founded on conquest or usurpation.[150] Hume implies too that those who reject the lessons of history in favour of *a priori* natural rights are to be condemned. Few changes in government can ever be wisely carried out on such "philosophical" grounds. Established government bears a sacred authority by the very fact that it is established. Resistance to it is always unwise and must be considered only as a last resort since nothing is more terrible to contemplate than the anarchy that would result from a complete dissolution of government:

> Did one generation of men go off the stage at once, and another succeed, as is the case with silk-worms and butterflies, the new race, if they had sense enough to choose their government, which surely is never the case with men, might voluntarily, and by general consent, establish their own form of civil polity, without any regard to the laws or precedents, which prevailed among their ancestors. But as human society is in perpetual flux, one man every hour going out of the world, another coming into it, it is necessary, in order to preserve stability in government, that the new brood should conform themselves to the established constitution, and nearly follow

150. It is interesting to note that the future *monarchien* Pierre-Victor Malouet quoted Hume's authority in rejecting the contract theory in 1777. See Jean-Baptiste-Antoine Suard, *Mélanges de littérature,* Paris, 1803–4, I. 277.

the path which their fathers, treading in the footsteps of theirs, had marked out to them. Some innovations must necessarily have place in every human institution, and it is happy where the enlightened genius of the age gives these a direction to the side of reason, liberty, and justice: but violent innovations no individual is entitled to make: they are even dangerous to be attempted by the legislature: more ill than good is ever to be expected from them: and if history affords examples to the contrary, they are not to be drawn into precedent, and are only to be regarded as proofs, that the science of politics affords few rules, which will not admit of some exceptions.... [151]

Hume may not have been entirely sure that the old gods existed but, in the best sceptical tradition, he held that they ought to be worshipped. An acquiescence in the *status quo,* a shrinking from change, a pessimistic desire to retrench, to set up comforting barriers against the "frenzy of liberty" permeates many of his personal comments on political events at this time. The course of history is cyclical; the new ideals of liberty and progress represent recurrent political delusions. In his answer to Turgot, Hume expressed a weary unwillingness to believe in man's ability to improve his lot by seeking such lofty goals:

I know you are one of those, who entertain the agreeable and laudable, if not too sanguine hope, that human society is capable of perpetual progress towards perfection, that the increase of knowledge will still prove favourable to good government, and that since the discovery of printing we need no longer dread the usual returns of barbarism and ignorance. Pray, do not the late events in this country[152] appear a little contrary to your system? Here is a people thrown into disorders (not dangerous ones, I hope) merely from the abuse of liberty, chiefly the liberty of the press; without any griev-

151. "Of the Original Contract" in Green and Grose, op. cit., I. 452–53. The passage just quoted, which first appeared in the 1777 edition of Hume's essays, corresponds with the increasing conservatism he expressed in the later revisions of his *History.* Hume found that the first editions of that work were still too full of "those foolish English prejudices" and he tells us in *My Own Life* that in "above a hundred alterations, which farther study, reading, or reflection, engaged me to make in the reigns of the two first Stuarts, I have made all of them invariably to the Tory side." (See Greig, op. cit., I. 5.)

152. The "Wilkes and Liberty!" riots.

ance, I do not only say, real, but even imaginary; and without any of them being able to tell one circumstance of government which they wish to have corrected: They roar liberty, though they have apparently more liberty than any people in the world; a great deal more than they deserve; and perhaps more than any men ought to have.... You see, I give you freely my views of things, in which I wish earnestly to be refuted: The contrary opinion is much more consolatory, and is an incitement to every virtue and laudable pursuit.[153]

With all the idealism and moderate optimism which he shared with the Enlightenment's better political prophets, Turgot returned Hume a frank rebuttal:

If my departure allowed me a few moments, I would add a word or two in defence of my ideas on the perfectibility and the perfecting of our poor species. These minor disorders now taking place before our eyes do not shake my confidence one whit; and I say, with more justification than the General of the Jesuits—*alios ventos alias tempestates vidimus....* [we have seen other winds, other storms]. Good government will not come without crises, and these will be accompanied by disorder. Should we blame enlightenment and liberty for guiding us through this turbulence to a happier state? Obviously not. Injuries will be suffered during our passage, of course! But will these be more harmful than the injuries suffered under the rule of tyranny and superstition that seeks to smother liberty and enlightenment, and strives to do so through means that, once things have progressed beyond a certain point, are either totally useless or entirely abominable, and often both one and the other? I doubt that you think so any more than I do. The people preoccupied with their necessities, the great with their pleasures, have no time to be savants and to shake off their prejudices on their own; but a consequence of the progress in knowledge is that one does not need to be a savant to have good sense and to popularize truths that today can be made convincing only with work and effort. Adieu, Monsieur—time is short and I must hurry....[154]

In fact time was running short; there were many important reforms to carry out; perhaps even, for others if not for Turgot,

153. Greig, op. cit., II. 180–81, letter of 16 June 1768.
154. *Letters of Eminent Persons,* p. 163, letter of 3 July 1768.

there was a revolution to prepare. Not long after, the unsuccessful minister Turgot would warn in fateful words his young King, Louis XVI, about the dangers of ineffective political leadership: "Never forget, Sire, that it was weakness that placed the head of Charles I on the block; ..."[155]

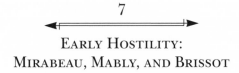

7

EARLY HOSTILITY:
MIRABEAU, MABLY, AND BRISSOT

Perhaps the earliest work by a future revolutionary expressing open dissatisfaction with Hume's political conservatism is Mirabeau's *Des lettres de cachet et des prisons d'état*. Himself a victim of the *lettre de cachet*, Mirabeau, composing this work in prison in 1778,[156] protested against all forms of ministerial despotism. Both natural and positive law, he affirmed, condemned arbitrary imprisonment.

Although, especially when dealing with the medieval period, Mirabeau occasionally cites Hume's authority and even refers to him as "this philosopher who was the first modern historian to rival the ancients,"[157] he cannot accept the timid reservations Hume seems to have concerning the protection of *habeas corpus*. Like Montesquieu in the *Esprit des Lois* (Book XII, ch. 19), Hume believed that there were times of crisis in the affairs of men when certain civil liberties should be suspended. There is even much to suggest that, had he been alive, he would have heartily approved the suspension of *habeas corpus* in England during the period when Mirabeau was actually composing his work.

155. Letter to Louis XVI, 30 April 1776, quoted in *Journal de l'Abbé de Véri*, publié par le baron Jehan de Witte, Paris, 1928–30, I. 455. See also Jean-Louis Giraud Soulavie, *Mémoires historiques et politiques du règne de Louis XVI*, Paris, 1801, II. 55; III. 165; VI. 518–19.

156. I have found no serious evidence to support the once-current opinion that this work is not by Mirabeau.

157. *Des prisons d'état*, in *Oeuvres de Mirabeau*, Paris, 1835, VII. 443.

"The celebrated Hume," Mirabeau writes, "in giving an account of the *Habeas Corpus* Bill, states: '... it must be confessed that there is *some difficulty* to reconcile with such extreme liberty the full security and the regular police of a state, especially the police of great cities'...."[158] Hume, Mirabeau adds, is guilty of excessive circumspection in the defence of liberty: "This equivocal style of writing, to which this famous author is a little too prone in all matters relating to government, almost leaves us to question whether he unreservedly approves or disapproves of this famous law. The great philosopher certainly forgot himself most strangely if it is true that he seriously hesitated on this occasion."[159]

Mirabeau admits that Hume in a preceding passage had seemed to call this law necessary for the protection of liberty in a mixed monarchy and had seemed to say that, since it existed nowhere but in England, it alone was a consideration sufficient to induce the English to prefer their constitution to all others. To this Mirabeau adds the following comment:

> If the law which prohibits all forms of arbitrary imprisonment is *essentially requisite for the protection of liberty*, it is forever sacred and irrefragable; for what is the benefit of government if not the protection of liberty? And what can authorize it to commit evils it must prevent? The supposed disadvantages that this much slandered liberty entails for the police are manifestly, and could not be other than, the consequences of an administration's clumsiness, its lack of vigilance, firmness, and integrity. In any case, if the sole object of government is not to guarantee our liberty and property, what care we for its fine police; what care we for the advantage of society that serves as a pretext for all forms of individual injustice if that advantage can only be obtained at the cost of the rights and benefits whose protection and enhancement formed the original purpose of our uniting with our fellow-creatures.[160]

Habeas corpus, contrary to Hume's fears, has not produced great disorders. The lesson, Mirabeau concludes, is obvious: France

158. *Des lettres de cachet,* op. cit., VII. 184.
159. Ibid., VII. 184–85.
160. Loc. cit.

could do away with its system of *lettres de cachet* and its complicated apparatus of despotism which induced foreigners to laugh at Frenchmen as poor, down-trodden slaves. The *raison d'état,* moreover, can never be legitimately invoked to suspend such measures of legal protection:

> Let us not then abuse this word *necessity,* capable of authorizing every act of tyranny, as well as arbitrary imprisonment. Never let it be introduced into a legal cause, or in any circumstance that is anticipated in the law. When this deadly necessity exists in fact, it requires no explanation: no one will call it into question.... This supposition of a state of emergency is thus entirely irrelevant to the present discussion; we have asked the question: Is the use of *lettres de cachet* just? Is it beneficial? We are given the answer that there are circumstances when they become necessary.
>
> Why this ridiculous evasion? Do such circumstances exist? No, they do not, and if they did, it is highly doubtful that the *lettres* would be obeyed; for orders so arbitrary can have force only in times of the most peaceful and complete obedience.... [161]

Mirabeau, who, like Turgot, shows unbounded admiration for Rousseau's political writings, goes on for an entire chapter defending *habeas corpus* against Hume's objection. He hints that practical observers like Hume are guilty, through their pride in being "empirical politicians," of a certain scholarly charlatanism. Mirabeau does in fact condescend to cite facts to support his arguments but, in the typical radical tradition of many later revolutionists, he prefers to talk of principles rather than precedents. History is somehow irrelevant in a question of right:

> Polemical details should never be more than a secondary consideration in politico-philosophical writings, if I may employ that term, and the principles of natural law must be given first place ... for natural law is the only law that men have not the power to abrogate. Arguments of reason are always infinitely stronger than those of any other authority and in political and philosophical matters they render historical dissertations that are subject to interminable

161. Ibid., VII. 205.

debate quite superfluous. Everyone will agree that it would be most unfortunate if a nation's liberty and rights hinged on a point of grammar. . . . [162]

Besides rejecting history altogether, another possibility open to the revolutionary who finds the evidence of history in apparent contradiction with his principles is, of course, to rewrite history or at least to find historians whose ideas are more in keeping with those principles. We shall see that Mirabeau attempted this last solution as well when he set out later, partially, no doubt, because of dissatisfaction with Hume, to translate and publish the "republican"-inspired *History of England* by Catherine Macaulay-Graham as well as some of the political doctrine of Milton. But more on that later. Let us now examine the work of another radical theoretician who found it necessary at this time to attack the historian Hume.

Although Mably in 1757 had called Hume the economist "a man of genius,"[163] he was unable, later, to find any words of praise for Hume the historian. In the work *Des droits et des devoirs du citoyen*, this disciple of Rousseau, who tended in his own writings to defend a primitive form of idealistic communism, gives us a fairly good idea why. History, first of all, must be a source-book of liberalism: "Let it show the rights of peoples; let it never stray from that primary truth from which all the others are derived." Pre-requisite to the writing of history is the study of natural law or of just political theory which is based on "the laws that nature has established for providing mankind with the happiness she has made them capable of." These laws, Mably tells us, are invariable and "the world would have been a happy place had it observed them."[164] History then has an explicit propaganda purpose: ". . . the object of history is not simply to enlighten the mind, its function is also to guide the heart and give it an inclination for the good."[165] Thus it is that Mably judges Rapin-Thoyras, the Huguenot historian of England who was generally seen as biased against France and in every way

162. Ibid., VII. 388.

163. *Collection complète des oeuvres de l'Abbé de Mably*, Paris, An III, V. 197.

164. *De la manière d'écrire l'histoire* (1783), in *Oeuvres*, XII. 379.

165. Ibid., p. 397.

inferior to Hume, as in fact superior to the Scottish historian: "...his views are upright, he loves justice, and his politics are based on the principles of natural law."[166]

Unusual too in France at this time is Mably's emphasis on the love of liberty rather than on the fanaticism shown by the seventeenth-century Puritans.[167] Beginning as he did with these revolutionary premises, it is perhaps only to be expected that Mably found Hume wanting: "His own reflections are commonplace, and too often based on false politics that morality cannot sanction."[168] In some parts of the *History* Hume is even judged to be "unintelligible," and Mably, contemptuous of the great praise given Hume in France only twenty years earlier, asks: "...and how can I approve of a work that, whether because he was ignorant of his art, or lazy, or slow-witted, the historian has only sketched out? All these unconnected facts slip from my memory, I have wasted my time...."[169]

During this same period we find the future revolutionary leader Brissot de Warville largely agreeing that history should be, first and foremost, a school of liberalism. Discussing the duties of an historian in 1783, Brissot takes up a position similar to that of Mirabeau and Mably: "...his purpose is to instruct his times, posterity, princes especially, and ministers; for it is they who can profit from history. Who among them will not amend an inclination for arbitrary government after contemplating the fate of Charles I and James II?...The first duty of the historian is thus to be courageous and fearless, if he wishes to be useful...."[170]

Impartiality is seen by Brissot as a rather secondary virtue in the historian. In fact, Brissot makes it something of a sin for the historian to be impartial in the wrong way. Speaking of Catherine Macaulay's *History,* which was later to influence the revolutionary Brissot and several other leading Girondins to a surprising extent, he writes:

166. Ibid., p. 430.

167. Ibid., pp. 111, 226.

168. Ibid., pp. 430–31.

169. Ibid., p. 520.

170. *Correspondance universelle sur ce qui intéresse le bonheur de l'homme et de la société,* Neuchâtel, 1783, II. 54.

She has been blamed as an historian whose partiality for republicanism is too marked. But how could she have avoided partiality while depicting the tyrannical excesses that signalled the ministries of the Buckinghams, the Lauds, and the Straffords? Her partiality in favour of that system speaks highly of both her spirit and her intellect. Partiality for characters alone dishonours the historian.... Respect for the sacred rights that nature has granted to mankind is what distinguishes this history and places it well above that of Hume, whose fawning courtier spirit often alters or effaces the colours of truth.... Madame Macaulay has had the courage to...go off the beaten track that other historians have followed, to open up a new path, to censure the servile principles of Hume, to defy the body of public opinion he had managed to captivate.... And now I have but one wish: that her History be translated into French.[171]

8

DEFENCE AND DEFIANCE

The change in political climate which took place between the 1760s and the 1780s is well illustrated by earlier French reactions to republican interpretations of the English revolution. The *Journal Encyclopédique,* not the least liberal of *ancien-régime* periodicals, refused in its highly laudatory review of Hume's *Stuarts* in 1760 to go into any detail concerning the most guilty activities of Cromwell and his hot-brained parliamentarians: "Our readers would shudder if the bounds of this journal allowed us to place before their eyes portraits depicting some of the features of these tyrants."[172] Nor is it easy to find at this time in France a very much more favourable opinion of the English Protector and his Puritan sup-

171. *Journal du Licée de Londres ou Tableau de l'état présent des sciences et des arts en Angleterre,* Paris, No. 1, January 1784, pp. 33–34. A resident of London at this time, Brissot was personally acquainted with Catherine Macaulay. A letter of 30 January 1784 sent by her to his Newman Street address indicates that discussions concerning the translation of some of her work into French were already taking place (Archives Nationales, 446 AP2).

172. June 1760, IV. 25.

porters. The hostility expressed by Bossuet in the seventeenth century toward these fiendish regicides is still very much alive a century later. Rousseau speaks of Cromwell as irredeemably vile and perhaps best sums up the general view: "What has never yet been seen," he wrote in 1751, "is a hypocrite turning into a good man: one might reasonably have attempted the conversion of Cartouche, but never would a wise man have undertaken that of Cromwell."[173] Some further idea of the Protector's reputation in France as the most evil of men may be had from the fact that Crébillon found himself able to use parts of the first two acts of an abandoned tragedy on Cromwell in his *Catilina*.[174] An unsuccessful tragedy, *Cromwel,* by Antoine Maillet-Duclairon, was in fact performed by the Comédiens Français in June 1764, and depicts the prevailing view of the Protector as a murderer and usurper. The last two lines of the play, significantly, are spoken by the heroic General Monk:

> Et montrons aux Sujets que les premières Loix
> Sont d'aimer la Patrie & de servir les Rois.[175]

> *[And let us show our subjects that the first of all laws
> Is to love our country and to serve our kings.]*

The youthful poet François de Neufchâteau in a work of 1766 also displays this classic reaction to the leading figures in Stuart history. Charles I is seen as an "unfortunate and innocent" prince.[176] Cromwell, on the other hand, is looked upon as the supreme hypocrite:

> Personne mieux que lui sous l'air de la candeur
> N'a de ses grands desseins voilé la profondeur

173. *Réponse de J.-J. Rousseau au Roi de Pologne, Duc de Lorraine,* in *Oeuvres complètes de J.-J. Rousseau,* Paris, 1852, I. 492.

174. See *Oeuvres complètes de Voltaire,* XXIV. 359.

175. *Cromwel, tragédie en cinq actes et en vers.* Par M. Du Clairon. Représentée pour la première fois par les Comédiens Français Ordinaires du Roi, le 7 juin 1764, Paris, 1764. The play closed after the fifth performance.

176. *Lettre de Charles Ier, Roi d'Angleterre, de la Maison de Stuart à son fils le prince de Galles retiré en France,* par M. François de Neufchâteau en Lorraine. Neufchâteau, 1766. See the *Avertissement.*

Il a reçu du Ciel des talens en partage,
La valeur, l'éloquence, et même des vertus;
Mais ces présens des Dieux, il les a corrompus,
Il les a dégradés par un coupable usage:
Il déguise le crime et la rébellion
Sous le masque sacré de la religion:
Il veut être Tyran, sans jamais le paraître;
Ennemi sans retour, Juge sans équité,
Politique subtil, et Guerrier redouté;
Voilà quel est *Cromwel,* voilà cet heureux Traître,
Qui proscrit des Anglais le véritable Maître.... [177]

[None more cleverly than he with innocent air, did ever hide great schemes so deeply. Valour, eloquence, and even virtues were Heaven's gifts, but these he corrupted and degraded in guilty use. 'Neath religion's sacred guise he masked crime and rebellion: With purpose veiled he seeks a tyrant's throne, relentless foe, unjust magistrate, cunning politician, dreaded warrior; there you have Cromwell, this thriving traitor who denied Englishmen their true master.]

In 1764 the *Journal Encyclopédique* reviewing Catherine Macaulay's work in the English edition illustrates much the same attitude. It begins by translating (or, rather, "colourfully adapting") the "horrifying" introduction of this female historian, this "Amazon," whose "patriotic scoldings" would soon remind Burke of the "heroines in Billingsgate" and earn from him the designation "our republican Virago":[178]

From my early youth, I have nourished my mind by reading those histories which exhibit liberty in its most exalted state; the word Republic alone is enough to raise up my heart, and my soul rejoices every time I think of the independence of the Greeks or the free and noble pride of the Romans. Reading and studying the authors of those two nations nurtured in me an extreme love of Freedom, that intense and irresistible passion which is nature's gift to every ra-

---

177. Ibid., p. 6.

178. See letter to R. Shackleton, in *The Correspondence of Edmund Burke,* ed. Lucy S. Sutherland, Cambridge, 1960, II. 150. Bridget Hill has graciously adopted the appellation as a title for her excellent study, *The Republican Virago: The Life and Times of Catharine Macaulay, Historian,* Oxford, 1992.

tional being.... The mind of the historian must be similarly disposed, in my view, if he wishes to see the events he recounts in a manner that differs from the productions of most of our political writers, those outrageous and contemptible sycophants whose only talent lies in casting a seductive veil over the most monstrous vices;... insipid authors who lack even that discernment required to distinguish truly virtuous and exalted patriots from time-serving place-men who sacrificed the most essential interests of the public to the baseness of their private affections. I propose in my history to accord praise only to true virtue, paying no heed to the rank or fame of those who have dishonoured their name, etc., etc....

The *Journal Encyclopédique* editors, choking with indignation, seem scarcely able to believe that such a writer could exist. Still commenting on Catherine Macaulay's introduction, they warn their French readers of her seditious intent:

Miss Macaulay's purpose in this introductory speech is to predispose her readers in favour of the history, or rather the libel, she is about to present, and for which she pleads in advance.... She protests that she will say nothing that is improper, nothing that breathes licence or sedition; but does she speak the language of the good citizen, does she seem to love the public peace when she asserts that *whoever attempts to reconcile monarchy with liberty is a rebel in the blackest and fullest sense; he is a rebel to the laws of his country, the laws of nature, the laws of reason, and the laws of God....* We shall note only a few isolated passages in this History; our readers would be too outraged at the author's effrontery were we to give them an account of the criminal lengths to which she goes to inspire in her fellow-citizens a hatred of royalty and scorn for the memory of Great Britain's most respectable princes.

Significantly, the *Journal Encyclopédique* cites as an example of Catherine Macaulay's bias her portrait of James I and then adds: "what we have said about this monarch, following Mr. Hume, exempts us from having to recount here Miss Macaulay's observations... because, in this regard, we cannot possibly give an account of her inaccurate narrations and insulting commentaries."[179]

179. January 1764, I. 91–100. Brissot (*Mémoires de Brissot*, Paris, 1877, p. 422) was highly indignant on reading the following anecdote reported by Boswell in his *Life of Johnson*:

The next two decades were to witness a rapid evolution of French political attitudes. This same journal which in 1764 could not even bring itself to reproduce examples of Catherine Macaulay's criminally seditious republicanism for fear of shocking its readers (and, of course, the censors) was able to speak in 1778 of the "sound ideas, the solid judgement of Miss Macaulay, and the profound knowledge she has of human nature...."[180]

A similar evolution in political attitudes is reflected to some extent by the opinions of a few pre-revolutionary writers who take a more positive approach to the idea of Cromwell as the central figure in philosophical tragedy. Delisle de Sales, for example, ponders in 1772 the question of a *Cromwel* in which Locke would play

---

He (Johnson) again insisted on the duty of maintaining subordination of rank. "Sir, I would no more deprive a nobleman of his respect, than of his money. I consider myself as acting a part in the great system of society, and I do to others as I would have them to do to me. I would behave to a nobleman as I should expect he would behave to me, were I a nobleman and he Sam. Johnson. Sir, there is one Mrs. Macaulay in this town, a great republican. One day when I was at her house, I put on a very grave countenance, and said to her, 'Madam, I am now become a convert to your way of thinking. I am convinced that all mankind are upon an equal footing; and to give you an unquestionable proof, Madam, that I am in earnest, here is a very sensible, civil, well-behaved fellow-citizen, your footman; I desire that he may be allowed to sit down and dine with us.' I thus, Sir, showed her the absurdity of the levelling doctrine. She has never liked me since. Sir, your levellers wish to level *down* as far as themselves; but they cannot bear levelling *up* to themselves. They would all have some people under them; why not then have some people above them?"

For a somewhat different yet essentially good-humoured narration of this same incident, see Catherine Macaulay's own account of it in her *Letters on Education*, London, 1790, pp.167–68.

Dr. Johnson was not alone in criticizing Catherine Macaulay as is evident in the following passage from a letter addressed to her by Hume: "I grant, that the cause of liberty, which you, Madam, with the Pyms and Hampdens have adopted, is noble and generous; but most of the partizans of that cause, in the last century disgraced it, by their violence, and also by their cant, hypocrisy, and bigotry, which, more than the principles of civil liberty, seem to have been the motive of all their actions..."—Letter from Paris, 29 March 1764. (See *New Letters of David Hume*, ed. R. Klibansky and E. C. Mossner, Oxford, 1954, p. 81.)

180. *Journal Encyclopédique*, July 1778, V. 109. In December 1781, however, the editors, albeit more gently than in 1764, again chide her for her anti-royalist bias. (Ibid., 1 December 1781, VIII. 230–31.)

an important rôle.[181] Later, the future *conventionnel* Louis-Sébastien Mercier almost begs dramatic authors to treat the subject of Cromwell: "What can you tragic poets be thinking of? You have such a subject to deal with and yet you speak to me always of ancient Persians and Greeks, you give me novels in rhyme! Pray, bestir yourselves! Paint me a Cromwell!"[182] Mercier imagines himself at the theatre in the year 2440, just after attending an historical play on the Calas affair. He hears announced that the following day the tragedy *Cromwell, or the Death of Charles I* is to be performed: "... the assembled spectators," this visitor to the future informs us, "appeared extremely happy with the announcement. I was told that the play was a masterpiece, and that the case of kings and the people had never before been presented with such force, eloquence, or truth. Cromwell was the avenger, a hero worthy of the sceptre he had dashed from a treacherous hand that was guilty of criminal actions against the state. Kings inclined in their hearts to commit injustice had never managed to read through this drama without sensing that a deathly paleness had crept over their arrogant brow."[183]

Mercier's attitude, unheard of earlier in France, is still extremely rare even at this time. Not only, as we have seen, did the French of the *ancien régime* generally consider Cromwell to be one of the greatest of political criminals, they were also quite certain, and Monsieur Hume had not contradicted their belief in the matter, that the eighteenth-century English fully shared this view. Frequent allusions are made in traditionalist *ancien-régime* literature suggesting that the English nation still felt desperately guilty concerning the crime of regicide committed in its name in the seventeenth century—so guilty, in fact, that it annually held a commemorative day of national mourning for the tragic loss of Charles I. A typical expression of this belief is found in Pierre-Jean Grosley's *Londres:*

181. *Essai sur la tragédie:* Par un philosophe, 1772, p. 368.
182. *L'An deux mille quatre cent quarante,* nouvelle édition, Londres, 1785, I. 162, note A.
183. Ibid., I. 163.

January 30th is dedicated everywhere in the Anglican church to a lengthy annual service commemorating the martyred Prince. During the prayers of this service, worshippers beg for Divine mercy and implore God to never again ask England for the blood of the holy martyr who faced with calm serenity the outrages leading up to death, following in the footsteps of his Saviour who died praying for his assassins and executioners.[184]

So strong indeed were official French feelings on the subject that in 1779 Louis XVI's council, preparing a war manifesto against Great Britain, included among its accusations the charge that the House of Hanover held its power through usurpation and also reproached the English with the assassination of Charles I and Mary Stuart. Louis XVI in marginal comments on the draft manifesto typically pointed out that England was already sufficiently remorseful concerning those crimes and that it would be unwise to include such a reminder: "Regarding the assassination of King Charles and Mary Stuart, those are crimes for which England still feels such deep shame a century and more later, that we should not remind her with reproaches that would seem all the more bitter and humiliating since it is a King of France, enjoying the love of his subjects, who would be including them in a declaration of war. The House of Hanover, moreover, played no part in those crimes."[185] Where the manifesto pointed out that, since Cromwell's day, all English treaties had shown revolting and subtle traces of base and envious policy, Louis XVI further observed: "I would prefer to remove entirely the word *Cromwell* and replace it with the date of his government; the English also blame us for giving recognition to the regime of this odious man. I would remove the entire sentence; after all, since Cromwell's time we have acquired many territories and possessions."[186]

In total disagreement with such sentiments, Mercier sees the

184. *Londres,* Lausanne, 1770, I. 354–55. In fact the English seem to have had three days commemorating the Stuarts: January 30 in memory of Charles I; May 29 to celebrate the Restoration; and, paradoxically perhaps, November 5 to celebrate the expulsion of James II.

185. *Oeuvres de Louis XVI,* Paris, 1864, II. 49.

186. Ibid., II. 51.

English of the year 2440 as a wiser race and favouring a rather different attitude towards the Protector:

> The English are still the leading nation of Europe: they continue to enjoy their ancient glory for having shown their neighbours the kind of government that befits men who are jealous of their rights and their happiness.
>
> There are no longer solemn processions commemorating Charles I; people see more clearly in politics.
>
> The new statue of the Protector Cromwell has just been erected. ... The people's assemblies will henceforth take place in the presence of this statue, since the great man it represents is the true author of the glorious and immutable constitution.[187]

We will see that not even in the Convention a decade later was such an enthusiastic attitude to Cromwell anywhere to be found. Although during the Revolution his ostensible opinion was to be quite different, the pre-revolutionary Brissot also greatly admired Cromwell if we are to believe his own retrospective account of certain cherished youthful dreams:

> This notion of revolution, which I dared not avow, often occupied my thoughts. As can be easily imagined, I gave myself a leading rôle. I had been singularly impressed by the history of Charles I and Cromwell; I constantly thought of the latter, tearing up the portrait of his king while he was still a child, crowning his career by having him decapitated, and owing solely to his own genius the great rôle he had played in the English revolution. It seemed to me not impossible to renew that revolution.... [188]

Brissot in fact was, perhaps more than any other revolutionary figure, deeply influenced by the events of Stuart history. As in the case of Mirabeau, his favourite historian of those events, several years before the Revolution, was Catherine Macaulay. In May 1784 Brissot expressed the hope that she would also write the history of the American revolution so that Americans might learn how to avoid the faults of the English, who had allowed republicanism to

187. Mercier, op. cit., I. 382–83.
188. *Mémoires de Brissot*, p. 19.

die in their own country.[189] Hume, on the other hand, Brissot singles out as the great enemy; only the Capuchin friar, the Père d'Orléans, had written a worse history,[190] but Hume is judged, because of his popularity, to be much more dangerous. Brissot speaks of the need to diminish "the implicit political faith people have in him."[191]

In September 1784, on the occasion of the English publication of Hume's essays "Of Suicide" and "Of the Immortality of the Soul," Brissot devoted fourteen pages of his journal to a general review of Hume's reputation. He praises Hume's early philosophical essays and judges that they had been mistakenly neglected by the public since, after all, they contained a good deal of useful material against superstition and prejudice.[192] It was because he had failed to please with these, Brissot maintains, that Hume decided to prostitute his pen, vowing to succeed in history at any cost: "...and he succeeded. Perhaps he owed some of his enormous success to the party whose principles he embraced, the party of the Crown against the people; he espoused it in all his undertakings and made himself odious in the eyes of the partisans of republicanism; but philosophers forgave him his attachment, his devotion to the Crown of England, because of his philosophical observations which, moreover, he scattered throughout his History."[193]

Brissot thus admits that the early *philosophes* had admired Hume for his "philosophy," meaning his anti-clericalism. This was not in itself bad but French intellectuals had now outgrown that intermediate stage of enlightenment and needed something more. The struggle now had to be more political than religious in emphasis. Now was the time for history to attach itself to a loud and clear defence of the people's liberty; the long-neglected rights of humanity had to be avenged:

189. *Journal du Licée de Londres,* I. 335–36.
190. Ibid., July 1784, II. 150–51.
191. Ibid., p. 151.
192. Ibid., p. 159.
193. Ibid., p. 161.

Hume did not, in my view, advance that kind of philosophy far enough: clearly, he belonged to those times when one protested more against the influence of priests than in favour of men. That was Voltaire's failing as well; the step they took led to those we are now taking, and theirs was the more difficult: we must thank them for risking it, the word is not inappropriate, given the character of the English clergy. We must, however, blame Hume rather more severely for his apology of the Stuarts, as well as his unduly pompous encomiums on the English constitution and on Roman law; he must be censured as well for confounding too often the people and the populace.... [194]

Even Hume's arguments against immortality are cited by Brissot as additional proof of his callous insensibility: "Hume, one can see, had never been tortured by oppression. He had never heard the dismal, soul-wrenching sound of a prison gate closing behind him.... Hume had no need of such beliefs; his soul was desiccated and his character matched the cause he defended, a cause in which nothingness is a resource."[195] To complete the picture Brissot adds a note on Hume's *Political Discourses;* it is in these that Hume especially betrays his selfish character: "You will find such aridness, such insensibility, such *unfeeling*, if I may be allowed to coin this English word, in his discourses on commerce, luxury and money; he there declares himself to be an apologist of luxury, and why? Because as a recipient of pensions and great income he enjoyed drinking champagne and living the Epicurean life...."[196] How corrupt, how unclean the *sage Monsieur Hume* seems now! One almost hears in the distance, not the intellectual Brissotins of a decade later, but the ostentatiously austere and often frankly obscurantist followers of Robespierre.[197]

194. Ibid., p. 164.

195. Ibid., pp. 171–72.

196. Ibid., p. 172.

197. Some hint too of the *culte de l'Etre suprême* can be found in Bernardin de Saint-Pierre's virtuous charge of the same year concerning writers like Hume: "...reading them is such an arid, disheartening exercise.... Posterity will prefer Herodotus to David Hume ... because we still prefer to hear related the fables of the Divinity in the history of men than the reasonings of men in the history of the Divinity."—*Etudes de la Nature* (1784), in *Oeuvres complètes de Jacques-Henri Bernardin de Saint-Pierre*, Paris, 1830–31, V. 111–12.

9

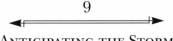

ANTICIPATING THE STORM

Such bitter attacks on the Scottish historian are still fairly rare before 1789. On the eve of the Revolution, proof of Hume's continuingly great historical reputation can be seen in the appearance of a new edition of the *Stuarts* in 1788—possibly the tenth separate French edition since 1760 of this the most popular part of the *History*. Additional proof of his enduring success is provided by the police records which show that on 20 June 1786 the Paris authorities seized in a book shipment from Marseilles the proof sheets of a counterfeit edition of Hume's *History*.[198] Quite obviously, book pirates do not go to the trouble of printing works whose popularity has run out.

Not only was Hume's *History* still popular on the eve of the Revolution, its authority continued to mould the opinions held by most Frenchmen, whether of traditionalist or liberal persuasion, on the English revolution. If we find, for example, a Mably attacking Hume at this time, we find also a Gudin de La Brenellerie defending him. In fact Gudin de La Brenellerie's important analysis of the British parliamentary system, published in 1789, follows Hume very closely, because, the author tells us, "he is the least partial of English historians, and the least opposed to the royal prerogative."[199]

Hume, moreover, could still appeal in the 1780s to the fashionable nobility he had pleased so much a quarter of a century earlier. The Comtesse de Boufflers's gracious letter to Hume on his *History*[200] should be contrasted with the following note by the same author to Gustavus III of Sweden concerning, not her great good friend the respectable statesman David Hume, but the rabble-

198. See "Journal des livres suspendus depuis janvier 1778," Bibliothèque Nationale, Fonds Fr. 21,934, f. 67.

199. *Essai sur l'histoire des comices de Rome, des Etats-Généraux de la France et du Parlement d'Angleterre*, Philadelphie, 1789, III. 111. See also Gudin de La Brenellerie's defence of Hume against Mably in *Supplément à la manière d'écrire l'histoire ou réponse à l'ouvrage de M. l'abbé de Mably*, 1784, pp. 113–14.

200. See *supra*, p. 11.

rousing, squalid Raynal: "... of low birth, lacking wit, driven out of France for having attacked with impudence and folly the very principles that hold society together and assure the safety of princes; and, on top of all that, a dreadful bore."[201] Hume, if nothing else, had never been found "dreadfully boring." We can especially appreciate the force of the comtesse's words when we learn that this famous salon hostess on one occasion had lovingly spent an entire day trying to equal in French translation *one* paragraph of Hume's elegant *History!*[202]

Our chapter on Hume's pre-revolutionary image can perhaps best be concluded with the quotation of an opinion expressed by Malesherbes late in 1788. At the time he was writing, all of France was waiting for the promised convocation of the States-General. Malesherbes, less than one year before the fall of the Bastille, runs over in his mind the intellectual achievements of the century and the titles of important works which, because of censorship restrictions, had not appeared in France with the express or sometimes even tacit permission of the authorities and yet which were *necessary.* Montesquieu's *Esprit des Lois* was one such work; another was Hume's *History of England:* "Mr. Hume is generally regarded in France as a paragon of wise and impartial historians, and now that the entire French nation is discussing the *Constitution,* and even expressly invited to do so by its King, we must find our instruction in this author's account of the constitution of his country, either to extract from it what might be useful to us or to reject what would not accord with our customs and laws."[203]

201. *Lettres de Gustave III à la comtesse de Boufflers et de la comtesse au Roi, de 1771 à 1791,* Bordeaux, 1900, letter 62.

202. See *Nouveaux mélanges extraits des manuscrits de Mme Necker,* Paris, An X, I. 202.

203. *Mémoires sur la librairie et sur la liberté de la presse,* par M. de Lamoignon de Malesherbes, Ministre d'Etat, Paris, 1809, p. 306. Additional evidence of Malesherbes's extremely high regard for the wisdom of Hume's *Stuarts* may be found in the following fragment of Abbé de Véri's *Journal,* dated 5 October 1788:

> After the removal of the two ministers, after the re-assembly of the Parlements and when the convening of the States-General had been decided, the King sent for Malesherbes and had a conversation with him lasting three quarters of an hour or an hour.

Someone once said of Malesherbes that he devoted his lifetime to pleading the cause of the people before the tribunal of the king and that he died pleading the cause of the king before the tribunal of the people. We shall see that once more, not long before his death on the revolutionary scaffold, while pleading the cause of his king, he would have occasion to deal with David Hume's *History*. In 1788 his plea is more general; it is for the peo-

---

Malesherbes related to me parts of the conversation which I shall reproduce here in his words without, however, pretending to equal his lively and eloquent style.

"I know of no situation," he told him, "more distressing than that of a king in your current position...

"You read a good deal, Sire, and you are more learned than is generally thought. But reading unaccompanied by reflection is of little consequence. I have recently been reading the section on Charles I in David Hume's History. Read it again and reflect on it. Your positions are similar. This prince was gentle, virtuous, and devoted to the laws; he was neither ruthless nor rash, but just and beneficent; and yet he died on a scaffold. Here, I think, is the reason. He came to the throne at a time when the prerogatives of the crown and those of the nation were being hotly disputed. If he had abandoned his prerogatives he would have been viewed as base by those who saw them as sacred through lifelong habit and because of the advantages gained by the nobility from these prerogatives. But, on the other hand, he was the weaker party in the dispute and he was constantly forced to make new concessions. Had he come to the throne fifty years earlier, his virtues would have made him a model king; if he had arrived fifty years later, when the question of mutual rights was more or less settled, he would not have transgressed those limits and his reign would have been long and happy.

"Your position is the same. The debate arises from the precedents of authority and the demands of the citizens. Fortunately, the quarrels of religion are not part of it."

"Oh! in that respect, very fortunately indeed!" the King answered, taking me by the arm. "And because of that the atrociousness of it will not be the same."

"Moreover, today's more temperate ways ensure that the excesses of those times will not recur. But little by little your prerogatives will be snatched from you. It is up to you to decide in your Council on a firm plan regarding which concessions you must make for the general good, and on what you must never surrender. Only your firmness can determine the success of such a plan. Without that firmness, nothing can be certain. I can promise you that what happened to Charles I will not happen here, but I cannot promise that there will not be all manner of other excesses. You must look to forestalling these...." (See "L'Abbé de Véri et son journal" par le Duc de Castries, *La Revue de Paris*, November 1953, pp. 84–86.)

ple as much as for the king and he speaks for that peculiarly sane group of moderates who worked actively for reform within the structure of the *ancien régime* and who followed Montesquieu rather than Rousseau. On the whole, it is also to this same group that Hume the historian—despite the extreme reactions of the Bergiers and the Brissots—appealed most during this period. After Montesquieu's death, Hume had been hailed as the only man in Europe capable of replacing the author of the *Esprit des Lois*.[204] With the arrival of the Revolution, the stars of both writers fell considerably. Both were eventually to recover their losses in prestige but at different times and in different ways. Montesquieu would take up his now permanent place as one of the eighteenth century's greatest political theoreticians. Hume, on the other hand, was to be recognized as one of the eighteenth century's most highly original philosophers. But before that, within only a few years, Hume the historian would play his greatest political role ever, as prophet of the French counter-revolution.

204. Greig, op. cit., I. 259.

II

————————

The Revolution and the
Rôle of History

1

————————

HISTORY AS A WEAPON OF
COUNTER-REVOLUTION

We have examined at the beginning of chapter I the prevailing eighteenth-century view of history. Some further general considerations on the subject are necessary at this point, however, since it is especially at the time of the Revolution in France that history's traditional rôle as the scientifically validating factor of all political speculation is seriously questioned.

Of course, with the conservatives, this traditional view of history's function still largely prevails, and, in fact, becomes, if anything, more intense. History shows us the stable facts of human nature. It represents, in a hard physical sense, the unchanging "nature of things." It has a certain Newtonian order to its predictably cyclical patterns of unfolding.

True enough, events in one century may differ from events in another: that is because of particular variations which characterize each nation and each century. One does not, therefore, become a helpless prisoner of the "science" of history; it does not repeat itself exactly. But history's essential aspect is its constant sim-

————————

ilarity from century to century. Since the human heart and the human passions do not change, the present and the future must resemble the past. If this were not true then history would have no purpose; the past is not studied for its own sake. History has its "lessons" to teach. It is the science, admittedly imperfect, admittedly based on analogy, of human social behaviour. One must be just as empirically minded, just as anti–*a priori* in dealing with this science as with any other. When one speaks of a "revolution" in man's form of government, for example, one must understand what can possibly be meant by such a term. A total change in the forms of man's social organization is a distinct physical impossibility. It is as impossible as miracles are in the universe of Newton. Neither human nature nor the law of gravity can be repealed.

History is thus the ordered apprehension of the moral nature of things. It condemns in advance any over-optimistic attempts to achieve ideal or drastically rational political change. It tells us that what has never yet been witnessed in man's behaviour in the past can hardly be expected to appear in the present or future. J.-H. Meister in 1790 sums up the view very clearly and with a certain irony not uncommon at this time in the writings of those who felt the reassuring weight of the centuries behind them as they attacked the impertinent *a priorists:*

> It may be that a great moral transformation has recently occurred in the world and that a marvellous revolution has suddenly turned all order and principles upside down. Before that memorable moment occurred, however, if we managed to have any confidence at all in the more obvious teachings of history and the experiences of the human heart, would we not have acknowledged without hesitation that what influences most powerfully the will of man is the force of things and circumstances; that this supreme power is counterbalanced only by the force of the passions, and that only for a short time; that the passions in turn have more force than habits, and habits more than prejudices, and prejudices more than life's ordinary interests, and these everyday interests more than the simple notions of justice and fitness; that, in short, of all the motives that determine our actions and our behaviour, the weakest of all is reason, no matter how splendidly logical it might be?

Now if the occult influence of some supernatural power had not magically transformed all of these relationships, could we really have imagined that the more or less haphazardly traced boundaries of a metaphysical notion are all that is needed to contain the volatile fluctuations of the human will and passions?...

Would we still be allowed to doubt that only a form of government that has never existed anywhere is incontestably the most perfect and most admirable?...

I have the greatest respect for pamphlet-philosophy revolutions, especially when they are backed by a coalition as terrifying as that formed by the rabble mob and the army; but no matter how decisive their progress may seem, I rather fear that a force which should never be overlooked must inevitably return, namely, the force of things and circumstances....[1]

The reformer of society must bear in mind not only man's unchanging passions in his lofty search for what is ideally right in government; he must pay attention also to more earthly matters, to what history, for example, has shown to be socially useful. Such is the opinion of the Abbé L.-S. Balestrier de Canilhac who in 1790 devoted well over a hundred pages of the *Bibliothèque de l'homme public* to a critically timed reprinting of Hume's political essays[2] and who subsequently provoked the angry protests of his fellow editor Condorcet by defending the historical empiricism of Burke against the *a priorism* of Thomas Paine:

Mr. Paine reasons in this work, like most of our modern legislators, in the manner of a simple philosopher, never departing from the principles of natural law and their most logical consequences. In

1. J.-H. Meister, *Des premiers principes du système social appliqués à la Révolution présente*, Nice, 1790, pp. 120–27.

Meister, one of the more original thinkers of late eighteenth-century France, gives proof, not only in this work but in several others, of having been generally influenced by the whole Humian doctrine of human nature. See *De l'origine des principes religieux*, 1768, pp. 5–49; *Lettres sur l'imagination*, Londres, 1799, *passim; Mélanges de philosophie, de morale et de littérature*, Genève, 1822, pp. 212–15, 243–44.

2. *Bibliothèque de l'homme public ou analyse raisonnée des principaux ouvrages français et étrangers*...par M. le Marquis de Condorcet..., M. de Peyssonnel..., M. Le Chapelier, et autres Gens de Lettres, Paris, 1790, I, tome 2. Balestrier was the major editor of this valuable compilation. See also his *Politicon ou choix des meilleurs discours sur tous les sujets de politique traités dans la première assemblée nationale de France*, Paris, 1792, and *Manuel des autorités constituées*, Paris, An IX.

contrast, Mr. Burke reasons in the manner of a wise politician who has made a study of men and of human passion's social effects in large societies. . . .

In politics one must consider not only what is *right,* but also what is *useful.* Reason unaided teaches us natural law; but only experience combined with observation can inform us with any certainty on what is truly useful. No one questions that the people, strictly speaking, have the right to elect their kings, and even to depose them at will. It does not take a great philosopher to prove that truth; but it takes more than a philosopher to decide the question on the basis of utility, and one of the great principles of politics is that *it is not always useful for the people to do what they have a right to do.* The truths that regard our rights are immutable; those relating to utility vary according to circumstance, and the situation of the world is always changing. From this we do not conclude that government must be constantly in the process of changing its principles but rather that it must take care to modify them only with that same wise and unhurried gradualism observed by nature in her own operations.[3]

The eighteenth century had indeed witnessed the production of a good many rather long, geometrically assembled, highly indigestible *ex professo* treatises on natural law, most of which, when all was said and done, proved impeccably in many languages that man should be *just.* One sometimes has, on reading such productions, the classic impression of watching mountains give birth to mice. The Age of Reason also spoke a good deal of natural rights, but natural rights, too, the empirical politician might object, seldom appear to be more than tautological fictions: there are no natural rights as such, there are only the historical adjustments of different men's conflicting claims. The reformer of society should be guided, then, by positive law rather than by so-called natural law. He should consult Hume and Montesquieu, not the reason of the Age of Reason. Cerutti, a member of the *Assemblée législative* and one of the warmest eighteenth-century admirers of Hume's *History* ("the history of English passions, as written by human reason") sums up the practical applications of this empirical view:

3. Ibid., 1791, IX. 247–48.

A principle is . . . the result of experience and calculation. Politics is not . . . an art based on sentiment, nor is it a systematic science. New ideas cannot . . . prevail over old ones solely by the fact that they are new. One does not become a legislator overnight. Those who scorn the notion of consulting the oracles of antiquity, those who look with pity on the Senate of Rome, the Areopagus of Athens, and the Parliament of England, the meditations of Montesquieu, the observations of Blackstone, the reflections of Hume, Robertson, Ferguson, and Delolme, may indeed be men of genius but their genius is most immature, most hasty, and, let us say the word, most infantile, if they dismiss in that way the wisdom of the ages.

All revolutions require courage; consequently, nothing hastens their progress more than the generous vitality of the young. But if youth excels in demolishing the present, it does not similarly excel in building the future. That is the work of maturity, of mature minds and mature ideas. Such maturity casts aside passions that are always extreme and always lacking in foresight, and concentrates instead on laying down solid foundations and on establishing proper limits.[4]

The counter-revolutionist Count Ferrand, future minister of Louis XVIII and another admirer of Hume's *Stuarts*,[5] gives in 1793 yet another conservative's view of the rôle of history. History shows how human nature can be "modified" but can never be "changed." Once he has a good understanding of the "nature of things," the reformer will automatically avoid all abstractions and general principles which always appear simple, since they ignore difficulties but which are, in fact, invariably based on false hypotheses:

He will not aim at mere simplicity or single methods, because nature is no more simple in moral than in physical man, because the goals and ends of society are so complicated that it becomes impossible to operate it by means of simple mechanisms that would be inadequate and consequently dangerous.

Well convinced of these general truths, the reformer will examine the particular situation of the State, but without claiming the

4. *Lettre de M. Cerutti adressée au café de Foix*, in *Oeuvres diverses de M. Cerutti ou recueil de pièces composées avant et depuis la révolution*, Paris, 1792, II. 3–5; see also I. 4–7.

5. See *L'Esprit de l'Histoire ou Lettres politiques et morales d'un père à son fils*, Paris, 1802, III. 400, 497–98.

distinction of having made great discoveries concerning morality, the principles of government, or the notion of liberty. The more his understanding acquires the habit of observation, the more persuaded he will be that the science of government, so practical and embracing so many objects, demands more experience than any man can acquire in a single lifetime. He will therefore seek assistance from the experience of centuries past; he will draw riches from this inexhaustible common treasure which funds the needs of all men; he will not look upon the antiquity of an idea, of a custom, of a prejudice even, as an infallible mark of its blameworthiness; he will accept that there are good prejudices whose preservation is useful and whose destruction would be harmful; that such prejudices, inspired by the initial reaction of a sentiment that advises and assents even before judgement comes into play, must constitute a powerful moving force for the majority of people who are always more capable of feeling than of judgement; and, accordingly, that the more ancient the edifice needing repair, the greater the reverence with which he will approach it, like a holy place where the majesty of the centuries has deposited in the care of experience the practical science of morality and justice; like an age-old establishment that has witnessed the passing generations, whose august and beneficent antiquity advances toward eternity. He will sense that a government possessing these characteristics is a precious hereditary asset, entailed by ancestors to those who must in turn transmit it to the succeeding generations who will inherit it, possess it, and leave it behind as they do life and property; he will sense that in this way *a political system is in perfect harmony with the order of the world;* that since the functioning of the State imitates the functioning of nature, it is *never made entirely new by what it acquires nor entirely old by what it conserves; ....*[6]

It is not difficult to hear in the preceding passages echoes of Montesquieu, Hume, and Burke. It would, moreover, be a comparatively simple matter to find scores of similar passages in the works of other conservatives of the period, all with essentially the same message: the facts of human nature, the lessons of history and experience, the moral nature of things, the science of man, in short, cannot be ignored. Revolutionary innovators who disre-

6. Antoine-François-Claude, Comte Ferrand, *Le rétablissement de la monarchie Françoise,* Liège, 1794, seconde édition, pp. 69–71.

gard what the great historical empiricists have written, who make up new men and new constitutions with the scissors and paste of mere logic, are condemned in advance to failure: "When one contemplates their political levellings and symmetries," writes Mallet du Pan, also a counter-revolutionary admirer of Hume, "one cannot help thinking of a band of lunatics attempting to line up the Alps in the pattern of Saint Peter's colonnade."[7]

Such being the case, what must one think of a "revolution" in the affairs of men or of those who claim to be placing man in an entirely new world where all the old problems, the old injustices will be eliminated? For the conservative the answer is not difficult: one has very little to think or to do except to wait and, perhaps, if circumstances permit, to smile ironically at such naïvely enthusiastic but completely wasted efforts. A "revolution" means exactly what it seems to mean etymologically: it is a wild and wasteful ride on a merry-go-round which, after going through the classical phases of saving everyone, ends up by, temporarily at least, enslaving everyone, and it ultimately leaves a nation in a social position much worse very often than the one it was in before the foolish political ride began. Revolutions go the full circle; they are "horizontal," and we shall see that even in the Convention the hope of many of the more history-minded radical members was not that such a view was untrue but that somehow history could be deceived, that the merry-go-round could be stopped at a half-turn. "Revolutions," one of them tells us, "do not follow a straight line, but progress in a circle.... Consequently, each step forward takes you in the direction of despotism, once you have reached the point that was diametrically opposite it...."[8]

All revolutions consequently resemble each other. If one has studied those of the past in the works of a good historian one can predict with accuracy and profit the course of present or future revolutions:

7. *Correspondance politique pour servir à l'histoire du républicanisme français,* par M. Mallet du Pan, Hambourg, 1796, p. xiii.

8. See *Opinion de L.-M. Revellière-Lépeaux,* député de Maine-et-Loire, 7 janvier 1793.

After two thousand years, Roman history thus becomes useful to the man of genius who analyses political events, determines their causes, and discovers their basic elements. By adopting this method, Montesquieu, in one volume on the Romans, provided more food for thought than all of the historians before him who chronicled even the tiniest details of Roman history. The majority of historians are like those gamblers who note and talk about the number of wins and losses, whereas the mathematician analyses the basics of the game, determines the odds, and has no need to know the game's events which, in a sense, he has predicted.[9]

So great are the resemblances between revolutions that the observer may be tempted even to believe that revolutionary leaders consciously imitate the actions of their predecessors. We shall see that extreme royalists did in fact make the charge that the French revolutionists were imitating, point for point, procedures of the seventeenth-century English revolution. Others seemed content with a less sinister account of similarities, explaining them as the unavoidable results of the "nature of things":

> ... vanity, self-interest, the spirit of independence, terror. These did not appear for the first time in this revolution; they will all be found recorded in history and will always be reproduced in a thousand varied forms by all those who undertake to attack governments.
>
> For convincing proof one has only to read Tacitus, Sallust, Livy, de Thou, Vertot, Hume, Velly, and in general any historian who has left us an account of the upheavals experienced by various empires.
>
> These similarities have been so striking that it has been commonly thought that the leaders of the revolution had made a special study of all those in the past, and that they had pondered these long and hard in order to avail themselves of every means employed by their predecessors to ensure success in this difficult career...; it must be acknowledged, on the other hand, that a great many of these similarities arise almost entirely from the nature of things which... could not have failed... to present such frequent parallels.[10]

9. Gabriel Sénac de Meilhan, *Des principes et des causes de la révolution en France,* Londres, 1790, pp. v–vi.

10. G.-M. Sallier-Chaumont de la Roche, *Essais pour servir d'introduction à l'histoire de la Révolution française,* Paris, 1802, p. 184.

Although he was not above occasionally playing the very popular game of historical *rapprochements* or parallels himself, the celebrated lawyer, Joseph-Michel-Antoine Servan, perhaps the eighteenth-century French political thinker who most admired Hume,[11] cautions that the sociology of revolutions is still in its infancy. It is undeniable, of course, that general laws governing human events exist: "No doubt," Servan concedes, "if we consider the matter from a very elevated perspective, we have to agree that all moral and physical events result from general causes. But how useful is that finding? Apart from the fact that these causes are extremely difficult to apprehend, their application to particular cases is very frequently impossible...."[12] Montesquieu's historical determinism, in particular, sometimes goes too far in making a science out of politics. The solution, although the end result still leads to political conservatism, lies in a Humian scepticism:

> I have discovered in the political essays of Mr. Hume certain reflections which, though seemingly paradoxical, provide us with what strikes me as an intriguing truth:
>
> "I am apt," he writes, "to entertain a suspicion, that the world is still too young to fix many general truths in politics, which will remain true to the latest posterity. We have not as yet had experience of three thousand years; so that not only the art of reasoning is still imperfect in this science..., but we even want sufficient materials upon which we can reason. It is not fully known, what degree of refinement, either in virtue or vice, human nature is susceptible of."[13]

What is the value of all these tantalizing analogies that come to mind when one compares the histories of mankind's various revolutions? Servan answers this question with another analogy:

> In conjecturing about the future, a man who possesses the greatest native sagacity, and who joins to it the most intense study and the

11. See, for example, *Lettre à Monsieur Rabaut de Saint-Etienne sur l'humanité, par un aristocrate sans le savoir* (April 1790), in *Oeuvres choisies de Servan, Avocat Général au Parlement de Grenoble*, Paris, 1825, III. 356–63; and, especially, *Correspondance entre quelques hommes honnêtes*, Lausanne, 1795, III. 136–78.

12. *Des révolutions dans les grandes sociétés civiles considérées dans leurs rapports avec l'ordre général*, in *Oeuvres choisies de Servan*, V. 70.

13. Ibid., pp. 76–77.

widest experience, is rather like a traveller...who, by dint of practice and habit, can estimate fairly accurately the distance between
himself and far-away objects, while a less experienced or less obser-
vant person will make serious mistakes; but this same man who, by
observing the effects of light and shadow and by comparing the size
of intermediate objects is able to determine with great accuracy the
distance to a certain mountain, a city, or other such elevated objects, will never be able to guess the existence of any intervening
crevasse that might impede his progress toward that mountain or
city or even cause him to lose his life should he attempt to cross
over it.

No matter how much we study we shall never learn more than a
little of the present, far less of the past, and almost nothing, perhaps even nothing at all, of the future.

The *torch of history* is a magnificent figure of speech; it shows up
well in a line of poetry or in a harmonious bit of prose, but when
one attempts to reduce it to an exact truth, it turns out that this
torch is little more than a dim candle....History, in short, provides
warning signals but not guidance; it is a light that alerts us to the
dangers of a reef ahead, but it is not a chart and compass.[14]

Servan's rather balanced if sceptical attitude is fairly rare
among French thinkers of the Right at this time. We shall have occasion to cite various counter-revolutionary texts that betray a great
deal more confidence in the prophetic value of history and draw,
in minute detail, historical analogies intended to condemn the simple optimism and criminal tampering of the revolutionary leaders.
This almost literal belief in historical parallels extended, moreover,
well into the early nineteenth century and is effectively illustrated
by the following anonymous and rather curious document pur-
porting to be a history of the session of 1828, written in advance by
the great Scottish prophet of prophets, David Hume.

The "editor" of the *ultra* work in question begins by telling
his readers that he had intended at first to write his own history of
the session, "when I noticed," he goes on to say, "that it had already
been written a long time in advance, and in the most exact detail,

14. *Correspondance entre quelques hommes honnêtes*, III. 72–78.

by David Hume, in his history of the Stuarts."[15] Happy at finding his work already done, the writer abandons his original project and begins to copy:

> ...I place before my readers an account of what has just occurred here, penned by a necessarily impartial hand. If by this striking parallel I am able to open the eyes of so many honest persons who are being deceived with fine phrases, I would be only too happy....
>
> They will see that in all times and in every country the progress of revolutions does not vary; that in this century of perfectibility, we have been at pains to invent nothing, and that we are merely slavish imitators of the seventeenth-century English....
>
> Could we not say today as the English royalists did in 1641: "Never was sovereign blessed with more moderation, with more justice, more humanity, or more honour? What pity that such a prince should so long have been harassed with suspicions, calumnies, and complaints! If there have been instances of abuse, is there no other way to prevent their return than by total abolition of royal authority?...Authority as well as liberty is requisite to government; and is even requisite to the support of liberty itself. What madness, while everything is so happily settled under ancient forms and institutions, to try the hazardous experiment of a new constitution, and renounce the mature wisdom of our ancestors for the crude whimsies of turbulent innovators!" (Hume, tome XIV)....The English historian gives us here the explanation of many fine speeches, the measure of many great men, and the key to many great mysteries.
>
> Men are indeed the same in all centuries and in all places; the cunning of some exploits the passions or the credulity of others, and the vile motto of 1789: *That's my place if you don't mind!* has been and always will be that of all revolutions.[16]

15. *Histoire abrégée de la session de 1828, écrite à l'avance par David Hume*, Paris, 1829, *Avis de l'éditeur*, p. 3.

16. Ibid., pp. 3–15. In his *Analogies de l'histoire de France et d'Angleterre ou 1828 et 1640*, Louis de Bonald also invites the French to study Hume at this time: "It is in the history of the last Stuarts, especially in that of the most unfortunate Stuart of all, that we must study our own history, that of our own times." Those who felt in 1828 that there was no danger of revolution were especially urged to re-read the events of Charles I's reign: "They will recognize in the two nations, for 1828 as for 1640, the same causes of revolution, the same means employed, the same effects...." (See *Oeuvres complètes de M. de Bonald*, publiées par M. l'Abbé

The prime examples cited in the preceding note suggest the extent to which the idea that the French revolution paralleled the English revolution and paralleled it not only closely but, for many, identically, caught hold of the conservative imagination in revolutionary France. It is, in fact, through the counter-revolutionists' all but total acceptance of this idea that the influence of Hume's history had its effect from 1789 to 1800. For most Frenchmen of the time, no other history of the Stuart period existed; and Hume's manner of relating the events of the English revolution, his frequent reflections on those events, the guaranty provided by his long-standing reputation for nearly superhuman impartiality were all factors which served to increase the authority of his account in support of the doctrines of the Right.

A careful examination of all types of rightist literature of this early counter-revolutionary period would show, I think, that Hume's influence, though in some ways more subtle and diffused, is greater before the turn of the century than even the sensational but somewhat speculative impact of Burke. Burke's shouting, cranky pamphlet on the Revolution caused more amusement than concern among those it was meant to annihilate. Jokes were made about the probable insanity or at least senility of this raving Englishman who had been considered a frank liberal in France until the appearance of his *Reflections*. Burke's new tone could convince only those who wanted to be convinced. On the other hand, Hume's *Stuarts,* widely read during the thirty years preceding the

---

Migne, Paris, 1859, III. 913.) Joseph de Maistre, much earlier, had already included as the final chapter of his famous *Considérations sur la France* (1796) a similar "posthumous" work entitled "Fragment d'une histoire de la révolution française par David Hume." That de Maistre considered it an important and integral part of his text is made clear in the following letter to de Bonald from Turin, 15 November 1819: "Everything you tell me in your last letter about the English Revolution compared to yours is perfectly true. I was right, therefore, to use it as the last chapter of my *Considérations* and even more right to be angry with that brute of a publisher who took it upon himself, by his own authority, to excise it from the latest edition." (*Oeuvres complètes,* XIII. 192.) See also de Bonald's letter to de Maistre in 1819: "That deplorable history is ours, point for point, and up to this stage the two revolutions were copied, one from the other." (Ibid., XIV. 348.)

Revolution had had what we might call a subliminal influence even on the hostile, on those who did not want to be convinced and who were forced by the resulting intellectual tension to rewrite history in a more suitable form or to reject its authority altogether.

Through his popular description and analysis of the English revolution, Hume had helped to condition the minds and to form the prejudices, both negative and positive, of the generation which was to be so vitally concerned with similar events. He had provided in advance an almost irresistible set of categories to impose on France's own revolutionary events—a formula of response most suited to conservatives, it is true, but which, even as late as the period in which Louis XVI was tried, a fair number of *conventionnels,* I will not say accepted, but at least felt obligated to consider. Mailhe's report is only the most outstanding example of the need that was felt by many to formulate revolutionary activity in terms of the parallel activity which seventeenth-century England had witnessed.

The many conservative parallels, and there are almost none which do not make specific use of Hume, were not thus just the fashionable and flimsy games of idle pundits. In most cases, historical analogies were pointed out with deadly seriousness and were consciously intended to provoke or encourage a vigorous counter-revolutionary response. I will cite here one of the earliest of these *rapprochements* which, brief as it is, serves as a good example. It is revealed in an anecdote that we find in Soulavie's *Mémoires* and though its author, Louis XVI's brother, did not express it in the form of a published document, many documents published subsequently make a similar point:

> On the day that M. Necker succeeded in doubling the representation of the third estate in defiance of the advice of the royal princes and the notables, the Comte d'Artois took down the portrait of Louis XV that was hanging in the King's chambers and replaced it with a likeness of Charles I. And on the day that Louis XVI asked M. Necker to remain in the Ministry, the same day that the people of Versailles demonstrated by their rioting their support for M. Necker, M. d'Artois removed the excessively mute portrait and substituted for it a recently published engraving that showed King Charles I on

the point of having his head chopped off by the executioner's axe. This second hint had no greater effect than the first.[17]

Indeed, as Soulavie also suggests, there is perhaps good evidence to show that such *rapprochements* may have had, at least on Louis XVI, an effect opposite to that intended. But not all the parallels were conceived so brutally. Some were published to lend hope to the royalists in their darkest hour, to console them by showing that history was on their side, that all would come out right in the end and that they should therefore continue their faithful support of the counter-revolution. Others were quite obviously published to shame the revolutionaries, to humiliate the pride of those who ignorantly proclaimed that the bonds of history had been broken, that their revolution was new and without precedent. Pointing to the Stuart parallels, the royalist felt he could prove conclusively that the revolutionaries were not at all original; they were not even original in their crimes, and their wasted and bloody efforts would be condemned to futility once the whole sorry mess had gone the full circle. Some parallel makers, with their studied analogies, seem even to have cherished the rather sanguine hope of converting the radical enthusiasts to conservatism. Chateaubriand tells us, for example, that it is important to show there is nothing new under the sun since a man "well convinced that there is nothing new under the sun, loses his taste for innovations."[18]

One last more general reason for the proliferation of parallels during this period should not be neglected. In addition to their polemical value, they obviously provided a certain intellectual and aesthetic satisfaction to the hundreds of amateur pamphlet-historians who sprang up everywhere and who found it understandably difficult to give immediate meaning to the confusion and chaos of contemporary events. For these, the obvious parallel with Stuart history furnished a readily available short-cut to the time

17. Jean-Louis Giraud Soulavie, *Mémoires historiques et politiques,* VI. 312–13.

18. François-René de Chateaubriand, *Essai sur les Révolutions,* in *Oeuvres complètes de M. le vicomte de Chateaubriand,* Paris, 1834, I. 202.

perspective and allowed the chronicler of current happenings to speak with the borrowed authority of the ages. Here for the asking was a pre-fabricated dramatic structure ready to be imposed on events only an hour old. Here, Hume seemed to say, was the beginning, there was the middle, and finally, there would be the happy conclusion. Some parallels end, in fact, with wistful invocations to General Monk! The making of historical parallels was not new at this time nor has it entirely disappeared from serious modern historical literature. One would probably have difficulty finding, however, a period in history in which such analogies were more widely used and in which they had more real influence.

2

HISTORY AS THE SUPERSTITION OF SLAVES

If we turn now to the opinions of the Left on this matter we will see that the revolutionary ideologists disagreed passionately with the basic assumption on which such historical conservatism rested: namely, the idea of a stable human nature, of an inflexible moral "nature of things."

True enough, if man at birth is shown to be a creature of innate principles, of unchanging passions, of totally predictable motivation, why then his range of potential behaviour would be strictly limited; nothing really new could ever be expected of him; his "original sin" would be the despair of all social reformers and all efforts to change and improve his form of social organization would be predestined to failure. But original sin, even in its naturalistic interpretations, had been driven out with the advent of Lockian epistemology. Man is not, Locke tells us, born with a human nature, his mind is a *tabula rasa;* his heart, too, others said, is a blank sheet. Man is merely what, not nature, but nurture makes him. Good education for the individual and for the society, good legislation, can change man, not overnight, of course, but at least in a generation. Thus the so-called nature of things is no longer a great stumbling block; history becomes bunk, and progress, even indefinite progress, becomes a real possibility.

No one, perhaps, argues the case for a rejection of history more cogently than the Abbé Sieyès:

> Let us leave it to others to think that they must go back to barbaric times to find laws for civilized nations. We have no intention of becoming lost in a labyrinth of random searches through antiquated institutions and archaic errors. Reason is timeless and it is made for man; it is especially when reason speaks to man of what he holds most dear that he must listen to it with respect and confidence....
>
> Ask a clockmaker to make you a clock and take note whether he wastes any time extracting from the history of clockmaking, true or false, the different methods the industry in its infancy may have thought up for the measurement of time....
>
> We are always so eager to take advantage, for our own enjoyment, of the slightest improvements in the arts of luxury and commerce: do we then turn our backs in shameful indifference when it comes to improvements in the *social art,* this most important of all the arts, on whose expert arrangements depends the happiness of the human race?[19]

We should note that, with the eighteenth century's empirical connotation for the word *science,* Sieyès prefers to speak of an *art social* and not a *science sociale.* The choice of words is highly significant for it is the conservative's privilege to speak at this time of history as a sacred repository of all the empirical data from which could be derived a science of human nature. It is the conservative who speaks also of general psycho-physical laws governing with Newtonian regularity the processes of moral phenomena. Those who reject history are forced, on the other hand, and not without considerable embarrassment, to resort to an almost pre-scientific moral indeterminism and to claim, paradoxically for this monistic age, an almost spiritually independent status for man's moral and political being:

19. Emmanuel-Joseph Sieyès, "Vues sur les moyens d'exécution dont les Représentans de la France pourront disposer en 1789," in *Collection des écrits d'Emmanuel Sieyès,* édition à l'usage de l'Allemagne, Paris, pp. 8–10.

Every day we witness the inane efforts of pedants confidently trying their hand at belittling philosophers who go back to first principles in their analysis of the social art. Useful, seminal meditations are viewed as nothing more than evidence of laziness by these pompous scholastics; and when a man of superior genius, as much from disgust as discernment, abandons the depressing chronicles of error bequeathed by our ancestors, mediocrity immediately sets about the material task of noting down assiduously every single page of history, seeing in the mere ability to read and transcribe a pre-eminent merit, as well as the answer to every question.

Unfortunately, the philosophers themselves, who in the course of this last century have rendered such signal service to the physical sciences, seem to lend credibility to this ridiculous presumption, as well as the authority of their own genius to these mindless declarations. Quite properly sickened by the systematizing mania of their predecessors, they devoted themselves single-mindedly to the study of facts, and proscribed all other methodologies; for this they deserved only praise. But when, leaving the physical sciences, they recommended and applied the same method to their study of the moral world, they were mistaken. Before prescribing a uniform treatment for all of the sciences, they should have examined their differences—both in essential nature and in subject matter.

Nothing is more sensible than the physical scientist's determination to limit himself to observing and gathering facts, and to trying to discover their interconnections. The physicist's object is to discover nature; and since he was not called upon to advise on or to shape the plan of the physical world, since the physical universe exists and continues on quite independently of his corrective meditations, he must obviously restrict himself to the experience of facts. Physics can be nothing other than knowledge of *what is*.

But the limits of science are not the same as the limits of art. Art takes bolder flight; it proposes to bend and accommodate facts according to our needs and enjoyment; keeping in view the benefit of mankind, it asks the question: *what ought to be....*[20]

The historico-scientific method in politics, Sieyès affirms, leads not to science but to superstition. It is true that history can provide some useful information to the legislator who has a meditative turn of mind, but he must also look beyond mere facts. Most historical facts are, moreover, entirely unedifying:

20. Ibid., pp. 40–41.

Oh! if the road of experience is long for the physical scientist, at least it promises a useful journey; at least he can be certain that by continuing to advance along that road he will increase his store of knowledge. How different is the situation of the legislator! How heavily events must weigh on his spirit! How pressed he must feel to leave behind at last the appalling accumulation of past experience....

Take care that your representatives are not influenced by the notion, already preached to excess by your learned philosophers, that morality, like the physical sciences, must be based on experience....

Never has it been more urgent to restore to reason its full authority, to take back from the facts the power that, unhappily for the human race, they have usurped from reason. I am governed by such considerations and, yes, I shall give free rein to my complaints and my indignation against that multitude of writers who are obsessed with asking the past what we should become in the future, who are consumed with a desire to search through the debris of miserable traditions composed of irrationality and falsehoods in order to find the legislation needed to restore health to the social fabric; who stubbornly dig away in the archives, inspecting and compiling countless reports, reverently seeking out for purposes of worship even the most minute fragments, however doubtful their authenticity, however obscure and unintelligible these may be. And all in the hope of discovering what? Old certificates of title, as if in their gothic rapture they dream of calling upon the entire nation to *show its proofs* of worthy ancestry.[21]

Legislators will find nothing useful searching in historical archives; the true archives of man lie in his heart:

...the light of reason must finally be joined to the sentiment of liberty. We are capable of finding the way to social order on our own; and once on that road, we shall not be so ridiculously weak as to choose for our guides people who know only how to look backwards to the past....

...let us hasten to abjure the superstition of slaves; let us cease our resistance to the light that surrounds us on all sides; and when the great day that is dawning for us comes, let us make clear to all that we are aware of our rights; let us not allow our Representatives who are charged with determining the destiny of twenty-six million

21. Ibid., pp. 42–45.

people to debase themselves in vain quarreling, offering to a world that is watching the ridiculous and shameful spectacle of a theological rabble fighting over texts, competing on how best to tear reason apart, and, after much noise and uproar, achieving in the end nothing more than the profoundest nullity.[22]

There are thus no lessons from the past worth worrying about. History is largely irrelevant. It is not, for example, a valid argument to point out that certain political institutions deserve respect because they are old and therefore good. All human institutions are old, and despotism is perhaps the oldest of all. The French would be wrong to follow the examples of past generations or of other nations. They must have the ambition and courage to strike out on their own, to develop independently the ideal forms of political government, and to serve, finally, as a model for other nations and for future generations.

Thomas Paine in 1791 stresses this same need for emancipation from the tyranny of old historical adjustments: "Every age and generation," he writes, "must be as free to act for itself *in all cases* as the ages and generations which preceded it. The vanity and presumption of governing beyond the grave is the most ridiculous and insolent of all tyrannies. . . . Every generation is, and must be, competent to all the purposes which its occasions require. It is the living and not the dead, that are to be accommodated."[23] Paine's own description of how he set about writing his highly influential pamphlet *Common Sense* is typical of this radical rejection of history: "I saw," Paine wrote in 1792, "an opportunity in which I thought I could do some good, and I followed exactly what my heart dictated. I neither read books, nor studied other people's opinions. I thought for myself."[24]

The inventory of Robespierre's Paris library seems to indicate that he too was not an avid reader of history.[25] It is not too far-

---

22. Ibid., pp. 50–53.

23. *The Rights of Man,* Part I, Everyman's Library, p. 12.

24. Ibid., Part II, p. 223, note 1.

25. See G. Bapst, "Inventaire des bibliothèques de quatre condamnés," *La Révolution Française,* July–December 1891, XXI. 534.

fetched, moreover, to see in the Incorruptible's famous diatribe on the *philosophes* an anti-history attitude, directed as much against their learning—which Robespierre seems to equate with sophistry—as against their religious disbelief. He praises Rousseau, on the other hand, for the *purity of his doctrine,* "drawn from nature and from the detestation of vice."[26] The virtue of unlettered patriots, he affirms, is to be contrasted with the craven neutrality of the once-celebrated intellectuals:

> Generally speaking, the men of letters have disgraced themselves in this Revolution; to the eternal shame of intellect, it is the people's reason that alone has made a contribution.
>
> Blush with shame if you can,[27] you vain little men! The miracles that will forever immortalize this period of human history have been wrought without you, and in spite of you; simple, honest good sense and unschooled genius have carried France to our present great heights that terrify your craven baseness and crush your nullity. While this artisan was displaying skillful knowledge of the rights of man, that scribbler of books, almost a republican in 1788, was stupidly defending the cause of kings in 1793; while this ploughman was spreading light in the countryside, the academician Condorcet—once a great geometer, they say, according to the men of letters, and a great man of letters, according to the geometers, but afterwards a cowardly conspirator scorned by every party—was working incessantly to obscure that light with his treacherous hotchpotch of mercenary rhapsodies.[28]

Ironically, Condorcet himself not long before, although he did not attack history *per se,* had assailed the old historians on much the same grounds:

26. "Sur les rapports des idées religieuses et morales avec les principes républicains et sur les fêtes nationales," séance du 7 mai, 1794, in *Oeuvres de Robespierre,* ed. A. Vermorel, Paris, 1867, p. 324.

27. At the risk of sounding facetious in defence of outworn perspectives, one might observe that it was no longer possible, thanks to the tidy efforts of this gentleman from Arras, for a good number of them to blush at this time.

28. Ibid., p. 325.

Until now, modern history has been corrupted: at times because of the need to deal tactfully with established tyrannies, at other times because of partisan bias....

... Even Voltaire, the greatest of modern historians, so outstanding in the moral portion of his historical writings, was not able in the political sections to give free rein to his genius. Obliged to spare one enemy of the human race in order to have the right to attack the other with impunity, he crushed superstition but opposed despotism only with the rules of personal justice and the cries of humanity; he reproached it for its crimes, but he left untouched in its royal hands the power to commit them.

We need, consequently, an entirely new history, one that is concerned essentially with the rights of man and with the vicissitudes that both the knowledge and the enjoyment of those rights have suffered over the centuries and in every place....[29]

Other republicans had even more severe recommendations. The reading of history, some suggested, should be sternly limited; that of the ancients and that of one's own country sufficed.[30] That of one's own country, agreed Mercier, provided it was first properly purged: "The history of France should be burned and begun afresh; it must be discarded along with all those massive tomes of *jurisprudence* and scholastic philosophy...."[31] In 1798, the *idéologues* in *La Décade* go even farther: "Every history book must be made over; every book dealing with political, civil, or criminal legislation must be rewritten; all books on moral philosophy, up until now uniformly tainted with mysticity, must be redone."[32]

Once history was burned it could of course be rewritten along republican lines for those who still felt some need of it. We shall see that such revolutionary figures as Mirabeau, Brissot, Condorcet, Mme Roland, and others did indeed actively publicize Catherine

29. *Sur l'instruction publique*, "5ème mémoire," in *Bibliothèque de l'homme public*, XI, tome 9, pp. 57–59.

30. See J.-J.-G. Levesque, *Essai sur la manière d'écrire et d'étudier l'histoire*, Paris, An III, pp. 79–80.

31. *De J.-J. Rousseau considéré comme l'un des premiers auteurs de la Révolution*, Paris, 1791, II. 194.

32. See *La Décade philosophique, littéraire et politique*, XVII. 493.

Macaulay's history of the English revolution as most suitable to replace the hated royalist account by Hume. For others, however, the history of former revolutions was totally irrelevant. Carra, speaking during the Convention debates on Louis XVI's trial, exemplifies the new attitude:

I shall try to present to your enlightened wisdom the findings of broad common sense, dispassionately calculated comparisons, simple and straightforward ideas, reasoning grounded in the human heart's inner conscience and in the intellect's sense of morality. I shall not quote from history, because history offers nothing that compares to our Revolution . . . ; because history, as I have observed it since the beginning of the Revolution, has done nothing but lead kings and ministers astray in the way they have applied it to future events; because our Revolution, being the product of decisive advances in universal reason and politics, can have absolutely nothing in common with the revolutions of earlier times, nor can it suffer retrograde interpretations or the application of empirical data taken from history. Everything in our Revolution is new. . . . [33]

Everything was new in Carra's revolution—a radical sentiment which was very neatly answered by Bancal who summed up in his reply the traditionalist defence of history: ". . . yes, everything is new, except for the human beings involved, who constitute the basic elements of a revolution, and who, no matter the country or the century, continue to be ruled by the passions."[34]

Saint-Just even implies that holding to the old cyclical view of revolutions was part of the Girondist conspiracy. In his report of 1793 to the Committee of Public Safety concerning the Girondins arrested after 31 May and 1 June, he made the following accusation: "Every step taken by the prisoners led in the direction of restoring the monarchy. . . . These cunning men, cunning and depraved, sensed in the end that they should follow the people, convinced as they were that revolutions progress horizontally and that because of the excesses, the misfortunes, and the reckless actions

33. *Discours contre la Défense de Louis Capet, Dernier Roi des Français,* par le Citoyen Carra, député de Saône-et-Loire, prononcé à la séance du 3 janvier 1793.

34. *Discours et projet de décret de Henri Bancal,* député du Puy-de-Dôme, p. 4.

that accompany them, revolutions eventually return to their starting point...."[35]

Quite to the contrary, revolutions progress vertically not horizontally; they are the instruments of man's moral ascent. To say that similar attempts had been made before and had necessarily failed, to identify the French revolution and the English revolution—these were counter-revolutionary ideas and a subtle form of treason: rather like pointing out that the total number of victims of the Bastille in all the centuries of its existence probably never equalled the number of prisoners confined in the Châtelet and the Abbaye during the first two or three glorious years of the *reign of liberty.*

35. "Rapport sur les trente-deux membres de la Convention détenus en vertu du décret du 2 juin," in *Oeuvres complètes de Saint-Just,* ed. Charles Vellay, Paris, 1908, II. 10.

III

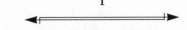

From 1789 to the
Trial of Louis XVI

PROPHETIC PARALLELS AND THE
COUNTER-REVOLUTIONARY LESSONS OF HUME

Abbé Maury figures most appropriately at the beginning of this chapter dealing in part with examples of Hume's influence on some of the early counter-revolutionary leaders. Maury, generally recognized as the leading orator of the Right in the Assemblée Constituante, had been since 1785 a member of the French Academy and was eventually to be named a cardinal of the Church. He seems to have been a witty, rather forceful person and an extemporary speaker of some brilliance. It is not too inappropriate to contrast him, as contemporaries often did, with Mirabeau, his opposite number on the Left.

Like his personal friends Gerdil and Bergier, Maury was fond of quoting Bossuet in defence of the *ancien régime* but, like them too, he occasionally found it useful to invoke also the authority of that new Bossuet, the historian David Hume. Long before the Revolution he had commended Hume as a loyal and impartial historian worth using to attack the "English bias" of the *philosophe* Voltaire. In 1777, for example, he quite happily pointed out that the Scottish historian disagreed with the great Voltaire on the quality of English eloquence.[1] Voltaire had devoted one of his famous philosophical letters to praising Bacon, and Maury points out at this time—as Joseph de Maistre was to later—that Hume had attacked the inflated reputation of this culture hero of the *encyclopédistes* and had rightly put him well below Galileo in importance. On at least one occasion we even find the Abbé adducing proofs from Hume in his sermons, as in his panegyric of Saint Louis delivered to the assembled members of the French Academy in the chapel of the Louvre on 25 August 1772.[2]

Hume is not infrequently mentioned in Abbé Maury's speeches delivered during the early revolutionary debates. Defending the rights of the throne in 1790, he accused the National Assembly of an illegitimate attempt to deprive the Crown of its traditional prerogative to declare war and make treaties. The rôle of the Assembly, as Maury saw it, was not to establish a new constitution but to correct with the help of the king any current abuses in government and to revive, to that end, the ancient constitution of France. History, he asserted, provides a warning to those who dare to attempt more radical reforms and who, wishing to extend illegitimately the powers of popular representatives, reduce the monarch's importance to that of being merely a "republican" figurehead:

> We know that Cardinal Mazarin, after the tragic death of Charles I, went to great lengths to encourage the English to adopt a purely republican style of government in their island, Mazarin . . . realizing as he did how that form of government, by its slowness of action and its internal divisions, would weaken the political power of the English nation; but the English, after trying, as Mr. Hume has said, *to do without a king,* realized that their parliament needed counterbalancing by royal authority; with patriotic hands they raised up the throne once more, and for a century now, they have not tried to shake the sacred foundations of their constitution. Is it possible,

1. *Discours choisis sur divers sujets de religion et de littérature,* par M. l'Abbé Maury, Paris, 1777, p. 132. See also *Oeuvres choisies du cardinal J.-Sifrein Maury,* Paris, 1827, II. 142–51.

2. Ibid., III. 361–62. Maury quotes Hume's portrait of the French king.

Gentlemen, that this assembly could forget the great lesson that England has taught Europe?[3]

A reader of the *Political Discourses* as well as the *History,* Maury cited Hume in July 1790 against the fiscal policies of Necker:

He alone, it must be acknowledged, by lending an outward appearance of prosperity to our finances, by maintaining the lie that he was able to sustain the costs of war without recourse to additional taxation, brought about the ruin of the kingdom through borrowing at exorbitant rates. The enticements he held out to investors strengthened considerably his own personal credit, which afterwards proved so disastrous for us. *Either the nation must destroy public credit,* writes Mr. Hume, *or public credit will destroy the nation....*[4]

Abbé Maury had already quoted Hume's testimony in his maiden speech of September 1789 on the question of the royal veto, again to the effect that the king's authority must not be weakened, that revolutions are basically futile, that Charles II, for example, had found the source of his restored power in the aftereffects of his unfortunate father's execution.[5] Maury's greatest Hume-inspired parliamentary triumph was to come, however, in 1790 during a verbal exchange with his noted enemy Mirabeau concerning the sovereignty of the people.[6]

3. *Opinion sur le droit de faire la guerre et de conclure les traités de paix, d'alliance et de commerce;* prononcée dans l'assemblée nationale le 18 mai 1790, ibid., IV. 99–100.

4. *Opinion sur les finances et sur la dette publique,* July 1790, ibid., IV. 172.

5. *Discours sur la sanction royale,* ibid., V. iv.

6. A note of caution is necessary here. That Maury was the only rightist orator at this time who could match the vigour of Mirabeau seems little in doubt. That such was the opinion of contemporaries is evidenced in the following not entirely biased "Anagram-Epigram concerning two very well-known party leaders," which we find in the *Actes des Apôtres,* 1789, I, No. 28, p. 16:

Deux insignes chefs de parti
D'intrigue ici tiennent bureau,
Chacun à l'autre est assorti,
Même audace & voix de taureau;
L'on pourrait faire le pari
Qu'ils sont nés dans la même peau;
Car retournez *abé Mauri,*
Vous trouverez *Mirabeau.*

Maury began his attack on the concept of the people's sovereignty with an appeal to the traditional arguments of Fénelon and Bossuet on the subject. The theory of contract is a fiction. Society took its origins in man's natural, that is, God-given, sociability. Authority and subordination are thus also divine in origin. Express or tacit consent of a primitively "free" people may *seem* at times to have been the source of government, but this is a fallacious appearance. Free consent is sometimes the *channel* of authority, it is not the *source*. "The consequence of this theory," Maury continues, "is that religion gives us a notion of authority that is both true and inspiring when it shows how it emanates originally from God. By presenting the Supreme Being as the direct author of sovereignty, the protector and avenger of the laws, it illustrates clearly in this perspective that every human society is a theocracy.... "[7]

[Two distinguished party chiefs
Scheme and hold forth here;
Well-matched to one another,
Both are brassy, both bellow like bulls;
One could almost lay odds
They are brothers under the skin;
For if you shuffle abé Mauri,
Out comes Mirabeau.*]*

There are many anecdotes attesting to Abbé Maury's quick wit. The following example of it is related by Montlosier, who describes how one day the future Cardinal was walking near the Halles market area: "Several of the local streetwalkers caught sight of him and accosted him: —'Good-day to *you*, my fine sturdy fellow!' —'Good-day ladies.' —'You've got wit enough, 'tis true, but no matter how you kick and struggle, you'll be f..... in the end!' —'Oh! ladies, as *you* very well know, one doesn't die from that!' At which they burst out laughing and rushed up to hug and kiss him." (*Mémoires de M. le Comte de Montlosier sur la Révolution française*, Paris, 1830, II. 314.) There is evidence to show, nevertheless, that Maury's powerful lungs and sharp wit were not always sufficient for the task of overcoming the increasingly impatient heckling of the opposition benches (see, for example, the *Journal des débats*, Nos. 153 and 382). Although he remained at his post until 1791, he more than ever took to publishing dictated versions of his speeches. It is thus very likely, as Aulard points out, that "the most celebrated speeches of Abbé Maury were never *delivered* by him." (F.-A. Aulard, *Les Orateurs de l'Assemblée Constituante*, Paris, 1882, p. 234.)

7. *Opinion sur la souveraineté du peuple,* prononcée dans l'Assemblée Nationale en 1790 par M. l'Abbé Maury et publiée sur les manuscrits autographes de l'auteur par Louis-Sifrein Maury, son neveu, Avignon, 1852, pp. 95–96.

Preparing to go on with the practical applications of this pious theory, Maury, as he tells the story, was interrupted by that foolish fellow Mirabeau who shouted:

—"You are making a mockery of the Assembly when you come here and peddle your lessons in theology. Only fanatical and ignorant theologians have ever professed such a doctrine regarding the supposed origins of sovereignty. I defy you to cite the name of even one person of sense who has ever argued such nonsense!"

Quite unruffled and wisely prepared in advance to answer such an impertinence, Abbé Maury took up the challenge:

—"I accept your generous challenge, Monsieur de Mirabeau, first, by pointing out that we should in no way be surprised that the human mind is obliged to have recourse to God in order to find an unshakeable support for sovereignty, since without divine intervention even a solid foundation for morality would be lacking. I shall therefore cite among the defenders of my doctrine, not a theologian but one of the most celebrated political writers of this century, an English philosopher whom no one has yet suspected of believing in pious superstitions. Here is what I read in the twenty-fifth moral and political essay of David Hume:..."

If we are to believe Maury's account, he then recited to the assembled representatives of the French nation the "theocratic" passage already used for a similar purpose in 1769 by his friend Cardinal Gerdil,[8] omitting, however, and hardly because of its length, the last half. His conclusion is triumphant:

—"Have you had enough, Monsieur de Mirabeau? I'll spare you ten other quotations just like that one. As you can see, even the greatest authorities support my opinion and have joined in these incontrovertible arguments, while you are left with making assertions that I disprove and issuing challenges that only advance my cause.

"Along with Mr. Hume, then, I say to all short-sighted philosophers that sovereign power emanates not from the people, but only from God. The magnificent and fertile nature of God which has created in the immensity of his thought all of his decrees has also

8. See *supra*, pp. 43–44.

created this tutelary authority by summoning mankind to the social state...."[9]

Abbé Maury leaves it to be understood that after such a complete answer his opponent Mirabeau was, momentarily at least, struck dumb with defeat. Of course, at least in this last example, Maury is merely continuing the practice of retortion in the tradition of Gerdil, Bergier, Nonnotte, and others, and it would be a mistake to imagine on his part anything more than a polemical attachment to Hume's statement. His perhaps more sincere opinion of Hume he confided privately years later to another counter-revolutionary ideologist, Count Joseph de Maistre, when they met in Venice during the winter of 1799. There they had an extensive conversation on various literary subjects and one of these was the question of Hume's merit as an historian. De Maistre notes without comment that Maury judged Hume to be "a mediocre historian who gained a reputation for impartiality by what he said of the Stuarts." The English were really superior only in their novels, of which *Clarissa Harlowe* and *Tom Jones* seem to have been the good Cardinal's favourites.[10]

It is not difficult to find other counter-revolutionary figures who make at this time less spectacular but undeniably influential use of Hume's writings. In this regard, his statements on the empirical nature of the British constitution, denying that before the seventeenth century it formed a "regular plan of liberty," were found of special interest.

Traditionalists were disturbed from the very beginning of the revolutionary debates by the radicals' claim that France had no constitution. It was of no use to speak, as Fénelon, for example, had spoken years before, of an ancient "unwritten" constitution. A constitution, as Thomas Paine wrote in 1791, "is not a thing in name only, but in fact. It has not an ideal, but a real existence; and

9. Ibid., pp. 96–98.

10. *See Oeuvres complètes de J. de Maistre,* VII. 503. Worth mentioning here also is the use made at about this same time of Hume's position on divorce by another representative of the clergy in the National Assembly, the Abbé Armand de Chapt de Rastignac, in his work *Accord de la Révélation et de la Raison contre le divorce,* Paris, 1790, pp. 332–33, 339, 347–48.

wherever it cannot be produced in a visible form, there is none."[11] A constitution, in short, had to be something that one could roll up and put in one's pocket. The English had no constitution until Magna Carta; France in 1789 was in rather the same position as England before the granting of the Great Charter.

Along with others on the Right, the extreme royalist de Montjoie took exception to this view. The revolutionists, he jeered, talked endlessly about constitutions without having even the most elementary understanding of what that word meant. Constitutions are not theoretical *a priori* constructions, they are as natural as gravity itself. It is impossible for a nation not to be "constituted" and France was no exception:

> Our *parlements,* our *assemblées du clergé,* our *provinces à états* and *sous-états,* were not a constitution; but the existence of these institutions, the way they were organized and connected to the whole of government, that was the constitution of France.
>
> It is my ardent wish that from the current anarchy a reasonable constitution will emerge, but it is not I who have dug this deep abyss of anarchy; it is those, rather, who misled Frenchmen in 1789 into believing that they had no constitution....
>
> Every civilized people has a constitution, for a civilized people could not exist without some form of government.[12]

What de Montjoie and others who took this position are really doing, of course, is rejecting the contract theory of the origin of government in one of its various manifestations. Hume's political empiricism helped to support this anti–*a priori* line of argument. His *History,* de Montjoie pointed out, underlines the fact that constitutions are nothing more than the products of time and circumstance. One cannot say that the British nation had a fixed constitution in all the years of its political existence following Magna Carta. The British constitution had been a fluctuating and ill-defined thing throughout the ages. Hume had in fact viewed the "usurpations" of the Stuart kings with more leniency than most

11. *The Rights of Man,* Part I, p. 48.

12. Félix-Louis-Christophe de Montjoie, *Histoire de la Révolution de France et de l'Assemblée Nationale,* Paris, 1792, cinquième partie, pp. 127–28.

historians precisely because of his belief in the extenuating circumstances provided by such constitutional variation. Speaking, for example, of the constitution under James I, de Montjoie asserts:

> ... it was fathered by violent innovations and bears so little resemblance to that of the English under James II that Mr. Hume describes them as two absolutely different constitutions. Here are his remarkable words on the subject:
>
> "The praise bestowed on those [patriots] to whom the nation has been indebted for its privileges ought to be given with some reserve, and surely without the least rancour against those who adhered to the ancient constitution."
>
> It is thus not because the English had a Great Charter in the thirteenth century that England's constitution is what it is today.[13]

From the *tabula rasa* political view of France without a constitution naturally followed for many revolutionary theoreticians the conclusion that the National Assembly was invested with the primary status of a *convention nationale* representing all the authority of the nation in its pre-constituted state. Radical attempts to grace the National Assembly with this title were of course vigorously opposed by members of the Right. Citing Hume on the question, both Calonne and Lally-Tollendal[14] insisted that to call the National Assembly a *Convention* would be to imply with impudence and quite erroneously that all preceding government had been entirely dissolved, whereas France's national parliament had in fact been convoked by the king in conformity with the "constitution" and with all the ordinary formalities "as have all of the National Assemblies since the time of Charlemagne. Consequently, we were not a *Convention Nationale*."[15]

The details of the semantic controversy just noted may seem trivial in retrospect. What was certainly not trivial, however, was the nature and amount of political power being hotly disputed, and it

---

13. Ibid., p. 127.

14. *De l'Etat de la France, présent et à venir,* par M. de Calonne, ministre d'Etat, Londres, 1791, pp. 360–61; *Mémoire de M. le Comte de Lally-Tollendal, ou Seconde Lettre à ses Commettans,* Paris, 1790, pp. 107–8.

15. Lally-Tollendal, op. cit., p. 109.

is significant, I think, that Hume's authority was brought into the question by two such important members of the Right. Also wishing to show that France before the Revolution was not entirely without legal foundation, another noted traditionalist, Jean-Joseph Mounier, quoted Hume's opinion that the privileges of English peers and the liberty of the English Commons had in fact originated in France. Consequently, Mounier asserted in 1792, if the French had adopted the British constitution they would only have repatriated what was to begin with their own.[16]

It can be easily seen that, with the parties of the Right, Hume's reputation and authority as an historian are in this period perhaps even greater than they were during the thirty years preceding the Revolution, when he was so widely read under very different circumstances. Barnave in 1792, for example, called Hume "the best of modern historians,"[17] and Lally-Tollendal in the same year recited Hume-inspired political lessons to Burke.[18]

Hume's interpretation of the Long Parliament's activities as a series of cunning usurpations seems to have been particularly useful to those rightists who at this time wished to attack the National Assembly's claim that it fully represented the true wishes of the nation. What was this *nation*, royalists liked to ask, this fantastic creature whose mandate was always being invoked, which was presumably all of France but which apparently made its wishes known only to a few and at the bidding of a few? Attacking a current practice of some parties in the National Assembly, the Comte d'Antraigues, who was later to play an active cloak-and-dagger rôle in the counter-revolution, quoted Hume against the demagogic use of *adresses* or petitions:

16. *Recherches sur les causes qui ont empêché les Français de devenir libres et sur les moyens qui leur restent pour acquérir la liberté*, Genève, 1792, I. 210. In this same work Mounier, quoting Hume's sentiment that despotism is preferable to popular anarchy, urges the French to rally round Louis XVI and place absolute power in his hands for the period of one year. (Ibid., II. 213–15.)

17. *Introduction à la Révolution Française* (1792), in *Oeuvres de Barnave*, Paris, 1843, I. 72.

18. *Seconde Lettre de M. de Lally-Tollendal à M. Burke*, Londres, 1792, p. 35. The French jurist J.-V. Delacroix also calls Hume "the most impartial of historians," in his *Constitutions des principaux états de l'Europe et des Etats-Unis de l'Amérique*, Paris, 1791, II. 206.

We know only too well how people go about generating bundles of petitions.

But I say to you that while these petitions may be flattering to the assembly that receives them, they can never be regarded as substitutes for the required and absolutely essential forms. Petitions received from even a thousand municipalities cannot be equated to the decree of a single bailiwick; it would be as if the partial and isolated consent of individuals who make up the national assembly was enough to form a decree.[19]

In a three-page note attached to this passage, d'Antraigues reproduces Hume's description of the similar abuse of petitions by the Long Parliament. The petitions were, Hume tells us, a fraudulent device of popularity, accepted only from groups favourable to the Puritan faction and used to incite the people to civil discord. All petitions favouring the monarchy or the Church were, on the other hand, immediately rejected. D'Antraigues concludes with the darkly prophetic comment: "I shall add no observations to the quoted passage but prudence alone requires that I prove it exists, that I did not invent it; and if presenting such tableaux is a crime, it is Mr. Hume who is guilty: see his *History of the Stuarts* for the year 1642 ... seven years before the murder of Charles I, eleven years before Cromwell was declared Protector."[20]

Comparisons such as that by d'Antraigues, viewing at the same time the activities of the Long Parliament and those of the revolutionary assembly, form the basis of most parallels drawn between the English and French revolutions published by conservatives at this time.

Fairly typical of these are the *tableaux* which appeared in the ultra royalist journal *Les Actes des Apôtres* in 1790. Beginning in January of that year and with a studied light-heartedness (since at first the *apôtres* seemed to believe that it would take no more than a

---

19. *Quelle est la situation de l'Assemblée Nationale?* (1790), pp. 41–44.

20. Ibid., pp. 43–44. The same passage from "the wise Hume" is quoted against the Convention in December 1792 by Dugour: *Mémoire justificatif pour Louis XVI*, Paris, 1793, pp. 119–21.

timely dose of *Hudibras* to push back the Revolution),[21] the editors presented their readers with the "Tableau parlant, Fragment de l'histoire d'Angleterre."[22] Although it is an account largely from Hume of the seventeenth-century revolution in England, the *tableau* is presented as an exact depiction of events taking place in revolutionary France: ". . . the plan was formed to do away with the Church and the monarchy. The monarch's council had acted in bad faith; the nation was irritated, and its representatives were ambitious and corrupt. The minister parleyed, the abyss grew deeper, and thickening clouds of blood darkened the horizon."[23]

At the end of this historical sketch the editors state its purpose and promise more of the same:

> We conclude at this point the first part of our introduction, which presents an authentic *living-image tableau*. Since those times, similar events elsewhere have fostered the same passions. We leave it to the reader to draw the lesson. By presenting to faithful subjects and enlightened citizens the picture of one great nation's past disorders, we hope to spare others seeking renewal the errors and horrors that will forever remain in the eyes of posterity a reason for proud Albion's shame.[24]

21. As in the following pastiche of the popular revolutionary song *Ça ira:*
Enfin de la folie
Le peuple guérira,
Et de sa maladie
Les auteurs punira.
Je crois qu'après cela
Tout se rétablira;
Je crois qu'après cela,
Ça ira, ça ira.
(*Les Actes des Apôtres*, No. 173, p. 16.)

[Finally, the madness of the people will be cured, and the authors of it punished; I think after that, everything will be right again; I think after that, 'twill be fine, 'twill be fine.]

Along with those of other conservative heroes, Hume's name figures in some of the *apôtres'* light verse against Robespierre. See, for example, ibid., No. 15, pp. 5–6.

22. Ibid., II. 5–25.

23. Ibid., II. 21.

24. Ibid., II. 22.

Volume III followed with the "Comparison Tableau" continuing the account of Stuart history from 1641. Written in April 1790, and still inspired by the wise prophet David Hume, the new sketch pictures the unfortunate king "struggling to defend his royal prerogative against a parliament made up of factious persons determined to build a republic on the ruins of the monarchy and the Church."[25] In Volume IV we are presented with the "Royal Tableau," which quotes in full Hume's portrait of Hampden, now seen as describing perfectly the typical French revolutionist: "We must only be cautious, notwithstanding his generous zeal for liberty, not hastily to ascribe to him the praises of a good citizen. Through all the horrors of civil war, he sought the abolition of monarchy and subversion of the constitution; an end which, had it been attainable by peaceful measures, ought carefully to have been avoided by every lover of his country."[26] Hampden's portrait is then contrasted with that of the virtuous Falkland whom another Hume disciple, Lally-Tollendal, had already seen himself as imitating when he resigned from the Assembly in 1789. In addition, the *apôtres* note the existence in both countries of a "national assembly simulacrum" which, "contemptuous of the existing constitution, did not fail, in order to shore up its authority, to decree as a principle that all sovereignty emanates from the people."[27] Finally less concerned with pointing out parallels, the editors optimistically attempt a number of predictions. They meditate without sorrow on the fate of Charles I's judges: "It is not without a certain secret pleasure that we anticipate events by announcing that twenty-seven of them were hanged when, ten years later, Charles II regained the throne of his ancestors."[28] Of course, bringing attention to this last fact was somewhat gratuitous. If the inexorable parallel between the two revolutions seemed to waver in one respect it was that the French in 1790 were too wise to rush headlong into the crimes of seventeenth-century England: "Louis XVI has already

25. Ibid., III. 5.
26. Ibid., IV. 15–16.
27. Ibid., IV. 28.
28. Ibid., IV. 29.

triumphed over the wicked; we hope that the monarchy will like-wise triumph over the republic, and that one day we shall have a translation into French of the constitutional hieroglyphics that are being randomly engraved on the national obelisk."[29]

To celebrate this anticipated happy change in the course of the French revolution, a fourth and final tableau was prepared, the "Tableau of Resurrection," depicting, of course, the restora-tion of the monarchy in England. Events in France at the end of 1790 stubbornly refused, however, to follow true to form. The *apôtres* ruefully concede in Volume V that the promised last instal-ment would have to be postponed for a time; the task, it seems, was even beyond the strength of *Hudibras* and renewed meditation on the darker parallels was necessary:

> Unhappy people ... they are trying to flatter your passions with the word *republic;* their aim is to make you desire it; they want the word to inflame your imagination, to lead you astray, just as the word *lib-erty* has already led you astray.... Listen carefully for a moment, learn what happened one hundred and fifty years ago to your neigh-bours, compare the events, the methods employed, and the results; compare and judge, so that, if possible, the misfortunes of others will not be lost on you.
>
> Cromwell and his parliament still inspire universal horror throughout the ages and they will continue to be held in execra-tion by posterity; and yet they were called *patriots, defenders of the laws, protectors of the people;* they said that everything they did, they did for the good of the people, to preserve the rights of the nation, and in the name of liberty. Inspired by such noble motives, they ravaged their country, erected scaffolds, and executed all those whose virtue offended them: they attacked the throne, harried the king, impris-oned him, protesting all the while their respect and love for his per-son: finally, ... these many crimes placed sovereign power in the hands of forty petty tyrants, and ended with the odious Cromwell being declared *protector of the good people of the republic.*
>
> But listen still: scarcely was the monster in his grave when the spell was suddenly broken, and the eyes of the English people were opened. They pursued his accomplices, and wreaked vengeance on his memory; in every town, they hanged and burned the usurper's

29. Ibid., IV. 31.

effigy; they disinterred his corpse, dragged it through the filth and mire, and finally left it swinging on the gallows, a worthy reward for his wickedness and treachery.... People of France, spare yourselves these crimes; they bring in their wake misery and shame, remorse and slavery.[30]

We have in the last quotation a good average view of Stuart history as interpreted by the French of the Right. Important to note also, it is seen as David Hume's view. Even when the parallels do not quote him explicitly—and this is exceptional—his tremendous hold over French conservative opinion is still felt and his explanation of events a century and a half old also becomes the explanation of what is seen as the eighteenth-century French version of a similar evil cycle in the course of human history. The *apôtres* have suffered only a temporary delay in their presentation. The "Tableau of Resurrection" is already prepared; its turn would come, just as day follows night: "history has already presented the same causes, the same effects."[31]

Very similar to the *tableaux* of the *Actes des Apôtres* are the parallels drawn also in 1790 by Angélique-Marie Darlus du Taillis, Comtesse de Montrond, in her work *Le Long Parlement et ses crimes, rapprochemens faciles à faire*. The book is a 143-page history of the Long Parliament, again summarized from Hume and illustrating the harmony of his account with a royalist interpretation of "equivalent" events in France. With regard to the causes of the two revolutions, in both cases the antecedent actions of the reigning monarch are exonerated. The Countess underlines, for example, Hume's statement that the allegedly unconstitutional levy of ship-money by Charles I proved subsequently to be very useful to the British navy in its encounters with the Dutch. As for the individual members of the Puritan parliament, Countess Montrond affirms that "the majority were ambitious schemers and hypocrites who called not for the renewal of the state but for humiliation of the king and abasement of the crown."[32] Later her work draws a fur-

---

30. Ibid., V. 43–44.
31. Ibid., V. 63.
32. *Le Long Parlement et ses crimes, rapprochemens faciles à faire*, Paris, 1790, p. 9.

ther parallel between the English patriots and the French revolutionary leaders: "These diabolical impostors laid claim to saintliness, just as our demagogues pretend to humanity."[33]

The suffering multitude is deceived by such unintelligible slogans: "*Happy the English!* writes Mr. Hume, *had the commons proceeded with moderation* and been contented in their plenitude of usurped power to make blessed use of it. Happy the French! one day the Tacitus of our misfortunes will say; but who today can judge these misfortunes heaped on a deceived people!"[34]

Holding to a cyclical view of history, the Countess invites her French readers to compare events in both revolutions and to reflect seriously on them. The results of France's upheaval must inevitably be the same: "The misguided French will feel remorse, soon to be followed by a resurgence of love for the best and most courageous of kings; with mingled feelings of repentance and love they will rush to throw themselves at the feet of this Monarch, so sensitive, so *self-denying,* and their very error will fortify the ties that shall forever bind their devotion to their generous Sovereign."[35]

Rarely, if ever, do the people gain anything from revolution; the new government is likely to be worse than the old one: "On no occasion," writes Monsieur Hume, "was the truth of this maxim more sensibly felt, than in the present state of England."[36] The English had managed to pull down the throne but, far from finding themselves happy, they were soon crushed with an unprecedented burden of taxes and subjected to a tyrannical administration in which there was not even the shadow of justice and liberty.

History cannot be deceived. Inevitably the French revolution too would go the full circle and a Cromwell would appear on the scene. A deadly experiment had proved that to the English. Again she quotes from Hume: "By recent, as well as ancient example, it was become evident that illegal violence, with whatever pretences it may be covered, and whatever object it may pursue, must in-

33. Ibid., p. 108.
34. Ibid., p. 16.
35. Ibid., pp. 84–85.
36. Ibid., pp. 100–101.

evitably end at last in the arbitrary and despotic government of a single person."[37]

Comtesse de Montrond's *rapprochements* clearly illustrate how the parallels were not just idle works of analysis and prediction. Hers is a work heavily charged with emotion:

> The spirit in which I find myself writing this History has caused me constantly to see Louis XVI at the side of Charles I, in terms of both similarities and contrasts; such a flood of sympathy for the misfortunes of Charles I and gratitude toward Louis XVI wells up in me that I am forced to suspend my arduous labours, and I know not whether I shall be able to continue my account up to the time of the English king's death; if my tears are cruel, if they flow in such abundance, they at least raise up in me a consoling thought! I, a Frenchwoman, am not alone in my fervid devotion to my King.... [38]

There is even some hint in her book that if Louis were to choose, as Charles had chosen earlier, to raise the Royal Standard against these vile usurpers, he would not be lacking in support: "Remember, oh! remember always, that thousands of Frenchmen adore you, that they are silent only to be united with you in your resignation and in that of your companion whom they honour and cherish; that if your interests required it, or even allowed it, countless legions would fly to your rescue...."[39]

Another of the "écrivains noirs," François-Louis Suleau, published more *rapprochements* in 1791 and 1792, again with the intention of rousing the French and especially Louis XVI to more vigorous counter-revolutionary action.

Side by side, in two columns of his journal, he compared what he called the "English drama" and the French "Imitation that exceeds the bounds of parody." Throughout the running account of the "Imitation" column we find added comments such as the following: "These parallels are striking," "Exactly the same has happened here," "The circumstances are precisely parallel," "The very same verbiage." Suleau seems, in fact, to believe in an almost com-

37. Ibid., p. 143.
38. Ibid., p. 103.
39. Ibid., p. 45.

plete identification of the two revolutions: "Our demagogues," he wrote, "have slavishly copied all of these stratagems and I need not add that they have obtained the same results. *Nil sub sole novum.* [There is nothing new under the sun.]"[40] We are not surprised to learn, even, that the Puritans had their own Faubourg St. Antoine: "The comparison holds up with amazing exactness, even in the most wretched details...."[41]

As he draws his parallel, Suleau is no less explicit and no more innocent of purpose than the Comte d'Artois had been in performing the portrait antics to which we have already referred. His is a hawkish warning to princes "who, when they believe themselves to be following only the advice of prudence, are in fact giving in to the ever deadly vertigo of bewilderment and faint-heartedness."[42] Pointing to Charles I's initial "co-operation" with the Puritans, Suleau warns:

> Guided by terror, he resolved to appease them with various acts of indulgence. He judged the torrent too strong to resist, he acquiesced in all their measures and was even prepared, it seems, to make peace with the factionists.
>
> We know how well that strategy succeeded for Charles I! Louis XVI would be ill advised to adopt such a humiliating policy. There are no doubt circumstances so critical that stiff resistance must inevitably end in deadly consequences; Louis XVI is in that situation; but at least he must preserve his honour and abandon himself to events with dignity.
>
> All this is so horribly similar.[43]

Citing Bossuet rather than Hume but delivering essentially the same message, the Abbé Marie-Nicolas-Silvestre Guillon published in 1792 his *Parallèle des Révolutions*—a work which went through at least four editions during that year.

Guillon praises Charles I as a just, moderate, and magnanimous prince, perhaps the most honest man of his century and one

40. *Journal de M. Suleau,* Paris, 1792, No. XII, p. 78.
41. Ibid., p. 85.
42. Ibid., p. 77.
43. Ibid., pp. 82–83.

whose only fault was an excess of clemency. He minutely notes parallels between the French and English revolutions, using a highly emotional, breathless style, reminiscent, not of Bossuet, but of a bad eighteenth-century *drame:*

> O the courage to flee! O my King, how virtuous you are in your misfortunes! But...dreadful forebodings: he too, the ill-fated Charles I, departed...and Strafford and Montrose!...Palace of Whitehall! theatre of gloom, soaked still with the fresh warm blood of a murdered king, sacrificial victim of his people; are there Cromwells among us? No, no!...scheming underlings, incapable of either his artful hypocrisies or his potent atrocities that defy understanding, that require genius to devise and heroism to execute; a Bradshaw, yes, or a Chabroud; an Ireton or a Grégoire, a Fairfax or a Lafayette,...hideous memories! Parallels until now only too similar!...[44]

Abbé Guillon makes parallels with other revolutions as well as with that of the Puritans, but all his evidence is chosen to prove the cyclical nature of such violent occurrences. Like the Comtesse de Montrond, he predicts the eventual replacement of popular anarchy by a dictatorship. History shows no exceptions to the rule that the usurpations of the multitude are followed by the tyranny of one man.[45] There is nothing new in the French revolution. It is a base imitation from start to finish:

---

44. *Parallèle des Révolutions,* Seconde édition, Paris, 1792, p. 297. In fact, the denigrating title *Cromwel* had been used rather generously and indiscriminately from the very beginning of the Revolution by both the Right and the Left as the supreme political insult. Within the space of only a few years it was applied variously to, among others, Necker, Mirabeau, Lafayette, Dumouriez, Danton, Robespierre, the entire Directoire, and, of course, Bonaparte. Curiously enough, it is the royalists who most often saw Cromwell as a great genius, albeit evil, and far superior to the revolutionary leaders, the "vile lowlifes," of the Convention. (See, for example, the Comte d'Antraigues's *Adresse à l'ordre de la noblesse de France,* Paris, 1792, p. 99; also the opinion of La Harpe expressed in December 1794: "...Robespierre and his henchmen! You compare Cromwell to them! There is not one (and history will bear me out) that he would have wanted, even as a sergeant in his army...." —*Lycée ou cours de littérature ancienne et moderne,* VIII. 17.)

45. Ibid., p. 292.

If we examine the succession of heresies that have threatened the tranquillity of empires by shaking the pillars of the church and of truth, we see, right down to the smallest details, a picture of the same events we are witnessing today. Change the names, change the setting; what remains of our revolution? Only its acts of cowardice and its heinous crimes. Nay, even here they are plagiarists! Whether in their persecutions or their political schemes, they have not even been original in their crimes![46]

One critical detail of the French parallel with the English revolution was still seen as different in 1792, but Guillon, with a certain grisly tenacity (for most of the "Stuart prophets" avoided before January 1793 going this far), does not fail to note it: "the records of Whitehall," he writes, "will indicate that to complete the resemblance, the revolution needs one additional crime, and that this crime is perhaps not far off."[47]

We shall deal later with other specific *rapprochements* made for various purposes by counter-revolutionary writers during the trial of Louis XVI and after the Reign of Terror. Those that we have noted for the period from 1789 to 1792 by no means exhaust the bibliography on the subject but they are fairly indicative of the sort of thing commonly done at this time.[48]

46. Ibid., p. 414.

47. Ibid., p. 417.

48. Mention should perhaps be made here of what seems to have been a veritable Strafford cult at this time among some French conservatives, directly inspired, I think, by Hume's extensive and highly favourable account of Charles I's minister. Already in 1788, Linguet, drawing the parallel between a French trial of that year and that of Strafford, had exclaimed prophetically: "God grant that subsequent events not be the same! ..." (*Annales politiques, civiles et littéraires du dix-huitième siècle,* 1788, XV. 339; see also his *La France plus qu'Angloise,* Bruxelles, 1788). At about this same time, Lally-Tollendal with the parallel of his hapless father in mind, gave private readings of his tragedy *Le Comte de Strafford* at Versailles: "My tragedy became a literal prophecy; I was urged to have it performed. ..." But his *Strafford* was not made, he tells us, to compete with such admonitory *school-for-tyrants* tragedies as *Brutus, César, Guillaume Tell,* or *Charles IX.* (See his dedicatory remarks in *Le Comte de Strafford: Tragédie en cinq actes et en vers,* Londres, 1795, in which Hume is praised as "especially dedicated to impartiality" and is contrasted with Rapin-Thoyras, "whose only talents lay in being a Presbyterian and a rebel" —pp. 327–28.)

It is possible that Strafford's execution was tacitly used as a convenient eu-

Perhaps the entire spirit of the parallels can be best summed up iconographically. The frontispiece of an anonymous work entitled *L'Angleterre instruisant la France ou Tableau historique et politique du règne de Charles Ier et de Charles II,* published in Paris early in 1793, provides a good contemporary example. The legend of the engraving reads: "England teaching France, 8 February 1649," followed by:

> Je commis un grand crime.
> Prenez bien garde de suivre mon exemple.
> Si du Dieu de bonté vous voulez implorer la clémence,
> Ouvrez les cachots, et brisez les fers de l'innocence.
>
> *[I committed a heinous crime, Take care not to follow my example. If you wish to implore a beneficent God's mercy, Open up your dungeons, and free the innocent of their chains.]*

Pictured are two women standing; one is showing the other a book on which can be read the words "Read and tremble."

It is an irony of history that this same idea of England teaching France could have changed so much in meaning in the sixty years since Voltaire's *Lettres philosophiques.* At that time, England's "lessons" were feared by traditionalists in France. These were the

---

phemism symbolizing the most dreaded possible consequences of revolution for those royalists who, before Louis XVI's close arrest, wished to avoid indelicate references to regicide. Cazalès, another faithful Hume reader, refers in 1790 to Strafford as "this minister who possessed so many talents and virtues, yet was shamefully executed; but England mourned his loss and the whole of Europe honoured his memory, and today his name is venerated by all subjects of this now peaceful empire. Such is the example that must be followed, such is the model to be imitated by those who are called upon in these difficult times to administer the affairs of state." (*Discours et opinions de Cazalès,* Paris, 1821, pp. 114–15.) In 1792 Barnave in yet another parallel of the English and French revolutions wrote: "There were, in both countries, three classes of patriots. In England, Strafford, the Presbyterians, and the Independents; here, Mounier, the constitutionalists, and the republicans. M. de Lally with his tragedy *Strafford* seemed to have had a premonition of this analogy by the importance he gave to a man who had occupied a place corresponding to his own." (*Réflexions politiques sur la Révolution,* in *Oeuvres de Barnave,* Paris, 1843, II. 69–70.) Lally-Tollendal tells us, however, that he saw himself as a Falkland. (See *Seconde Lettre à ses Commettans,* January 1790, p. 169.)

lessons of Voltaire. Now traditionalists almost religiously sought out other examples from across the Channel. These were the lessons of David Hume.

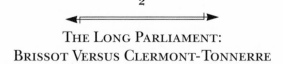

2

THE LONG PARLIAMENT: BRISSOT VERSUS CLERMONT-TONNERRE

To illustrate the intensity of the revolutionary debates provoked by differing views of Stuart history and, what is more important, to show how Stuart history influenced in an immediate sense the formulation by both sides of many political problems of the day, let us examine at some length a controversy on the subject which raged during the summer of 1790 between the two important figures, Clermont-Tonnerre and Brissot.

Brissot is a particularly good example to choose here as representing the Left, since he was probably influenced more than any other French revolutionary strategist by the examples of English civil-war history. We have already noted in our chapter on Hume's pre-revolutionary fortunes that the Girondin leader was one of the first in France to reject Hume's royalist interpretation of that period. His own admiration for English parliamentary heroes knew no bounds. His very name, Brissot de Warville—anglicized from the French place name Ouarville where his family held property—is a youthful tribute to his long-standing political anglomania. In its essentials, this anglomania remained as one of his most notable characteristics until his death by decapitation in Paris in 1793.

Also destined to be a victim of the Revolution, Stanislas Clermont-Tonnerre represents equally well, as a constitutional monarchist, that section of the rightist opposition most strongly influenced by the familiar Hume version of Stuart history.

A dispute over the famous *Comités de recherches,* the new tribunals that Burke would also attack as likely to extinguish the last traces of liberty in France and bring about "the most dreadful and arbitrary tyranny ever known in any nation," was the original issue that sparked their important debate, especially valuable to us as an illustration of how the lines of battle on the current significance of the English revolution were drawn up. The controversy also shows the extent to which Hume's account for many traditionalists had come to be more than merely one man's history of that revolution but rather a body of essential, undeniable political facts, the profound appreciation of which was absolutely necessary for a correct understanding of the revolution in France.

The *Comité de recherches* of which Brissot was a member had been established by the Assembly in October 1789 and authorized to receive denunciations and evidence of conspiracies as well as to arrest, to question, and to hold suspects. Brissot had already defended his committee on several occasions against the accusations of various critics.[49] In August 1790 he found it necessary to return once more to this defence against charges made by Clermont-Tonnerre that such committees represented an inquisitorial device of despotism and had a public effect rather similar to what might be expected from a re-establishment of the Bastille.

Quite to the contrary, Brissot maintained, the powers of the committee were legal and constitutional, the popular party approved of them, they did not in any way resemble those of the Inquisition or the horrors of the Bastille and, finally, such extraordinary measures of security were necessary in a time of crisis when the Revolution had so many enemies. "How could you have believed," he asks Clermont-Tonnerre, "that men stripped of their ill-gotten privileges which they had been enjoying for many centuries would, with heroic patience, simply submit to the will of those they had formerly oppressed? How could you not have seen that they would rebel against an equality of rights that brought them down to the level of other men?..."[50]

Brissot continued his self-apology by giving Clermont-

49. See, for example, *Le Patriote Français,* 25 November 1789, 30 January and 25 February 1790.

50. *J.-P. Brissot, membre du Comité de Recherches de la municipalité à Stanislas Clermont (ci-devant Clermont-Tonnerre) membre de l'Assemblée Nationale...,* Paris, 28 août 1790, p. 8.

Tonnerre one of those classically familiar revolutionary lessons on how people sometimes have to be forced to be free and even killed to be made equal: "Remember the axiom, so trivial and so true: *if you desire the end you must also accept the means.*"[51] Then, having on other occasions already told his readers that there was great merit in the English idea of defining the crime of *lèse-nation*, that the Long Parliament had *many* salutary lessons to teach the National Assembly on how to choose its ambassadors, deal with king's ministers, et cetera,[52] he proceeded to justify the *Comités de recherches* on the same authority: "And the Long Parliament of England, during a time when it was inspired by the purest form of patriotism, did it not also have its committee of safety or committee of investigations? More than once, the republic would owe its salvation to that committee. And so I ask you, was France in 1789, is France today, not caught up in a sufficiently violent crisis to justify the institution of these committees of safety?"[53]

Clermont-Tonnerre's answer, the *Nouvelles Observations sur les comités des recherches,*[54] was not long in making itself heard:

> I shall attempt to repress the horror that the English Long Parliament inspires in me and examine for a moment this monster of politics and immorality in order to discover along with J.-P. Brissot *the precise instant during which it was inspired by the purest form of patriotism.*
>
> The loathsome history of the Long Parliament displays for us two phases: we see it obsessed first with its Presbyterian fantasies and exploiting these as a vehicle for the private ambitions of several members; we see these men cleverly seizing upon and manipulating for their own purposes the natural tendency of every political body to seek power and to act; we see this insane body in turn usurp all royal prerogatives, form and sign a league and covenant, appoint to office, raise an army, declare war on the king, purchase him from the Scots whose protection he had sought, place him on trial, abolish the upper chamber which refused to participate in these crimes,

51. Ibid., p. 11.

52. *Le Patriote Français,* 10 August 1789, 8 and 22 January 1790.

53. *Brissot à Stanislas Clermont,* p. 7.

54. See in *Oeuvres complètes de Stanislas de Clermont-Tonnerre,* Paris, An III, volume III.

and then proceed to carry out the heinous act on its own: there you have the *crimes* of the Long Parliament. I come now to its *infamy:* after the king's assassination, stricken with shame at its crime, it becomes an object of contempt and ignominy; the army insults it, the people defy it; Cromwell, weary of it, speaks but one word and the Long Parliament is gone. Now I ask J.-P. Brissot, which of these moments exemplify his notion of the purest patriotism? When was the Long Parliament patriotic? Was it when it trampled underfoot the bloody head of its king? Was it when it too groveled at the feet of the usurper? Does J.-P. Brissot see approaching in the distance this Cromwell whose culpable power was the certain consequence of the Long Parliament's crimes? If he does see him, it is his duty to expose him so that we may smother the monster in his cradle.

What times must these be? What notions of liberty and patriotism do we harbour, if there can exist among us a man who dares to promote as a model the Long Parliament of England, this cowardly assembly of regicides which with seven years of disorder and anarchy made the English pay dearly for the privilege of living afterwards under despotism?[55]

Brissot in a prompt reply showed that he had long since been emancipated from such a view of the English revolution, that he had read historians other than Hume:

My worship of liberty, my political credo, dates from a time when Stanislas Clermont was still part of the slavish herd of servile courtiers who bowed and scraped in the antechamber of the King's bedroom at Versailles, who were then pleased to ridicule the philosophical and political ideas that today they bravely parade, because these ideas are now victorious.

When I despaired of ever seeing the destruction of despotism, too proud to bend under its insolent yoke, too much the enemy of inequality to allow my children to witness such an odious spectacle, I set off for America to settle in a republican land.[56]

We remember that Brissot in 1784 had expressed the wish that the history of this new republic in America would be written by that most patriotic of English historians, Catherine Macaulay. It

55. Ibid., III. 341–42.
56. *Réplique de J.-P. Brissot à Stanislas Clermont,* Paris, 8 octobre 1790, pp. 8–9.

is with her account of the English revolution that he now answers Clermont-Tonnerre:

> The English Long Parliament inspires horror in you. I believe it: it is not surprising that the history of a republic jars the nerves of a courtier.
>
> You call it a *monster of politics and immorality.* You are astonished that I find in its *loathsome* history a moment when *it was ruled by the purest patriotism.* You see in its history only two phases: that of its crimes, when Charles I mounted the scaffold; that of its infamy, when Cromwell dissolved it.
>
> One can see from such observations that you have read the history of this monster only in *Hume,* a writer who prostituted his talents to monarchism and betrayed so frequently the cause of liberty. Had you studied the history of the immortal *Macaulay,* a work so well suited to rouse our indignation against tyranny, you would doubtless not have been so ready to slander one of history's most brilliant epochs, a time when England produced its greatest profusion of virtues and talents.[57]

After setting his opponent straight on that all-important point, Brissot gives the radical view of Stuart history and a litany of answers to Clermont-Tonnerre's accusations:

> You ask when was this parliament patriotic? It was patriotic when . . . it *rebelled.*
>
> It was patriotic, when it determined to put an end to the tyranny of a *Strafford;* of a perverted priest, *Laud;* of an inquisitorial court called the *Star Chamber;* of Charles I, who summoned parliaments only to obtain money for his dissipations and debaucheries, who dissolved them when they refused to satisfy his criminal lusts, who imposed taxes without the consent of the people, who imprisoned those who refused to comply, &c.
>
> It was patriotic, when it refused to disperse until all of the abuses that England had been subjected to for centuries were reformed.
>
> It was patriotic when it ordered the criminal indictment of the ministers who had given pernicious advice to the king; when, after

57. Ibid., pp. 44–45.

itself engaging zealously in that prosecution, it secured their condemnation and execution for crimes against the nation.[58]

It was patriotic, when it decreed the exclusion of the bishops from the upper chamber and required that the commanders of the army and the navy be *chosen by the House of Commons;* when it took precautions to ensure that ministers and ambassadors were selected who were *sympathetic to the revolution* and also that the education of the presumptive heir to the throne was entrusted only to hands that were pure, that is to say, *the hands of the people.*

It was patriotic, when it disbanded the foreign troops; when, because conspirators were plotting to gain Hull as a stronghold for the king whence to begin a war, it ordered the governor to shut the gates and refuse admittance to the king himself.

It was patriotic, when, wishing to avoid a civil war, it offered proposals of peace to the king, who was first in erecting the standard of war against the nation.

It was patriotic, when it armed the nation to resist the king's aggression; when it armed the London national guard (*trained band*);[59] when it did not give up on the public's cause after its troops suffered three consecutive defeats; when, in spite of those defeats, it ordered the impeachment for high treason of the queen, who had urged the king on in this criminal war.

It was patriotic, when, in the midst of this civil war, it adopted the

58. Two weeks after writing this, Brissot, in *Le Patriote Français* of 25 October 1790, attacked the paragraph (see *supra,* pp. 121–22, n. 48) praising Strafford in Cazalès's speech on the dismissal of the ministers: "M. Cazalès has frequently reminded us in this speech of the history of Charles I. We know to what end royalists quote these passages: they wish to frighten the head of our nation and to compare the National Assembly to the Long Parliament...." Brissot contradicts Cazalès on the following points: "(1) Strafford possessed no virtues; (2) Strafford had few talents and those that he had were disastrous for the nation; (3) England, in fact, rejoiced at his death; (4) Europe does not know his name, and veneration of this name will be found only in the brain of M. Cazalès." Camille Desmoulins the very same day also rebutted Cazalès's Hume-inspired account with a republican appraisal of Charles's minister by Milton. (*Révolutions de France et de Brabant,* IV. 404–7, 25 October 1791.)

59. "Mme Macaulay observes that everyone during that time breathed the spirit of liberty. The artisan deserted his workplace, the merchant his shop, even the women abandoned their domestic chores to engage in politics: all talk was of reform, of the destruction of tyranny. Is that not the picture of our own revolution?"—*Note by Brissot.*

most vigorous measures to establish republicanism; when it abolished the upper chamber and established a single class of lawmakers.[60]

To praise the next accomplishment of the Long Parliament was still a matter of some delicacy in France in October 1790, but Brissot, who at this time was recommending hair-cuts *à la round-head*[61] as superior even to the *coiffure à la Brutus,* does not hesitate in the slightest:

> It was patriotic, finally, when it abolished the monarchy. You will no doubt cry shame, pronounce an anathema, and ask me if it was also patriotic when it condemned the king to death? Will you hear and understand my reply, you who have so recently come to know liberty! But I will be heard and understood, I have no doubt, by all those who, convinced of the principle, do not cravenly capitulate when confronted with the consequences; by those who refuse to kneel before the idols they have shattered.
>
> Answer me this: a man guilty of the greatest of crimes, should he be punished, or should he be exempt from punishment by the very fact that his crime is so great? If this last opinion is one of ignorance, of slavery, of denial of man's dignity and good sense; if you are obliged to agree that no criminal on earth can be exempt from punishment, that his punishment must be in proportion to his crime; if you are obliged to concede that the greatest of crimes is to plunge a nation into slavery, to substitute whims for constitutional laws, to crush the people under a burden of taxes to which they have not consented, to dissipate in debauchery the monies received, to mock justice and morality; if, finally, the greatest of crimes is to provoke a civil war, to shed men's blood in order to enslave them; if, I say, you avow all these truths, you have yourself passed judgement on Charles I, for there is not one of these crimes that he did not commit.[62]

Before going on to defend the Long Parliament's actions under Cromwell, Brissot adds a note on the supposed inviolability of kings: A king, he maintains, can be judged—as Milton, Sidney,

60. Ibid., pp. 45–47.
61. *Le Patriote Français,* 31 October 1790.
62. *Réplique de J.-P. Brissot,* pp. 48–49.

Locke, Mrs. Macaulay, and other patriots have shown.[63] As for Cromwell, the French republican maintained that one had to make distinctions between the victor at Naseby and the usurper. To be added to Brissot's current recommendations on hair-styles are his revolutionary toasts. One of these is: "To the rights of man and to the true friends of liberty who tried to establish republican government in England in the last century; to Ludlow, to Ireton, to Saint-John!"; it is followed, however, by an equally clear "Anathema to the Cromwells and to all the hypocritical scoundrels who would disguise their ambitious designs under a cloak of sham popularity. May they all, like him, devoured by remorse and terror, descend into the darkness of the tomb amid the execrations of the people."[64] In concluding his answer to Clermont-Tonnerre, Brissot feels he can do no better than once more cite Mrs. Macaulay, now to the effect that it was precisely because the Long Parliament had been doing so well in its reform programmes that Cromwell, fearing a possible loss in his military prestige, decided to dissolve that assembly. If Clermont-Tonnerre were to read Mrs. Macaulay instead of Hume, he would no longer be surprised that men exist "who cite as a model (not in everything) this long parliament. Oh! woe betide humanity, woe betide liberty if such men, consumed with a burning passion for freedom, do not multiply; if everywhere we do not renounce the ideas—so degrading to men, so offensive to God—of those vile courtiers who raise up the grandeur of one man on the backs of the oppressed millions...."[65]

Clermont-Tonnerre's reaction, which followed in print within only a few days, was one of complete horror. The extent to which Brissot's unheard-of views on Stuart history must have seemed po-

---

63. See also Brissot's speech of 10 July 1791 on this subject, in F.-A. Aulard, *La Société des Jacobins. Recueil de documents pour l'histoire du Club des Jacobins de Paris,* Paris, 1891, II. 608–26; also *Le Patriote Français,* 15 July 1791. In a February 1792 issue of this last work, Brissot rather gratuitously reminded his readers of the anniversary of Charles I's execution. Later, however, his vote in the Convention on Louis's trial was in favour of the *appel au peuple* (ratification by referendum) and a suspended execution of sentence.

64. *Le Patriote Français,* 12 July 1790.

65. *Réplique de J.-P. Brissot,* p. 51.

litically insane to him is made clear by the fact that he obviously felt it more necessary to reproduce without alteration Brissot's defence of the Long Parliament than he did to attempt a detailed refutation of the republican's "principles, as dangerous as they are culpable":[66]

> If J.-P. Brissot were alone in professing such views, I would not fear the consequences; but J.-P. Brissot is associated with a party, a party whose members would have already caused us to curse liberty were it possible to mistake it for the licence in favour of which they have prostituted their names. J.-P. Brissot is a member of the most accredited of these clubs whose existence and influence was regarded by J.-J. Rousseau as destructive of the true general will; it is possible that the doctrine attributed to it is no more than hearsay and without wishing formally to accuse all the so-called patriots gathered there of sharing in it, I think I am authorized by this consideration to appeal to the opinion of the public regarding this abominable doctrine.[67]

After citing Brissot's text in full, a text which he obviously feels is enough to hang any man politically, Clermont-Tonnerre concludes:

> France is a monarchy or it is nothing. Monarchical government in this country has two unshakeable foundations: national character and size of territory. If the first of these causes is momentarily altered, the second will sooner or later take effect in a decisive manner. England, after the assassination of Charles I, became the captive of a usurper's despotism, and soon after his death, returned to the rule of Charles II. England achieved freedom only by adopting a constitutional monarchy. . . . In vain will you preach republicanism to us, for if that political fanaticism were to triumph, our lives would be subjected for the next twenty years to tortures and dissension, all in the interests of advancing the private ambitions of a few and turning us once more perhaps into slaves. . . .
>
> P.S. I advise J.-P. Brissot that I shall no longer reply in future, no matter what insults he chooses to heap upon me. However, I also advise him that he is sadly misinformed as to the facts: he may wish, for example, to consult the patriotic courtiers, and there are such; they

66. *Sur la dernière réplique de J.-P. Brissot,* 14 October 1790, in *Oeuvres complètes de Clermont-Tonnerre,* III. 382–92.

67. Ibid., III. 382–83.

will tell him that they saw my face only at the first Paris assemblies, hardly the antechamber of the king's bedroom at Versailles![68]

For Clermont-Tonnerre the debate ended with the postscript just quoted, which Brissot immediately interpreted as a sign of defeat: "To those who are not deceived by fine words, it must be clear that he has demonstrated his inability to answer me."[69] After ironically thanking his royalist opponent for helping to advertise the merits of the Long Parliament, Brissot concluded with words that forewarned of things to come:

> England, free during the Long Parliament, lost most of its liberty on the restoration of Charles II: it recovered a portion of it by driving out James II in 1688, then lost it gradually through corruption and the parliamentary majority's coalition with the king under the current, very *unconstitutional,* monarchy....
>
> ...Frenchmen can be no more than slaves under an *ancien-régime* king, only half emancipated under a king of the 1790 regime, and ...they will be entirely free only when they no longer have any king at all.[70]

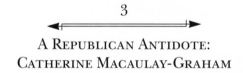

3

A REPUBLICAN ANTIDOTE: CATHERINE MACAULAY-GRAHAM

If the debate between Clermont-Tonnerre and Brissot gives proof of the continuing importance of Hume's *Stuarts* in France at this time, it also makes clear the fact that the *History* of his republican

68. Ibid., III. 391–92.

69. *Le Patriote Français,* 21 October 1790, p. 3.

70. Ibid., p. 4. Brissot on another occasion (see *Le Patriote Français,* 11 February 1790) also complained about Lally-Tollendal's use of Hume's authority in his arguments against Abbé Sieyès's theory on the powers of a *convention* (see *supra,* p. 110). There seems little doubt that Brissot consciously based some of his own political action on the precedents established by the Long Parliament. See, for example, his speech urging sterner measures against the *émigrés,* 20 October 1791; also his various statements of 1792 on war policy for the Republic.

rival, Catherine Macaulay-Graham, had begun to play an equally important role in countering its conservative effect.

Five years before the Revolution Brissot had already expressed the hope that Mrs. Macaulay's work would one day be translated into French,[71] and in his *Mémoires* he speaks of having discussed at that time the feasibility of such a project with Mirabeau.[72] In fact, although there are some few doubts still remaining in the matter, it seems clear that Mirabeau undertook the initial responsibility for the translation, the first five volumes of which were published in the years 1791 and 1792 after his death.[73]

71. *Supra,* p. 65.

72. *Mémoires de Brissot,* Paris, 1877, pp. 327–28.

73. Catherine Macaulay-Graham, *Histoire d'Angleterre depuis l'avènement de Jacques I, jusqu'à la révolution. Traduite en français, et augmentée d'un discours prélimi-naire, contenant un précis de toute l'histoire d'Angleterre, jusqu'à l'avènement de Jacques I: et enrichie de notes. Par Mirabeau.*

Brissot states in his *Mémoires,* but somewhat unreliably, I think, that Mirabeau knew no English and that others did the work under Mirabeau's supervision. (See preceding reference.) Marie-Joseph Chénier also expressed doubts that Mirabeau translated the first two volumes (the last three were publicly avowed by Guiraudet), since he found the style quite bad: "...the language in no way reveals the man of talent: perhaps Mirabeau translated this part of the work too hastily, or, more likely, perhaps he did not translate it at all and it is the result of an all too common practice whereby mediocre writers or greedy booksellers speculate fraudulently on a famous name." (*Tableau historique de l'état et des progrès de la littérature française depuis 1789,* 3eme édition, Paris, 1818, pp. 186–87.) An undated letter by Mirabeau, probably written in 1784, indicates that he considered the history an important one and that he highly approved, for example, of Catherine Macaulay's portrait of James II; it implies, nevertheless, that J.-B. Durival and Guiraudet were to do the actual work of translation whereas Mirabeau would lend his "plebeian aristocrat" name to ensure success in the undertaking which is also described as "an affair of money." (See *Mirabeau's letters during his residence in England,* London, 1832, II. 230.)

On the other hand, it seems equally clear that Mirabeau was not such a complete stranger to the English language as Brissot implies. In 1778 we find him quoting from Hume's *History* in the original and complaining that the Abbé Prévost had made many alterations in his translation of the *Stuarts* (see *supra,* p. 60). The following quotation from d'Escherny also suggests that Mirabeau may have been actively involved in the translation: "I saw a good deal of the Comte de Mirabeau in Switzerland during the time that he was having his *Lettres de cachet* printed there. I can visualize him still, a fugitive from the prisons of France, wandering through Holland, lacking food and shelter, hiring out to a bookseller and, in order to put bread on the table, undertaking the translation of a work without

Even before the appearance of this long-delayed translation other notable revolutionary figures had commented favourably on Mrs. Macaulay's views. Condorcet, in July 1790, for example, contrasts the reactionary activity of Pitt and Burke with the potentially great rôle this republican historian could have played were she herself a member of the British House of Commons: "Although as enthusiastically in favour of liberty as Mr. Burke is of tyranny, would she, in defending the French constitution, have come anywhere near the absurd and disgusting gibberish this celebrated rhetorician has just employed in attacking it? ..."[74]

Hume rather than Burke, however, soon became the political writer whose villainy was most often opposed to the virtue of this female patriot. The *Journal des Savants,* announcing in 1791 the appearance in translation of her first two volumes, stated quite explicitly that they represented a "corrective" to Hume.[75] The *Moniteur,* giving notice of the *History* in the same month, added the promise to publish a full review of the work which it called "one of the most important that has been undertaken since the start of the revolution."[76] Mirabeau himself is quoted by the editor of the Macaulay *History* as having stated in the following terms that he considered its translation to be a task of patriotism and good citizenship: "In our present circumstance, this translation is no ordinary work. There are so many points of contact, so many connections between those events, those personages and us, that merely by pointing these out in simple notes becomes in a sense the equivalent of writing the history of both revolutions."[77] We see that re-

---

understanding its language; acquiring a grammar, a dictionary, and learning English at the same time as he translated the work into French. (It is Mirabeau himself who told me this.)" F.-L. d'Escherny, *Correspondance d'un habitant de Paris,* Paris, 1791, p. 469.

74. *Sur l'admission des femmes au droit de cité,* 3 July 1790, in *Oeuvres de Condorcet,* X. 123–24. Catherine Macaulay was herself attacking Burke at this time in England. (See *Observations on the Reflections of the Right Hon. Edmund Burke on the Revolution in France, in a Letter to the Right Hon. the Earl of Stanhope,* 1790.)

75. October 1791, p. 627.

76. *Gazette Nationale, ou le Moniteur universel,* No. 282, 9 October 1791.

77. *Histoire d'Angleterre,* Avis de l'éditeur, I. ix.

---

publicans were given to making parallels too, but to do this they needed a different historian, one who could avenge the "outrages" of Hume.[78]

Mirabeau's "Discours préliminaire" underscores some of these. The French parliamentary leader begins by attacking Hume's outrageously conservative premises:

> Hume claims that when we consider the distribution of power among the various constituted bodies, there is rarely any other question to ask than this: What is the established order?
>
> But if the established order is bad, must we respect as constitutional the usages that prevent it from being good? Even if this order is excellent, what human authority can prevent a nation from changing it? Hume's question implies that everything is as it should be, which is diametrically opposed to the historical record he himself has produced; it supposes that one need only be the strongest to transform one's might into right; it supposes that there are certain small groups of men, and even simple individuals, to whom entire nations must be indentured.[79]

A passage from Hume, already cited enthusiastically by the royalist de Montjoie[80] and showing very little admiration for political innovators but recommending a warm attitude of understanding toward their opponents, provokes another burst of indignant eloquence from the great French orator:

> What! *we are not to show rancour toward oppressors?* But even when the strictest and most demanding of religions saw fit to order the forgiveness of private injury, it required public chastisement of those monsters who persecute and dishonour entire nations.
>
> *Praise must be bestowed on the reformers of abuses only with some reserve!* What a confusion of ideas! What a disgrace! Who then, should be crowned by glory if not those who have given their all for her? Let ancient institutions be respected when they are not pernicious; but when they are deadly, why not proscribe them? And if mere antiquity is meritorious, how then can error compete advantageously in this respect with eternal truth? How can one not acknowledge that

78. Ibid., p. vi.

79. Ibid., "Discours préliminaire," I. cv.

80. *Supra*, p. 110.

while the lowest of men is able to carry out the functions of a grand vizier, it requires a combination of all the talents of both nature and art to prepare and bring to maturity a revolution, and to naturalize liberty in the souls of men accustomed to slavery!

O Hume! It was not enough to combine the profundity of the English with the good taste and elegance of the French; it was not enough to be the man of all times and all places, the lover of all the arts, the faithful painter of manners, the impartial recorder of all facts, of all opinions. It was incumbent upon you to push back the enclosures within which your compatriots confined civil and political liberty; it was incumbent upon you to be indignant about crime, to be passionate for virtue, to thunder against oppressors; had you done so, the illustrious Mme Macaulay, whose talents, though distinguished, are undeniably inferior to yours, would not have wrested from you, or even disputed, the palm of history.[81]

We see that in this frankly hostile but not entirely unflattering passage Hume's famous impartiality is not questioned; what is impugned is impartiality itself. Revolutions, of course, have little use for impartiality and the French revolution was no exception. Fairness to all sides would have implied a criminal indifference not to truth, for that was a secondary consideration, but to justice. Neutrality as such was scorned. Robespierre was to sum up his chief accusation against the *philosophes* of the eighteenth century with the words *lâche neutralité* (cowardly neutrality). Brissot, attacking Clermont-Tonnerre's professed love of moderation, made the comment that "*moderation, impartiality,* in these troubled times means, in gaming terms, seeing all the hands, or betting on certainties. The words also mean," he added, "protecting ancient abuses from useful innovations."[82] Mercier too shows his contempt for this once-honoured attribute, the one most often attached in the pre-revolutionary period to Hume's *History* and which had now come to be associated with the monarchist party. His anecdote on the subject is worth quoting:

"Impartiaux."
The name given at the beginning of the revolution to those men

81. *Histoire d'Angleterre,* "Discours préliminaire," I. cvii–cviii.
82. *J.-P. Brissot à Stanislas Clermont,* Paris, 28 August 1790, pp. 51–52.

who, having no opinion of their own, lacked the courage to adopt the opinion of others, for fear of compromising themselves, becoming in the end the laughing-stock of every party.

Some individuals were, or pretended to be, at a loss (in 1789) to know how much was six plus six. They asked a representative on the Left: he replied: "Six and six make twelve."

"Listening to only one party is of no value," exclaimed one thinker; "let us hear what a deputy on the Right has to say."

The question is asked of the Honorable Member. After lengthy reflection he replies: "Six and six make fourteen."

More perplexity. A centre deputy of the Assembly is consulted.

"What," he asked, "did they tell you on the Left?" —"Twelve." — "And how much on the Right?" —"Fourteen."

"In that case, six and six make thirteen: as you can see, I am impartial."[83]

So much for the *impartiaux, monarchistes, monarchiens,* and *moyennistes.* So much too for Hume's proud claim—recognized as just by so many until then—to being neither Whig nor Tory, neither patriot nor courtier. With Catherine Macaulay there was no room for doubt on these matters, and the *Moniteur,* reviewing her *History* at length in February 1792, gratefully elaborates in her defence an intricate dialectic of partiality. The historian must show more than just that imaginative sympathy which makes the past intelligible to the present. Imaginative sympathy must be one of his characteristics but he must also show himself able to preach the good cause:

It is already a commonplace truth for us, although we became aware of it very recently, that only free nations can have a genuine history. Another truth, equally undeniable, is that even in the case of a free people, the truth of its history can be altered, either by private interest and ambition, by a desire to please or to harm, by partisan sentiments, or, on the contrary, by the historian's taking special pride in a kind of imperturbability, allowing him to view with total composure the crimes perpetrated by vice against virtue, by despotism against liberty, and to relate as ordinary events and simple facts what he ought to have depicted as abominations. Take away from

83. *Paris pendant la révolution (1789–1798) ou le nouveau Paris,* Paris, 1862, I. 268–69.

Tacitus the verve of indignation that rouses his spirits against tyranny, and perhaps still more against servitude, and he could have provided an account of the same atrocities, the same contemptible actions, but the truth would have been altered by the very fact of his seeming to be impassive.

Let us not be deceived then by this notion of impartiality, so properly commended to the historian. He must not be passionate to the point of not seeing clearly, but he must be passionate enough to depict in a spirited manner what he does see, this being the only way he can properly convey it to his readers.

Today it is recognized, even in England, that in the section on British history dealing with the dispute between the people and their kings, a dispute in which the people were victorious as they always are when they wish to be, the celebrated Hume was partial, as it were, by dint of impartiality. This is a charge that cannot be levelled against Madame Macaulay. An ardent friend of liberty, she has viewed in a true perspective the crimes of the Stuarts against the English constitution, the connivance of the House of Lords, and the steadfastness of the Commons during this stormy period that extends from the accession of James I to the abdication of James II, an interval of eighty-four years.[84]

The *Moniteur* concludes by noting that not only was Catherine Macaulay's work important in itself, it had also been transmitted to the French by one of the founding fathers of their liberty; together these two facts formed a sufficient reason for all amateurs of history and all lovers of liberty to read the work carefully.

That the lovers of liberty did read it and that Catherine Macaulay played an important rôle in supporting, against Hume, the ideology of the revolutionaries is beyond any doubt. Let us examine one last example of her revolutionary success which we find to be notably important especially among the Girondins: her influence on Madame Roland.

A letter of November 1790 from Madame Roland to Bancal illustrates again the fact that Catherine Macaulay was being read in English by patriots in France before the appearance of the Mirabeau translation: "If I can devote a few moments this winter to

84. *Gazette Nationale, ou le Moniteur universel,* No. 45, 14 February 1792, p. 184.

the study of English," she writes, "it will be in order to read Madame Macaulay's *History*. After the historians, I shall turn to Rousseau's moral writings which are in such perfect conformity with civic duty.... "[85] It is probably fairly safe to assume also that Catherine Macaulay's *History* was being discussed at this time in the influential Roland salon.

Several years later, in 1793, we find Madame Roland in prison, drawing up a list of books she would like to be made available to her:

> ...I made a note of the titles: first of all, Plutarch's *Lives* which, at the age of eight, I took with me to church instead of a Holy Week prayer book, and which I had not thoroughly reread since that time; the *History of England* by David Hume, along with Sheridan's *Dictionary*, to strengthen my command of that language: I would have preferred to read Mme Macaulay's, but the person who had lent me the first volumes of this author was certainly not at his house, and I would not have known where to ask for the work, which I had already been unable to find at the booksellers.[86]

With all lovers of liberty presumably following the *Moniteur*'s urgent advice to read this work, it is perhaps understandable that it was in short supply. The shortage was soon remedied after the Terror, however, for we find the Ministry of the Interior recommending in July 1798 that Catherine Macaulay's *History of England* be included on the list of books distributed as prizes "at end-of-school ceremonies and on national holidays."[87] Meanwhile, in prison, Madame Roland must do with second best. In her *Mémoires particuliers* we find yet another great tribute paid to the English republican historian who, we remember, had been seen as defamatory, seditious, and criminal in France thirty years earlier: "Had I been allowed to live," Madame Roland concedes, "I would have had but one temptation: to write the annals of the century, to be

---

85. *Lettres de Madame Roland (1788–93)*, 1ère série, Paris, 1902, II. 191.

86. *Mémoires de Madame Roland*, Paris, 1905, I. 37–38. It was, in fact, Brissot who had lent Madame Roland the first volumes of Mrs. Macaulay's *History*.

87. See *La Décade*, lettre du 24 messidor, An VI, XVIII. 309.

the *Macaulay* of my country; I was about to say, the *Tacitus* of France, but that would not be very modest on my part. . . . "[88]

Madame Roland wrote these words in prison; soon she would be condemned to die by the hatred of the Montagnards, and we remember her famous remark as she mounted the revolutionary scaffold: "O Liberty, what crimes are committed in thy name!" It is perhaps worth noting that, thirty years earlier, Hume had already expressed the identical sentiment in a letter to the Englishwoman Madame Roland had most wanted to emulate.[89]

88. *Mémoires de Madame Roland*, II. 264.

89. *Supra*, p. 69, n. 179. Not to be neglected too is the important rôle of Milton's political writings during this period. Also translated under Mirabeau's name and similarly the honoured recipient of Brissot's revolutionary toasts, Milton is cited enthusiastically along with Catherine Macaulay by Camille Desmoulins as an ardent defender of liberty. (*Révolutions de France et de Brabant*, 12 December 1789, I. 125, 130; 19 December 1789, I. 180–81; 25 October 1790, IV. 404–7.) The *Annales patriotiques* of Mercier and Carra commend him as well (see No. 640, 4 July 1791, p. 1534). Administrators of the Département de la Drôme even ordered the official reprinting (Valence, 1792) of his refutation of Saumaise in anticipation of Louis XVI's execution. It is interesting to note too that Milton figures as a virtuous republican member of Parliament opposed to another M.P., a sinister character named Burke, in M.-L. Tardy's *Cromwel ou le général liberticide* of 1793. It was, of course, especially during Louis's trial that his political writings took on the greatest significance and he is quite frequently cited in the Convention. Royalists, on the other hand, showed a very distinct tendency to denounce him as a regicide, despite his Christianity, in favour of the conservative "atheism" of Hume. Abbé Guillon, for example, points out with horror the rôle of Milton in both the English and the French revolutions. (*Parallèle des Révolutions*, 1792, p. 303.)

IV

The Trial of
"Le Stuart Français"

1

LOUIS XVI AND CHARLES I:
A CONDEMNED KING'S MEDITATIONS

We remember that during Hume's visit to Versailles in 1763 the historian of the Stuarts had been complimented on his great reputation in France by a nine-year-old boy, the future king, Louis XVI. As it turned out, the young prince was to remain an avid and faithful reader of history all his life. No study, everyone agreed, was more suited to form part of the education of a future ruler:

> The second way to gain knowledge of men is to compare them to men of the past, and that comparison is made by reading history. Of all the sciences, history is the one that a prince must study most.
>   ...He must read it as one who seriously wishes to discover the true principles of government and to learn how to know men. He will derive far more enlightenment from the history of monarchies than from the history of republics, which are driven by mechanisms that he will be unable to make use of in a monarchy....[1]

1. *Réflexions sur mes entretiens avec M. le Duc de La Vauguyon,* par Louis-Auguste, Dauphin, in *Oeuvres de Louis XVI,* Paris, 1864, I. 310.

The history of the Stuart monarchy, in particular, was of special significance:

> If the prince wishes to become familiar with the spirit of an ill-governed people, and to know to what extremes it can go, he has only to read Lord Clarendon's *History of the Rebellion and Civil Wars in England.* He will discover that all weak princes conduct themselves like the unfortunate Charles I, that every people in ferment and rebellion are like the people of England; that every factious and venturesome man possesses the inclinations of a Cromwell, and that, if he lacks Cromwell's talents, he will at least have his hotheadedness and malice.[2]

It was not long before Louis XVI was to see his own kingdom in the grip of similar revolutionary upheaval. His former rather scholarly meditations on the lessons of Stuart history were suddenly transformed into something much more urgent. In fact, as the time of his trial approached, one can almost say that his preoccupation with the events of Charles I's reign, Hume's account of which he seems finally to have preferred above all others,[3] had become a veritable obsession.

2. Ibid., I. 314. Louis XVI was not limited to reading English history in translation. His own knowledge of English was apparently excellent and he had even translated Walpole's work on Richard III (published later as *Règne de Richard III, ou Doutes historiques sur les crimes qui lui sont imputés,* Paris, 1800), as well as fragments of Gibbon and other English historians. With regard to Louis XVI's reading habits, Necker notes the following in 1792: "I have always seen the King reading, diligently and by preference, the great works of history, politics, and morals, written in French or in English." (*Réflexions présentées à la nation française sur le procès de Louis XVI,* in *Oeuvres complètes de M. Necker,* publiées par M. le baron de Staël, Paris, 1820–21, XI. 363.)

3. The official inventory of Louis XVI's books, made at the Temple after his execution, shows that Hume's was the only work of English history in the imprisoned king's possession. (Archives Nationales, F. 17, 1200, No. 70: see Bapst, op. cit., *La Révolution Française,* XXI. 533.) Delisle de Sales, who had his information from Malesherbes's son-in-law, the *président* Rosanbo, stated in 1803 that Louis XVI "had his former minister (i.e. Malesherbes) obtain from Nyon the bookseller David Hume's *History of the Stuarts,* in order to look at the trial and execution of Charles I." He goes on to add, however, that Louis returned the work to Malesherbes after reading it and that "this copy, made precious by such use, was in the library at the château of Malesherbes when the revolutionary vandals invaded." (See Delisle de Sales, *Malesherbes,* Paris, 1803, p. 268.) It thus seems prob-

The obsessive nature of Louis's interest in Stuart history is emphatically pointed out by various contemporary eye-witnesses. Madame Campan, for example, tells how the king consented to wearing a plastron as protection against assassination during his obligatory attendance at the July 14th ceremonies in 1792. He had agreed to wear the device only to comply with Marie-Antoinette's wishes: "...they will not assassinate me," Madame Campan quotes the king as saying, "their plan has changed; they will have me killed another way." The queen's reader then continues:

> The queen saw that the king had lowered his voice to speak to me, and as soon as he left the room she asked me what he had said. I hesitated to reply but she insisted, adding that nothing must be kept hidden from her, that she was resigned to every eventuality. On learning what the king had said, she told me that she had guessed as much; that for a long time now, he had been saying to her that everything that was happening in France was an imitation of the revolution in England under Charles I, and that he had been constantly reading the history of that unfortunate monarch in order to avoid making the same mistakes in a similar crisis.[4]

Madame Campan refers also to the king's prolonged state of mental depression at this time: "—a despondency that extended to physical prostration. For ten days he said not a word, not even in the privacy of his family.... The queen brought him out of this state, such a dangerous one during a time of crisis when every moment brought with it the need for action.... She even went so far as to tell him that if they had to perish, it should be with honour and without waiting for both of them to be smothered on the floor of their apartment."[5]

---

able that Louis actually had two copies of the *Stuarts*. Cléry, the king's valet during his captivity, explicitly states that Louis read Hume in English during that time. (*Journal de ce qui s'est passé à la tour du Temple pendant la captivité de Louis XVI, Roi de France,* Londres, 1798, p. 96.)

4. Mme Campan, *Mémoires sur la vie privée de Marie-Antoinette,* Paris, 1822, II. 214–15.

5. Ibid., II. 205. This would be around June 1792.

It is nevertheless quite possible that the idea of being assassinated was in fact less forbidding to Louis XVI than the fear of being dishonoured by a criminal trial like that imposed on Charles I. Bertrand de Molleville, who as minister for the navy was in close touch with the king at this time, also suggests that Louis's reading of Stuart history was closely related to his prolonged depression and his generally fatalistic inability to take decisive action:

> He was not at all concerned about protecting his own life; ever since the Varennes misadventure, this unfortunate prince was firmly convinced that he would be assassinated, that all measures taken to guarantee his safety would be useless and might even place his family and the friends who had remained faithful to him in greater danger. Dominated by these gloomy forebodings, he awaited death with such heroic calmness that he seemed indifferent to life.
>
> He often read the history of Charles I of England, and concentrated his attention mainly on avoiding any action that might serve as a pretext for putting him on trial as a criminal.
>
> The sacrifice of his own life seemed of no importance to him. The nation's honour occupied all of his thoughts. The idea of being publicly assassinated in the name of the people affected him violently. He would have preferred to die by the blade of an assassin whose murderous deed would be seen as the crime of a few individuals rather than an act of the nation.[6]

In a later work Bertrand de Molleville comes back to this point, commenting with surprise on the fact that Louis learned so little from his haunted study of Charles I's career: "But what is most remarkable, is that the history of Charles I, which Louis XVI, from the beginning of the Revolution until the end of his life made part of his regular reading, instead of enlightening him on what measures he should adopt or avoid, became for him the most perni-

---

6. *Mémoires secrets pour servir à l'histoire de la dernière année du règne de Louis XVI, Roi de France.* Par Ant.-Fr. Bertrand-de-Molleville, Ministre d'Etat à cette époque, Londres, 1797, II. 259–61.

cious lesson of all."[7] It is Bertrand de Molleville's opinion, for example, that Louis never sought out any opportunity to use the army against the Revolution because he had been so impressed by the fact that such action had served to justify one of the chief accusations against Charles I during the English trial. Remembering the Stuart king's active resistance to Parliament, the former minister maintained, too, that if Charles I had been king of France in 1789 no revolution would have taken place. "On the other hand," he continues, "if one considers how lacking in jealousy Louis XVI was of his prerogative, or how disinclined he was to augment it by usurping the privileges and freedoms of the people, or, again, if one considers the readiness with which he consented to the reform of any abuses complained about in this regard, one might conclude with equal justification that if Louis XVI had been king of England when the revolution broke out there, his gracious and entire willingness to accede to all of the demands that gave rise to that revolution would have left the malcontents without the slightest pretext to act."[8]

Other contemporary accounts support Bertrand de Molleville's belief that Louis XVI had been harmfully affected by a too vivid appreciation of English revolutionary history. The younger Lacretelle, writing in 1801, tells how the king experienced as a result "the deadly qualms of a man who sees his certain ruin advancing toward him and dares not make any attempt to prevent it. He read constantly the history of Charles I and studiously adopted measures that were totally opposite in order to avoid, if possible,

---

7. *Histoire d'Angleterre,* Paris, 1815, III. 564.

8. Ibid., III. 565. In 1816 Mme de Staël expressed certain wise reservations concerning such a view in her *Considérations sur les principaux événements de la Révolution Française:* "It seems to me interesting," she writes, "to show those who are convinced that this or that man in France at the time could have prevented everything, that this or that firm decision would have sufficed to bring everything to a halt, it seems to me interesting, I say, to show them how the conduct of Charles I was, in every respect, the opposite of that adopted by Louis XVI and how despite this the two contrary systems led to the same catastrophe: such is the invincible force of revolutions whose cause resides in the opinion of the multitude!" (*Oeuvres complètes,* Paris, 1820–21, XIII. 89.)

the English king's fatal destiny. He consistently showed an excess of weakness where Charles I displayed an excess of confidence and inflexibility."[9] Jacob-Nicolas Moreau, Historiographer of France and librarian to Marie-Antoinette, also maintained that these obsessive Stuart readings were the cause of Louis XVI's being "the first to give up on the public enterprise." He also quotes the French king as saying as early as 1789, just after the march on Versailles: "I am threatened by the same fate; . . . if there is a way to avoid it, it is by doing the exact opposite of what that unfortunate monarch did."[10]

Personal sentiments expressed in various letters by Louis XVI also suggest that the example of Charles I was constantly before his eyes whenever he considered the possible courses of action available to him. "If I must step down from the throne," we read in one of his letters of 1791 to the Prince de Condé, "and mount the scaffold where Charles I was sacrificed, abandoning everything that I hold most dear in the world, I am ready to do so; *but no war! no war!*"[11] The words "I may suffer the fate of Charles I. . . ." occur also in another letter of 28 April 1792.[12] Interesting to note too is the fact that Louis was, on occasion, given to repeating Charles I's last words. When, for example, it was pointed out to him in 1791 that his use of the veto might have dangerous personal consequences, the king is said to have replied: "What will they do to me? They will kill me: well! *I shall acquire an immortal crown in exchange for a corruptible one.*"[13] It is quite possible even that his close knowledge of Charles I's statements to the English tribunal guided some of the feelings he himself expressed concerning the manner in which he wished to have his defence conducted. The following letter to

9. Charles-Jean-Dominique de Lacretelle, *Précis historique de la Révolution Française,* Paris, 1801, p. 242.

10. Jacob-Nicolas Moreau, *Mes Souvenirs,* publiés par Camille Hermelin, Paris, 1898–1901, II. 467–68.

11. Letter 49, 15 August 1791, in *Oeuvres de Louis XVI,* II. 157.

12. Ibid., II. 182.

13. See Le Marquis de Beaucourt, *Captivité et derniers moments de Louis XVI; récits originaux et documents officiels.* Paris, 1892, I. 385.

Malesherbes, written while Louis was a prisoner of the Convention, lends support to this conjecture:

> I have no illusions about my fate. The ingrates who have dethroned me will not stop in mid course; seeing their victims always before their eyes would shame them too much. I shall suffer the fate of Charles I and my blood will flow as punishment for my never having caused any to be shed. But would it not be possible to ennoble my last moments? The national assembly includes among its members the devastators of my monarchy, my accusers, my judges, and probably my executioners. Such men cannot be made to see the light, one cannot make them just, and even less can their hearts be softened. Weakness cannot save me; would it not be preferable then to put some spirit into my defence? I imagine that it should be addressed, not to the Convention, but to all of France, which would judge my judges and give me back a place in the hearts of my people that I never deserved to lose. Then my rôle would be limited to not recognizing the competency of the tribunal before which I am forced to appear. I shall maintain a dignified silence, and, by condemning me, these men who claim to be my judges would be no more than my assassins.[14]

There are distinct echoes of Charles I's own formal defence in the preceding letter. Whether these are the result of more than the similarity of circumstances in which the two monarchs found themselves is difficult to say. Other questions of an equally idle nature arise: one is permitted to wonder, for example, if Louis was inspired by the English king's actions when he showed an unaccustomed firmness in defending the established church, or, more trivially still, when he too, on hearing his sentence, asked for (but did not receive) three days' grace, wore the same colours to the scaffold, and attempted (again unsuccessfully) to address the spectators in the last few minutes before his execution. Such questions cannot of course be answered; indeed, there is some doubt even whether they can be properly asked. Perhaps one can speculate legitimately, however, on how pleased that style-conscious Scot David Hume would have been had he lived long enough to read in Cléry's journal a description of the following rather quiet scene:

14. *Oeuvres de Louis XVI*, II. 207–8.

The setting is the king's prison in the Temple; Louis has just learned that the Convention has voted the death sentence:

> He had been reading a logogriph in an old *Mercure de France* and asked me to guess the word; I was unable to find the answer.
>
> "Can you not guess what it is? And yet, it is so applicable to me in my present circumstance; the word is *sacrifice*."
>
> The king then asked me to get from the library the volume of the *History of England* containing the death of Charles I: he read it in the following days. . . . [15]

15. Cléry, op. cit., p. 203. In a somewhat cruel forgery of Cléry's journal, published in 1800, an editor's note insists that this part of Louis's final meditations was a salutary *pensum* imposed on the king by members of the Commune: "This historical work was not part of the small library at the Temple when Louis XVI arrived but it was sent there by the general council of the Commune, persuaded by Chaumette, Hébert, and others that it was improper for Louis XVI to be reading Latin poets which the council could not understand and to be asking that even more such works be purchased for him, instead of reading the trial of Charles I, which was more suited to his situation." (*Mémoires de M. Cléry ou Journal de ce qui s'est passé dans la tour du Temple, pendant la détention de Louis XVI; avec des détails sur sa mort, qui ont été ignorés jusqu'à ce jour.* Edition originale seule avouée par l'auteur. Londres, 1800, pp. 127–28.) The same work tells how on the eve of Louis's solemn appearance at the bar of the Convention, Marie-Antoinette spent many hours seated before her harpsichord merrily singing a collection of very naughty songs.

Curiously, the account concerning the Commune is a distorted version of an actual report on a meeting of its General Council, held on 23 November 1792, in which we read as follows: "At the beginning of yesterday evening's proceedings, a request from the commissioners on duty at the Temple was read out, stating that Louis XVI wished to have various books for himself and also for his son . . . ; in all, a total of thirty-three works in French and in Latin. . . . This application by Louis XVI sparked an extremely animated debate." Several members of the council were strongly opposed to the king's request, one objecting that the prisoner "could scarcely count on having two full weeks of continued existence, whereas the books he was asking for were enough to occupy the longest of lifetimes." Martin, demanding that at least the works in Latin be suppressed, added: "I ask that these be replaced with works entitled: The American Revolution, The English Revolution, The Life of Cromwell, The Life of Charles IX, including details of the Saint Bartholomew's Day Massacre." The militantly republican report goes on to say that unfortunately Martin's motion, "though supported by several members, was not acted upon." The application was finally approved. (See Le Marquis de Beaucourt, op. cit., II. 137–39.) A list of the books requested by Louis XVI may be found in M.-A. de Beauchesne, *Louis XVII; sa vie, son agonie, sa mort; Captivité de la famille royale au Temple,* Paris, 1852, I. 500–502.

2

DAVID HUME AND STUART HISTORY
FOR THE DEFENCE

Considerations drawn from Stuart history (and chiefly Hume's version of it) form a major part of many unofficial defences of the French king composed during his trial in 1792.

Undoubtedly one of the most important of these was the apology for Louis XVI published by his former minister, Jacques Necker, on 30 October of that year. In an eloquent plea to the Convention, Necker begged its members not to proceed with the trial, promising that they would thus avoid committing a crime even greater than that of the Long Parliament:

> An undertaking unique in the annals of the world, an atrocity that historians narrate with horror and that the English still atone for every year in solemn repentance, a public crime, the product of one man's ambitions: it is to this that they wish to accustom the French nation. You who have so carefully, and perhaps even with a kind of affectation, avoided modelling yourselves on those Englishmen, will you now make an exception only in favour of a barbarous action! No, not even that! You would be thinking that you were following in the footsteps of Cromwell's slaves, those judges pledged to his political passions... and you would be deceived still, for you would not even have their excuse. Would you indeed dare to compare the grievances only too legitimately cited against the hapless Stuart... with the accusations you are compelled to base on no more than conjecture, or that you strive to wring from a few papers found in the king's private office...? Here is what the English monarch did during his reign: a free constitution, defined in the most solemn enactments, prescribed his obligations and set out his prerogatives, and yet, scorning this constitution, he levied several taxes without the consent of the nation's representatives, he exacted forced loans, ... he exceeded his authority in the regulation of ecclesiastical matters.... Finally, urged on by events, he placed himself at the head of an army and initiated a civil war which ended in disaster for him. Where is the parallel? Where is the similarity between these various political offences and the conduct of a monarch who inherited pow-

ers with no known limits and who inaugurated liberty by voluntarily sacrificing a portion of his prerogatives that had belonged to the Crown for so many centuries?[16]

Necker's concessions concerning Charles I's real guilt are rarely expressed by members of the Right at this time but represent proof of the Swiss banker's political astuteness. He reveals an awareness, moreover, that in the preceding century of Anglo-French rivalry, the French had often shown pride in the claim that their own annals, at least, had never been defiled by the crime of regicide committed with all the hypocritical trappings of a legal trial. Now, Necker continued, the French would not even have England's excuse that the evil genius of Cromwell had urged on a small fanatic band of usurpers to this hideous crime. The French Convention, claiming as it did to represent openly the justice of the entire French nation, would, if it sentenced Louis XVI to death, make France the guiltiest nation of all.

Necker pursued his defence of Louis XVI by pointing out another consideration which Hume, Adam Smith, and, on different grounds, centuries of theocratic tradition had helped to establish in France as something of a dogma: the misfortunes of kings, he observed, have quite extraordinary and awesome effects on the feelings of the people. Kings are not ordinary creatures in this respect. Smith, in his *Theory of Moral Sentiments*, a work that was very well known on the continent at this time and which enjoyed three different French translations, had analysed in detail our feelings for the tragedies of the great. These feelings are often born of our admiration for the advantages of their high position. We like to serve the great in order to share in the completion of a system of happiness which seems so close to perfection. We ask for no other reward. Conversely, when the great suffer adverse fortune, we cannot help feeling that their situation merits more compassion on our part than what is normally provoked by similar mischance oc-

---

16. *Réflexions présentées à la Nation française sur le procès de Louis XVI*, in *Oeuvres complètes de M. Necker*, Paris, 1820–21, XI. 376–78.

curring in the lives of lesser men.[17] A like belief underlies the true
intent of Burke's rather over-romanticized passage in the *Reflections*
bewailing the disappearance of the age of chivalry. Strange things
happen when kings and queens are unceremoniously hurled from
their thrones; we are as awed by such disasters in the moral world
as we would be by a miracle in the physical order of things.

Arguing along such lines and citing Hume's *Stuarts* as proof,
Necker addressed the Convention in the following terms:

> O men of France! In the name of your past glory..., but especially
> in the name of Heaven, in the name of pity, be as one in rejecting
> the plans of those who seek to lead you to the ultimate act of in-
> gratitude, who want you to share in their violent passions and deadly
> thoughts. A king, they say to you, is only a man, and his destiny is
> owed no special regard. That assertion is not true; it is not true in
> respect of our feelings. A king whose fortunes have collapsed, a king
> who has fallen to the depths of misfortune, reminds us of every in-
> terest that attaches to him. By virtue of his power of guardian-
> ship over us, he has seemed to us for a long time morally part of
> ourselves, and his humiliation becomes our humiliation....Mo-
> ments of enthusiasm or passion may distract us from these thoughts
> and for a time even appear to disrupt the natural course of our sen-
> timents; but after the utmost limits of revenge have been reached,
> we look back at what has been done, and it is then that remorse and
> repentance begin. I do not present here merely speculative notions.
> Read in the history of the House of Stuart a philosopher's account
> of how every heart was thrown into convulsions by the ultimate ca-
> tastrophe suffered by the unfortunate Charles I. Let your attention
> dwell on that, if you can, then ask yourselves whether, in respect of
> our feelings, a king is only a man; whether, especially, he is only a
> man after having been for so long the object of our love, after hav-
> ing been for so long the symbol of the bonds that unite us. Yes! read
> that most horrifying of narrations and then try to consider without
> emotion the deadly notions to which these men seek to inure the
> French nation. Yes, read that horrifying narration, and see after-
> wards if you dare to entrust to the inflamed passions of the present

17. Adam Smith, *The Theory of Moral Sentiments,* the second edition, London, 1761; see Part I, Section III, Chapter II: "Of the Origin of Ambition, and of
the Distinction of Ranks," pp. 87–90.

moment the judgement of a prince reduced by fortune to the most absolute abandonment. . . . [18]

If the amount of attention accorded later by the Convention to the task of refuting Necker's points is any true indication, one must conclude that he had chosen arguments which were particularly effective. In another unofficial defence of Louis XVI, Lally-Tollendal also invited that body to meditate on Stuart history:

> Frenchmen, reflect carefully on this; remember that it means endless remorse and an eternal stigma. The English have been mourning for a century—and future centuries will see them mourning still—a regicide committed by a much smaller number of their fathers, with much less solemnity, and, it must be said, in circumstances much less odious than those that would mark in France today a re-enactment of that same crime. Men of France, you have been strangely abused; they have counted heavily on prejudice, or flightiness, or ignorance when, in your presence, they have been

---

18. Necker, op. cit., pp. 400–403. Necker then cites in full Prévost's translation of the following passage from Hume:

> It is impossible to describe the grief, indignation, and astonishment which took place, not only among the spectators, who were overwhelmed with a flood of sorrow, but throughout the whole nation, as soon as the report of this fatal execution was conveyed to them. Never monarch, in the full triumph of success and victory, was more dear to his people, than his misfortunes and magnanimity, his patience and piety, had rendered this unhappy prince. In proportion to their former delusions, which had animated them against him, was the violence of their return to duty and affection; while each reproached himself, either with active disloyalty toward him or with too indolent defence of his oppressed cause. On weaker minds, the effect of these complicated passions was prodigious. Women are said to have cast forth the untimely fruit of their womb: others fell into convulsions, or sunk into such a melancholy as attended them to their grave: nay, some, unmindful of themselves, as though they could not, or would not, survive their beloved prince, it is reported, suddenly fell down dead. The very pulpits were bedewed with unsuborned tears: those pulpits, which had formerly thundered out the most violent imprecations and anathemas against him. And all men united in their detestation of those hypocritical parricides, who, by sanctified pretences, had so long disguised their treasons and, in this last act of iniquity, had thrown an indelible stain upon the nation. (VIII, 137–38; —It should be noted that in his translation of this famous passage, the author of *Manon Lescaut* did full justice—and no more —to Hume's original.)

shameless enough to describe Charles I as infamous, a king who is still honoured with the name of martyr by an entire nation that by all appearances needs no one to teach it either its rights or a sense of dignity.[19]

Lally-Tollendal continued his plea for the king by assailing what we might now call the Macaulay-Brissot version of the English revolution—a version, moreover, which formed an important part of Mailhe's famous report. Lally preached, on the contrary, the familiar Hume account as he would again in 1797 in his *Défense des émigrés français.*[20]

Cazalès in his *Défense de Louis XVI* also defies the revolutionists to inquire of the English if they now approved of their ancestors' execution of Charles I. Their answer would not, he maintains, be comforting to a nation that seemed perversely bent on taking the same course. Only ask the English, Cazalès warns the Convention, "and you would no longer evoke a period of their history that they wish to forget."[21] Cazalès in 1792 was not a novice at this sort of thing. Long before the King's arrest he had warned France's revolutionaries that the English still maintained an expiatory cult for the Earl of Strafford; now that even Louis XVI's life was in danger, the "cult" of Strafford could become the "cult" of Charles I.

In yet another defence of the French king, the royalist de Montjoie addressed himself even more directly to the Convention, not more than forty members of which, he believed, sincerely wanted Louis's death. The best advice he could give to the others, to the vast majority whose opinions would decide the final outcome, was that they should study once more the lessons of Stuart history:

19. *Plaidoyer pour Louis XVI,* Londres, 1793, pp. 11–12.

20. A work about which the republican Jean-Jacques Leuliette contemptuously but significantly notes: "You seem to have borrowed Hume's brush in portraying the bloody denouement of January 21st. I admit that it was a sad day; but I cannot agree that it was the most horrifying day of the Revolution; the most horrifying day of the Revolution was the day the greatest number of heads fell; only one head was cut off on January 21st." (*Des Emigrés Français ou Réponse à M. de Lally-Tollendal,* Paris, 1797, pp. 91–92.)

21. *Discours et opinions de Cazalès,* Paris, 1821, p. 267.

Choose; there is still time: what image of yourselves would you have history hand down to posterity? Decide between crime and virtue, madness and wisdom....

Do not be deceived by that fatal sense of security shared by Cromwell's confederates.... Will you give in to intimidation? Will you allow the heinous crime to be consummated even though you loathe it in your hearts? What will you have gained by it? No sooner will the deed be done than a man of audacity will rise up, he will smash the instruments of the crime, after which he will proceed to enjoy its fruits. Open your history books: is that not the way of all usurpers? In order to attain supreme power they need accomplices; but once they have seized the sceptre, they wield it against the very ones who delivered it up to them.... Beware: the man of whom I speak is known to you....[22]

The warning about the dangers of a French "Cromwell" formed, no doubt, the cleverest part of this particular attempt to save Louis XVI's life. De Montjoie knew that the atmosphere in the Convention at this time was heavy with suspicion. Accusations and counter-accusations about hidden Cromwellian ambitions were being made with great frequency. Two dangers seemed especially imminent: that of a Cromwell or that of a Monk. As one reads the Convention speeches from September 1792 to January 1793 one even senses, I think, that the national representatives viewed a Cromwell as not only the more likely threat but as also the more horrifying of the two possibilities. De Montjoie hammered in this point: If the members of the Convention lacked the courage to be just with Louis XVI, their fate within six weeks would resemble that of the Cromwellian underlings who had sent Charles I to the scaffold.

A second major warning followed—this, too, taken from Hume's *History:*

Independently of that consideration, the interests of each of you forbid an iniquitous judgement.... No sooner would this blood have been shed than France, joined for so long to her leader, would cry out in pain and terror. Injustice would be followed by repentance.

22. *Avis à la Convention Nationale sur le jugement de Louis XVI*, Genève, 1793, pp. 6–7.

Repressed for three years, love and gratitude would well up violently; the conscience of all would accuse you, every voice would call out your names: There they are! There they are! thousands of Frenchmen will cry out; behold the murderers of Louis! Everyone will recall his virtues, his kindnesses, his forbearance, his heroic patience, the unfailing gentleness with which he suffered the outrages you allowed to be heaped upon him, under the burden of chains with which you weighed him down....

And your assembly once dissolved, what would become of its members?...Allow me to place before you once again the historical record, allow me to remind you of the pitiable end met with by all those who in times past contributed to the same judgement that Louis's recklessly unthinking enemies seek from you.... In England, the members of the court of iniquity that condemned Charles I to the scaffold perished in infamy and destitution....

Do not let yourselves stand deservedly accused of being unable to learn from the past even as you see recurring the same symptoms, the same crises, the same phenomena that preceded the deplorable era that England wishes it could erase from its annals.[23]

De Montjoie thus invoked the traditional lessons of history. He perhaps forgot them when he came to his last piece of advice for the members of the Convention: They were not to fear that they had gone too far to reverse their course; they were not to fear that kings are unforgiving: "Vengeance," he insisted, "is a passion Louis knows only by name;... *He can be blamed,* as Bossuet said of Charles I, *only for an excess of clemency....*"[24]

It would be possible to analyse other less important defences of Louis XVI published at this time but the basic pattern of these is not materially different from those of Necker, Lally-Tollendal, Cazalès, or de Montjoie. It is in such pleas for the French king that we find the use of historical parallels attaining a peak of intensity, a note of political urgency, unequalled by the many Stuart parallels drawn before or after Louis's trial. The belief was expressed more and more by royalists in these last few months of 1792 that the two

23. Ibid., pp. 9–12.

24. Ibid., pp. 17–18. See also the *Oraison funèbre de Henriette-Marie de France, Reine de la Grande-Bretagne* (16 November 1669), in *Oeuvres complètes de Bossuet,* Tours, 1862, I. 425.

revolutions had run along on exactly parallel courses, that Louis XVI would never even have been brought to trial if one hundred and forty-three years earlier, the English "Jacobins" had not executed Charles I. One last eleventh-hour defence of Louis XVI which repeats this sentiment is worth quoting from: "The course followed by the English seditionaries and that followed by their counterparts who have been devastating for such a long time our unhappy country are absolutely the same; if there is any difference at all, it is that the present revolutionaries have surpassed in hypocrisy, in viciousness, and in tyranny those who murdered the unfortunate Stuart."[25]

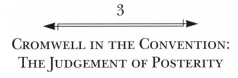

3

CROMWELL IN THE CONVENTION:
THE JUDGEMENT OF POSTERITY

The scores of published opinions emanating from the Convention during Louis XVI's trial and dealing with such questions as whether the King could be judged, how he should be judged, and what should be his punishment are all quite heterogeneous in their various tendencies and difficult to group in a significant manner. One common element becomes apparent, however, to anyone who has taken the trouble of going through these opinions: the parallel between the English trial of Charles and the Convention trial of Louis haunted the minds of all but a minority of those who were destined to judge the French king.

Significantly even Mailhe's *Rapport et Projet de Décret*,[26] the Convention's official pre-trial report which formulated so many of the members' reactions in subsequent debates, could not avoid going into the legality of Charles I's parliamentary hearing. Mailhe's re-

25. A.-J. Dugour, *Mémoire justificatif pour Louis XVI, ci-devant Roi des Français*, Paris, 1793, p. 123. (First published in parts, December 1792–January 1793.)

26. ...*présentés à la Convention Nationale, au nom du Comité de Législation*, 7 November 1792.

port was to conclude that Louis XVI could be judged by the Convention. The troublesome question of what legal forms to follow nevertheless remained. The English condemnation of Charles I was an obvious precedent; obvious too seemed the fact that history reproached the English for having violated legal forms:

> Charles Stuart was inviolable like Louis XVI; but like Louis XVI, he had betrayed the nation that had placed him on the throne. Being independent of all the bodies established by the English constitution, he could not be charged or judged by any of them; only the nation could do this. When he was arrested, the House of Lords was totally in his camp. It wished only to save the king and monarchical despotism. The House of Commons seized unto itself the exercise of all parliamentary authority; and no doubt it had the right to do so given its circumstances. But Parliament itself was no more than a constituted body. It did not represent the nation's full and entire sovereignty; it represented the nation's sovereignty only in respect of those functions that were determined by the constitution. It could thus neither judge the king nor delegate the right to judge him.[27]

Although this interpretation of Charles I's trial is far from being Hume's, it is no less certain that Mailhe's inability to avoid dealing with the question altogether is something of a tribute to the widespread success of the *History of the Stuarts* in France before 1789 and especially to the use made of Hume's work by the many defenders of the king and the *ancien régime* after that date.

Mailhe's report goes on to show that if the English had taken the same precautions as the French, their republic would have survived. The English Commons should have invited the nation to form a convention parliament:

> Unfortunately, the House of Commons was controlled by the genius of Cromwell, and Cromwell, who wished to become king under the title of protector, would have found in a National Convention only a tomb for his ambitions.
>
> It was therefore not any violation of the prescribed formalities for criminal prosecutions in England, but rather the lack of a na-

27. Jean Mailhe, op. cit., p. 20.

tional mandate, it was the protectorate of Cromwell, in short, that attached to the trial of Charles Stuart the odium which is evoked in even the most philosophical accounts of it. Charles Stuart deserved to die; but his execution could be commanded only by the nation or by a tribunal chosen by the nation.[28]

Many problems remained even though the Convention was seen as representing, in the words of the report, "entirely and perfectly the French Republic."[29] Could the Convention, for example, judge alone or should its judgement be ratified by all citizens in an *appel au peuple*? This question and others concerning the form of the king's punishment were to occupy the debates of that body and exasperate the impatient Robespierrists for many weeks to come.

In examining the Convention speeches during Louis XVI's trial I shall try to classify my sampling of opinions according to three admittedly rather personal headings which relate to the speaker's apparent attitude toward history generally and, more particularly, toward Stuart history. My first grouping will include those whose attitudes imply a fundamental belief in the traditional cyclical view of revolution. It will include those who, speaking often of the lessons of history, closely identified the French and English revolutions. This same group emphasized the conservative implications of the parallel and as a polemical tactic often called attention to the possibility that Louis XVI's execution would automatically leave the way open for an ambitious French Cromwell. Those whom I speak of next comprise members of the Convention who, although they seem to believe to some extent in the ideological identity of the two revolutions as well as in the general value of history's lessons, rejected the validity of any parallels drawn between the two trials because the English court had been influenced by Cromwell whereas revolutionary France did not have and could not possibly have any such monster in its midst. Lastly, I have found it useful to classify in a third group those who made it quite clear that not only Stuart history but all of history was totally irrelevant

28. Ibid., p. 21.
29. Ibid., p. 22.

to the deliberations, that no historical precedents were necessary, indeed that no trial was necessary, and that the sooner justice (i.e. decapitation) was carried out, the better.[30]

Fear of a "circular" revolution ending inevitably with the usurpation of a Cromwell heads the list of reasons cited by the moderates of the first group and underlies their use of the Stuart parallel. The following opinions represent typical examples: "It is perhaps not difficult to prove, as the experience of every century shows, that the violent or judicial death of a tyrant has never truly served the cause of liberty and has resulted only in the transfer of tyrannical power to other hands."—P. Marec. "I am unable to vote sovereignly and without appeal for the death of Louis XVI, because I cannot compromise either with my principles or my con-science...; because I abhor royalty even more than dethroned kings, because I see waiting in the wings a Cromwell who is plotting for my country the fate suffered by England after the death of Charles Stuart."—F.-C.-P. Garilhe. "And who will provide us with a guarantee, citizens, that some ambitious person, taking advantage of the trust he has acquired through his popularity, will not seize on the occasion of Louis XVI's trial to attempt an assault on lib-erty? Will anyone dare to swear that there are no Cromwells in the Republic; and if there is only one, you have traced out the path for his ambitions by following that of the parliament of England."—J. Guiter. "I see no Cromwell behind the curtain; but there are still men with the soul of Cromwell; and who can assure me that criti-cal circumstances are not favourable for conceiving and hatching plots to murder liberty?"—J.-B.-D. Mazade. "Citizens, listen to his-tory.... Consider the fate of the parliament that put Charles on

30. I must point out that I make no claim here to a systematic analysis of the divisions along traditional party lines of opinions expressed in the Convention during the trial. I am concerned only with a sampling of opinions in which the Stuart parallel was actually made whether in a positive or negative sense. I shall also make no distinctions between successive opinions delivered on different but related issues, for example, on the advisability of judging Louis XVI, on the *appel au peuple,* on the king's guilt, or on the form his punishment should take. With a few unavoidable exceptions, the quotations are taken from the original versions printed at the time of the trial by official order of the Convention. (B.N.Le[37].2.G.)

trial; it gave in to the passion of revenge, and overlooked the general good; it did not establish a constitution, and it allowed the republic to perish.... Charles I had to die on the scaffold, not because he was very guilty, like Louis, but because he lived in a superstitious century and he was judged by the faction supporting the usurper Cromwell who wished to reign in his place."—H. Bancal. "Cromwell managed to build up his power on the blood-soaked wreckage of Charles I's throne; and those same persons who had urged the king's death were afterwards moved to tears by his fate. Representatives of the people, do not lose sight of this example." —F. Buzot. "Republicans beware! you are too trusting; Cromwell was a fatal exception to English liberty! And I see all too clearly that one does not need his genius to have his audacity."—J.-B. Louvet. "Yes, we could have drawn some very useful political lessons from history:...A nation is never closer to despotism than when it surrenders to anarchy; the people grow tired of having a thousand masters, tired of being both tyrant and tyrannized, and in the end it seeks the protection of one man. When Cromwell, hiding behind the agitators,..." et cetera.—J.-P. Rabaut.

There are many other opinions in the same vein. Let us look at one last example, that of Vergniaud:

> When Cromwell, whose name has already been mentioned here, set out to dissolve the parliament he had used to overthrow the monarchy and place Charles I on the scaffold, he made several insidious proposals to it.... Parliament gave way to him. General unrest soon followed; and Cromwell easily smashed the instrument he had employed to gain supreme power.
>
> Have you not heard within these precincts and elsewhere, men angrily shouting: "if the price of bread is high, the fault lies with the Temple; if money is scarce, if your armies are lacking in supplies, the fault lies with the Temple; if each day we must suffer the sight of indigence, the fault lies with the Temple"?
>
> Those who say these things know full well that the high cost of bread, the shortages in the supply of provisions, the unsatisfactory administration in the armies, and the indigence we are all grieved to see around us, have causes that have nothing to do with the Temple.... Who can assure me ... that, once Louis is dead, these same

men will not begin shouting with the greatest of violence: "if the price of bread is high, the fault lies with the Convention...."[31]

Inspired by the Stuart parallel, other moderates added the fear of history's condemnation to their fear of a Cromwell. Mennesson warns of "the opprobrium that still haunts the English parliament of 1648" and adds: "The judgement of posterity!... Legislators, reflect on that word: one day, you too will be summoned to appear before that court...: remember, O my colleagues! Remember all those voices conspiring to hasten your ruin and their triumph by demanding that the execution of the tyrant be decided by acclamation and without his being heard.... They know that if the model republican Brutus freed his country simply by driving out the Tarquins, the model usurper Cromwell succeeded in erecting his throne over the tomb of the Stuarts."

Pierre-Florent Louvet also refers to the "reputation that, even a century and a half later, still hangs over the English parliament of 1648." It was not, as Mailhe had attempted to prove, because the English parliament had lacked the powers of the Convention that posterity judged it guilty but rather because Charles I's trial had, in every respect, been conducted illegally: "Imagine then," Louvet continued, "since you have been asked to go even farther than the parliament of England by judging directly yourselves, and without allowing witnesses—something that was not done in the trial of Charles Stuart—imagine then, I say, how much more blame you should expect to incur if you accede to the proposal of the committee."

Also objecting that the members of the Convention should not be Louis's accusers, judges, and executioners all rolled into one, Antoine Girard expressed the concerned belief that a loss of international esteem was as much to be feared as the judgement of posterity: "The English were no doubt right with respect to the sub-

31. Vergniaud's final vote despite these high-minded sentiments seemed, in the end, contradictory and disappointing to moderates: although in favour of the *appel au peuple* he later voted for the death-sentence and against the *sursis*, or reprieve.

stantive issues of the hearing but the procedural illegalities and the monstrous tribunal that served as a framework for the guilty monarch's trial impaired commercial and political relations with other nations...." Even Brissot, who had evolved somewhat since his debate with Clermont-Tonnerre ("the Brissot of 1791 is not the Brissot of 1793," as the elder Pinet scornfully informed the Convention), now warned that the European powers would ask for nothing better than Louis's execution, "because for them it represents a guarantee that the monarchy will be resurrected; because the death of Charles I won for his son the throne and the hearts of his subjects.... Yes, Citizens, the same farce that was played out in England when Charles I died has been repeated in our time. The French cabinet of the day seemed to be interceding on the king's behalf, and at the same time it was subsidizing the Cromwellians who put him to death." Perhaps even, Brissot concluded, the sinister politics of the English cabinet was behind the bloodthirsty cries of the Paris *cannibales*.

Not infrequently mentioned also by those who during the trial debate cited the lessons of Stuart history was the question of a dangerous popular reaction to the King's execution. The Convention was not, of course, excessively concerned with the number of simple women who might, as Hume suggests, cast forth the untimely fruit of their womb or, more simply still, fall down dead on hearing the fatal news. It was, on the other hand, very much concerned with the possible effects of pity which might prepare the way in France for a restoration of the monarchy. To the hearty guffaws of the assembled members, one earnest *conventionnel* even suggested the possible danger that Rome might canonize Louis. The following opinion by Armand-Guy Kersaint clearly shows that Necker's quotation of Hume on the subject had not been lost on all of Louis's judges:

> ...true republicans rightly fear the reaction to vengeful attacks on persons who have long been respected; they fear the pity that the human heart naturally feels for the unfortunate and especially for those who seemed destined to attain the pinnacles of happiness and who are instead brought down by great misfortunes. The profound

and judicious observation that *Charles I had successors while the Tarquins had none,* has prompted them to adopt a moderate course....

The same danger seemed equally evident to Jean-Jacques Thomas:

> Monk would never have found so many hands to help him place Charles II on the throne of England, if he had not been assisted by the memory of the father's execution. The effects of pity and commiseration, both within France and abroad, must be feared....Have you ever seen people on their way back from an execution not feeling sorry for the culprit, even though they still have in their minds a fresh impression of his crimes?...Scorn, nothingness, and oblivion for the individual, that is what can save the nation....

Agreeing with Kersaint and Thomas, Jean-Baptiste Girot added his own corresponding sentiments on the matter: "The death of Charles inflicted a deep wound on liberty; it put an end to the hatred his crimes had inspired. It left regrets; it revived fanatical royalist sentiments that survive still and continue to corrupt the nation's sense of liberty." Thomas Paine's opinion, the reading of which was objected to by Marat on the grounds that a "Quaker" should not be allowed to vote in a case involving the death penalty, pointed out essentially the same warning: the Stuarts returned to the throne of England after Charles I's *execution* but fell into obscurity after the *banishment* of James II. Pierre-Joseph Faure concurred with the American Quaker: "The death of Charles I was the chief cause of the restoration of royalty among a people too enlightened to love kings. The execution of the father pleaded the cause of the son. The people are sometimes moved by compassionate impulses—the frenzy and violence of which cannot be calculated—that work against their own interests. The revolution that deposed James II, who also had a son, adopted other measures; he was allowed to escape, and his son's later efforts to regain the throne were entirely unsuccessful. That is precisely your situation...."

Many other *conventionnels* appealed in their opinions to the

lessons of the Stuart parallel.[32] Not all drew from it the same conclusions but they nearly all agreed on the similar goals of the two
revolutions. Charles-Antoine Chasset, for example, insisted particularly on this last point: "And let it not be said that the English at
that time were insufficiently enlightened; let us not deceive ourselves, they were well versed in the principles of government. Their
history shows that they overturned the throne and founded a republic—short-lived, it is true—in accordance with the same maxims as ours." Like Chasset most of the speakers we have been
referring to were, of course, sincere republicans. It is nevertheless
important to note that they held at the same time a view of history
not too inconsistent with that which had prevailed among traditionalists during the *ancien régime* and which had allowed Hume's
account of the reign of Charles I to become an almost integral part
of French historical culture. A Hume, republican in practice as
well as in principle and viewing the French revolution at this stage
of its development, would probably have found little to object to in
the following passage drawn from the opinion of Jean-François
Barailon:

> It seems to me, all things considered, that prudence, forethought,
> and sound policy command us to defer, to distance ourselves from
> this judgement, to amend our current political system, to rectify, to
> suspend, to abandon even our would-be *revolutionary power....*
>
> It is not our wish to found a republic only for a few minutes,
> as the English did; it is not our wish to have a Cromwell succeed
> a Charles; to substitute a tyrant for a despot; to unleash count-
> less proscriptions, to shed even more blood and encourage new
> massacres....
>
> The discord that prevails and grows among us as the hour of
> judgement approaches, invites our immediate attention and also
> counsels the greatest caution. The violent haste of the English, their
> heedlessness in the matter of Charles Stuart, had the most terrible
> consequences: the destruction of their republic, the loss of their

32. See also, for example, the opinions of Bailly, Baudin, Birotteau, Bodin,
Bordas, Chasset, Guyomar, Lambert, Marey, Meynard, Morisson, Prunelle, and
Riffard St. Martin.

liberty, and the execution of the judges who had been cowardly enough to lend themselves to perfidious insinuations and stupid enough to abet the ambitions of a scoundrel.

4

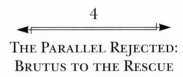

THE PARALLEL REJECTED:
BRUTUS TO THE RESCUE

Let us turn now to what we have arbitrarily set aside as a second group and consider those members of the Convention who, although they seem to hold a view of history not altogether incompatible with that of the group whose opinions we have just examined, maintained nevertheless that the much-quoted parallel with the seventeenth-century revolution in England was entirely invalid.

We find a good example of this attitude in the opinion of Sergent, one of the *députés* for Paris. He expresses utter amazement and disbelief at the hesitations of his colleagues who adduced parallels and who warned the Convention of great lessons to be drawn from the English experiment:

What are you afraid of? The example of England sacrificing Charles Stuart! But, as you have already been told, Charles was sacrificed to the ambition of Cromwell; and Louis will be brought to his death by his treacherous actions; Charles was judged by a commission chosen by the usurper himself, but you are chosen by the People who are Louis's accusers. Charles had no defenders attached to his tribunal, whereas Louis has found advocates even in our midst. . . . So much the better, our judgement will be all the less suspect, all the more irreproachable. We are told, finally, that the death of Charles was the shame of the English people. And what is the source of that claim? It is History! But is History written by a divinity immune to fear? No, the history of Charles's last days was written by MEN; these men wrote under the shadow of BASTILLES. They had to choose between deceiving future generations or expiring in some dark dungeon. Kings persecuted thought even under the humble roof of the philosopher who thought himself sheltered there with what is most sublime, Nature and his own soul. Times have changed; the men who today record in stone the events that will amaze posterity are free, no longer oppressed by the burden of kings.

Philippeaux similarly questioned the veracity of certain histories of the English revolution which seemed to have impressed too vividly the imagination of "a few quaking spirits" in the Convention:

> ... the historical tradition regarding this great period has been given an odious colouring as a result of the constant efforts of kings and their lackeys, who have sought to protect themselves from the same fate by representing it as a time of criminal culpability. In a monarchy, all affections are turned in the direction of idolatry; the throne's structure becomes a composite of illusion and wonder. All those whose interests lie in maintaining the throne and who have it in their power to mould public sentiment could not but succeed finally in their self-serving efforts to misrepresent as horrifying the act of justice that displeased them most. But we republicans, we who condemned tyranny before condemning the tyrant, we are in an entirely different situation: ghosts and disguises can no longer terrify our imagination; it is only the hideousness of the crime and the fact that it has gone unpunished that can sadden our hearts.

Several *conventionnels,* moreover, were not long in pointing out that not all historians of the Stuart reign preached the usual servile principles. The myth of a guilty English nation was nothing more than a revisionist fabrication of fawning historians since the time of the Restoration, affirmed Michel Azéma:

> ... England's so-called dishonour was nothing more than the effect of popular prejudice, error, and blindness, especially on the part of the trusting, generous, frank, and loyal people of France who idolize their kings however little they may deserve it. Most of the historians, authors, and learned contemporaries of this event, far from seeing it as England's shame, praise, on the contrary, the nation's energy, courage, and justice, especially Milton, the author of *Paradise Lost,* and several others.
>
> Ever since the revolution in thinking that has now taken place nearly everywhere among men enlightened by reason and philosophy, the old prejudices that had been formed with regard to Charles

Stuart's tragic death, prejudices that were carefully and shrewdly nourished and fostered by every despot, have totally changed.[33]

The view that no Cromwell existed or could exist in France formed the basis of most rejections of the Stuart parallel. We find this judgement summed up briefly in the opinion of Nicolas Hentz:

> They have tried to frighten you with the spectre of remorse; the example of Charles Stuart's trial has been cited.
>
> Listen carefully while I explain to you that our situation is entirely different. Who was it that sought the death of Charles Stuart? It was a man who himself aspired to the throne and who possessed the means to achieve his goal; ... He succeeded in usurping royalty in England. In other words, royalty never ceased to exist in England; it no longer exists in France.

Dubois-Crancé felt provoked to indignation on the same subject:

> What a comparison! Are we usurpers, then? Were the people ignorant of the mission they entrusted to us? Have we not sworn to avenge and to obey the people? Have we chosen among us a special commission corruptly dedicated to the purpose of beheading the enemy of a conspirator? Is it, finally, the will of one man that commands us, or is it a sense of the legitimate vengeance and compelling need of 25 million oppressed individuals? You have decreed that if a Cromwell exists in France, his head belongs to the lowest of citizens; and to lop it off, one need not be a Brutus. Let us therefore not dishonour our august functions with a comparison fit only for the Brunswicks and the Condés.

Directly refuting Vergniaud, Claude-Nicolas Guillermin also could see no rhyme or reason to the parallel:

> I confess that I am highly perplexed with respect to applying the example. I look in vain for a *Cromwell* in our Revolution, I see none; that is to say, I can see no Frenchman with Cromwell's great popularity in the armies and among the people generally (for it cannot

33. Rühl makes the same point and adds that in Milton's work the Convention would find "strong arguments for condemning Louis XVI"; see also the opinion of François-Siméon Bezard.

be just the people of Paris who constitute only a Section). I can see no Frenchman who commands the universal trust enjoyed by Cromwell, who possesses his powerful means, his beguiling virtues, his military talents, his political adeptness, his courage, his shrewdness, his vices even, all of which were so many rungs in the ladder that allowed him to mount the throne from which he had deposed Charles.

But I see, on the other hand, many who would play the rôle of *Brutus* should even one *Cromwell* be found lurking in the shadows.

Brutus of course! Here was the answer to all rascally Cromwells! Also claimed, but feebly, by the Right as the patron of all those who defended the ancient constitution against revolutionary usurpers,[34] Brutus was a hero the details of whose career[35] were sufficiently obscured by antiquity to permit his serving as an unassailable example to true republicans when even Sidney, the martyr to Liberty, had to be cast off because he was English.[36] Only the bust of Brutus and that of Rousseau managed to survive the years of progressive iconoclasm at the Jacobins, and it was his again that dominated the chair of the president of the Convention. No revolutionary hair style, not even that of the Round Heads, ever equalled in fashion the *coiffure à la Brutus*.

Brutus is also Louchet's answer to the threat of a Cromwell: "I ask you! What man would be sufficiently insane to attempt to seize royal authority in France once the sword of justice severs the tyrant's head. Oh! if such a man could exist, the Faubourg Saint-Antoine is there; it is everywhere in the Republic; would not the land of liberty and equality... bring forth a thousand Brutuses who would vie for the honour of striking the first blow against this new Cromwell?" Moïse Bayle was of the same confident opinion: "Have

---

34. See the Comte d'Antraigue's *Adresse à l'ordre de la noblesse de France*, Paris, 1792, pp. 124–35.

35. Revolutionary orators did not always distinguish between the earlier and the later Brutus.

36. See *La Décade,* 20 December 1794, III. 543.

you not decreed that any man who speaks of a king[37] will be punished with death? Are you afraid that this decree might not be carried out and that in the whole of France not a single Brutus would be found?"

It is in the opinion of Claude-Charles Prost that we find this position most clearly summarized:

> Let us reject any comparison of Charles Stuart's trial and that of Louis; the fundamental data and the results are not necessarily the same; Charles was a tyrant, but he was condemned by judges who assumed an authority not conferred on them by the nation; in contrast, your mandate is explicit: Charles was the victim of an ambitious hypocrite; we have no Cromwell in this republican parliament and I can see more than one *Brutus*. The death of Charles did not advance the cause of liberty for the people; the nobility survived the monarch, and everywhere that parasitical plant is to be found, one can expect the poisonous regrowth of a king or an oppressor by another name.[38]

The political image of Cromwell in France during the last three centuries would provide the basis of a long and interesting study. One fact would emerge certainly from such an investigation with respect to the Convention period, namely, that few revolutionaries[39] found it either in their conscience or in their political interests to express anything but the greatest horror for the leader of the English revolution. The subtitle of M.-L. Tardy's tragedy of 1793, *Cromwel ou le général liberticide,* typically sums up the current attitude although, as we have already noted, the Puritan general had been occasionally viewed as a hero by a few avant-garde thinkers before the Revolution. Robespierre frequently defended

37. It must be conceded that the modest Bonaparte used only the word *empereur.*

38. See also the opinions of Baudot, Cledel, Deleyre, Guyton, and Gertoux: the last refers to Louis XVI as "le Stuart français."

39. One might possibly except such men as Deleyre and Jean-Bon Saint-André, perhaps even Saint-Just who, it is worth noting, possessed in his small collection of books a biography of the Protector. (See Bapst, op. cit., *La Révolution Française,* XXI. 535.)

himself against the accusations of Jean-Baptiste Louvet and others who charged him with harbouring the malign ambitions of a Cromwell. Danton, interrupted in a speech of 1 April 1793 by the cry "And Cromwell?...," furiously demanded, to the wild applause of his supporters, that the "scoundrel who has had the effrontery to say that I am a Cromwell be punished: have him locked up in the Abbaye!"[40] After the Terror, the Convention found it wise to decree a *mention honorable* for Dugour's *Histoire de Cromwel* of 1795 and added the recommendation that the work be referred to the Comité d'Instruction Publique.[41] The *Moniteur* commented with a sigh of relief on 1 May 1795 that Dugour's book could not have been published at a more opportune time: "It is in the conduct of this tyrant that our recent oppressors found the means to enslave us anew. Read his biography and you will discover the same system of oppression, devised in almost the same manner; it is as if one were reading the history of our present times; the resemblances are so striking that one would be tempted to question the historian's veracity were it not for the fact that everything he narrates is recorded in the accounts and memoirs of contemporary authors."[42] Later still the parallel was frequently applied—perhaps with greater accuracy—to Bonaparte. But no matter what circumstance or which party is involved, the image of the Protector remains constant: Cromwell was as ostensibly odious in 1793 in the Convention as he was in Louis XVI's marginal notes of 1779.[43] A *hero* of any kind was feared and a Cromwell was feared perhaps most of all; for, to transpose a sentiment already expressed by a zealous English republican in 1649, if a *king* was desired, the last was perhaps as proper as any gentleman in France.

40. *Oeuvres de Danton,* ed. Vermorel, Paris, 1866, p. 188.

41. See *La Décade,* An III, V. 174.

42. *Gazette Nationale, ou le Moniteur universel,* No. 222, p. 902. See also *Journal de Paris,* No. 202, 11 April 1797.

43. See also Alexandre Tuetey, *Répertoire général des sources manuscrites de l'histoire de Paris pendant la Révolution française,* IV, Nos. 1125, 3342, 3458, 3643; VIII, No. 1403; X, No. 2102; XI, No. 28.

5

PRINCIPLES VERSUS PRECEDENTS

Finally, let us consider those *conventionnels* whose opinions concerning the relevance of history, expressed during the trial of Louis XVI, allow us to classify them as a third group. These last were, of course, no less politically earnest than the others but they showed a greater amount of impatience to get on with a revolution that had, in their view, vertically outgrown history and was destined to lead the French nation to unprecedented heights of virtue and justice. For these true radicals, the Revolution had rendered the old interpretation of history and all of the cyclical parallels meaningless.

Admittedly, some of the Convention parallel-makers had been infuriatingly didactic; Birotteau's triple comparison provides us with a good example: "Stuart died on the scaffold, and England continued to have kings. Rome, on the other hand, drove out the Tarquins, and Rome became the most stable and prosperous of republics; and, finally, the tyrant Dionysius, sent into exile at Corinth where he became a schoolmaster, saw no new tyrants succeed him in Syracuse."

For our third group this was too much! We are told that as the sober Birotteau prepared to leave the tribune the mocking voice of Jullien was heard to shout: "Honourable mention!"[44]

To many, such parallels seemed indeed a practice more suited to the pretensions of over-eager schoolboys than to the leaders of the world's greatest revolution. Mont-Gilbert boasts that his opinion will be unusual, that he will quote no obsolete authorities from history:

> What do free Frenchmen have in common with Cromwell's henchmen? ... This obsession with finding grandiloquent comparisons is unworthy of us.
>
> I shall come right out and say it (and may I be forgiven for doing

---

44. See *Journal des débats et des décrets*, No. 102, 29 December 1792.

so), this assembly, in my view, will never achieve its full majesty until, along with other reforms, we get rid of a certain importunate erudition which, to invest us with greatness and virtue, goes digging through the ruins of Athens and Sparta to find models. Woe betide us if to achieve great things we need to be encouraged by great examples! How feeble these virtues of imitation are when they do not derive their strength from the moral character of those who profess them!

If at all costs Louis's judges wanted to imitate a virtue of the past, let it be, added Mont-Gilbert, the laconism of the Spartans.

The familiar idealist's cry of principles not precedents was heard also from several other members: "What does it matter," asked Ichon, "that England put Stuart on trial! ... Basing on such comparisons the right of the people to overthrow kings is an outrage committed against the nation's majesty. It is from the very nature of social organization, it is from the principles of immutable justice, it is from the nation's code of sacred rights, that must be derived ... the power to judge a king. ..."

Bernard Descamps, attacking Rabaut's Stuart-parallel, made a similar objection: "I will simply point out that it is very easy to draw parallels, and that these are certain to lead you into error. It is not a question here of what has been done, but rather of what must be." What *must be*, he continued, does not depend on the bugbears of history: "We have been shown here the bloody head of Charles I, and the Convention Nationale of France has been compared more or less to the executioners who did Cromwell's bidding; we have been harangued here, not about justice, but about politics; not about duty, but about accountability."

Moderate appeals to the allegedly prudent lessons of history were nothing more than ill-disguised counter-revolutionary delaying tactics in the opinion of Marc-Antoine Jullien:

> The trial of Charles Stuart has been cited in order to justify the slow and complicated procedures that have been recommended to you, and you have been told that it was because such measures were not taken that the English nation incurred the censure of the most philosophical writers. Be undeceived, Citizens; do not mistake that excuse for a reason. If the English, instead of merely truncating and

abridging the sceptre of kings, had, like you, broken it up and melted it down; if the government that they adopted had been purely republican, and if the history of their revolution had been written only by republicans, you may be certain that it would never have occurred to anyone to find fault with how they judged their tyrant. In the eyes of true republicans, there are no inappropriate ways to destroy the usurpers of the people's sovereignty; but the best, in their opinion, is the shortest, it is the way of men like Scaevola and Brutus. Either your republic will survive, in which case the horror that the memory of your last king must inspire in you will be recorded in all historical writings, or else the monarchy will resuscitate, and then, no matter what formalities you employ to dress up the trial of Louis XVI, there will be vile courtier slaves who, in order to flatter new tyrants, will find ways to stigmatize your glory, to dishonour your virtues, and to depict you in odious colours to posterity as the most sacrilegious of regicides. Make haste then to settle with the executioner's blade a question that has already for too long taken up our time; make haste to found an eternal republic, do not hesitate to cement it with the blood of a perjuring king, and be not afraid that his execution will ever be imputed to you as a crime.

To satisfy their vanity, certain philosophers hoping to establish erudite theories, certain orators seeking to compose sublime speeches, have attempted to persuade you that this cause is difficult and of the greatest importance. Pay no heed to these sinister enlighteners and follow as I do the pure guiding light of reason; it will show you that there has never been an easier question to decide.

There are obviously no tiresome schoolboy pretensions in Jullien's opinion any more than in the following one by Robespierre, which probably served as Jullien's model:

Without realizing it, the Assembly has allowed itself to be led astray, far from the real question. There is no trial to proceed with here.... To suggest that Louis XVI should be tried, in whatever manner, is to retrogress to royal and constitutional despotism; it is a counter-revolutionary notion, for it is putting the revolution itself on trial....

The people do not judge in the manner of judicial courts; they do not pass sentence, they hurl thunderbolts; they do not pass judgement on kings, they annihilate them, and that form of justice is as good as what the courts offer....

We have allowed ourselves to be misled by foreign examples that have nothing in common with us. Cromwell had Charles I tried by a commission that was at his disposal . . . it is natural that tyrants immolate their own kind, not for the benefit of the people, but for their own ambitions, seeking all the while to deceive the common people with illusory formalities: it is not a question in such cases of either principles or liberty, but rather of scheming and imposture. But what laws can the people follow other than reason and justice, backed by their own omnipotence? . . .

I for one would be ashamed to devote any more serious discussion to these constitutional quibbles. I consign them to the classroom or the law-courts, or better still, to the cabinets of London, Vienna, and Berlin. I cannot find it in me to stretch out discussions when I am convinced that it is scandalous to debate at all.

We have been told that the case is very important and that it must be judged with wisdom and circumspection. It is you who are making it an important case: What am I saying! It is you who are making it into a case of any kind. . . .

Louis had to die so that the nation might live—such was Robespierre's conclusion. Saint-Just was equally frank: "One day, people will be amazed to learn that the eighteenth century was less advanced than Caesar's day: then, the tyrant was immolated right in the Senate with no other formality than thirty blows of the dagger. . . ." One is not obliged to cite legal or historical precedent to prove that kings are guilty. Kings are guilty by definition. All formalities to prove this guilt are vain. Every king is a rebel and a usurper. In Saint-Just's celebrated words: *"It is impossible to reign innocently. . . ."*

Quite obviously it would be a fruitless task to search for the influence of Stuart history in these last opinions. One is almost tempted to say that the influence of historical precedent is completely absent for, with these men, the Revolution seemed at last to have outgrown all history.

If, however, one detects no influence, one at least senses in the words of Robespierre and his supporters a quite intense and highly revealing mood of exasperation. The debate over the wisdom of the Long Parliament in judging Charles I had gone on a very long time, far too long in the opinion of these men who wished to make haste. If at worst the question of the Stuart parallel and the closely related issue concerning the *appel au peuple* represented nothing more than a clever device invented by those moderates who wished to save the king's life (and I believe it was much more than that), it clearly was a question on which a high proportion of members felt urged to speak or publish[45] their sentiments.

The seventeenth-century revolution in England had provided the only really significant modern European precedent to the French revolution. How, so many *conventionnels* felt obliged to ask, did this precedent affect the new French Republic? What lessons could be learned from it? Hume, through his long established positive influence on conservative thinking up until the time of the trial and through his specific impact on the writings of the king's chief apologists, had generated an important and not always totally negative reaction among Louis's judges. The Mailhe report and the many "Stuart" opinions delivered during the trial can be interpreted to a substantial extent as bearing witness to the intensity of this reaction. Many in the Convention were apparently willing to admit that there existed an ideological relationship between the events in England and those in France. But they were obliged to admit also that the English revolution had ended in counter-revolution and, finally, in the restoration of the monarchy. What course of action would best prevent the occurrence of a similar failure a century and a half later?

As it turned out, of course, the bloody spectre of Charles I was not enough to save Louis XVI from the guillotine. It is true, nevertheless, that this spectre remained to haunt even those who pretended to feel only contempt for it. The symbols of Stuart history continued to present a threat of potential counter-revolution to France's revolutionary leaders. The following incident, recorded during the Reign of Terror, though trivial in itself, is sufficient, I think, to illustrate this point. Late in December 1793, a certain Amable-Augustin Clément, clock-maker by profession and living in the rue Montmartre, was condemned to death by the revolutionary tribunal. He had been denounced as an aristocrat and partisan of

---

45. After a time there were so many *opinions* that they could not all be delivered orally.

Lafayette, charged with having wickedly and intentionally fired on the patriots during the day of 17 July 1791, and also with having voiced counter-revolutionary sentiments tending to restore the monarchy. Part of the damning evidence heard by the examining judge Etienne Foucault was an admission by the accused that he had in his possession several prints: notably a picture of Charlotte Corday and another of the execution of Charles I of England.[46]

46. See Alexandre Tuetey, op. cit., IX. 293–94.

V

The Aftermath

1

REPUBLICAN QUALMS

The counter-revolutionary use of Hume's *History of the Stuarts* as a bible of unshakeable prophecies, complacently illustrating the irrationalism and ineradicable sins of human nature, the implacable "force of things," and the inevitable failure of all revolutions, continued with perhaps even greater intensity in the last five years of the century. Disheartening to some revolutionists too was the fact that political events as they progressed seemed to lend a new respectability to the fashionable science of historical analogies as more and more of the royalist predictions were, in appearance at least, fulfilled.

On the whole, however, few republicans showed signs of discouragement. Although leaders of the Right flattered themselves with the hope of restoration and pointed again and again to the failure of the English republican experiment, those on the Left, now publishing parallels of their own, staunchly denied the validity of such royalist hopes.

Much of this republican optimism seems to have been based on the belief that the established church, acknowledged as the throne's chief support, was now gone forever. Such, for example, is the opinion of Jean-Jacques Leuliette, writing in 1797: "...if I could hazard an opinion, I would say that the return of the monarchy is impossible in France, that its very foundations have been overturned, that if this colossus were to rise again one day, it would stand, like the statue of Nebuchadnezzar, only on feet of clay. James Stuart once uttered a profound maxim: *no Bishop, no King* and there is no likelihood that the reign of superstition will be easily restored...."[1]

Republicans were generally confident on this last point. Neither the Church nor the monarchy could ever return to power. Also writing in 1797, the *idéologue* Roederer explained just why there was no need to fear a religious revival. His reasons, given only a few years before the appearance of the *Génie du Christianisme* and the ratification of the Concordat, are worth noting and invite certain reflections on the advantages held, temporarily at least, by the empirical conservatives of the opposing camp who spoke so lovingly of the inertia in the nature of things and who went on making their hopeful historical parallels:

> Do you know that in France there are two million copies of Helvétius, Voltaire, Rousseau, and Montesquieu, and that every day one hundred thousand pages of philosophy are read in France? Do you not think that it would be difficult to destroy entirely the power of these men, even if their works were no more than part of the personal furniture of a host of people? No one likes to see his library, the books that adorn his room, degraded. Certainly, the morocco leather, the vellum bindings, the gold tooling of our Voltaire and Montesquieu volumes weigh in our favour. Ask the old lawyers who looked on with such regret as some of the worst laws were being abolished if part of their concern was not because of their libraries.[2]

1. *Des Emigrés Français ou Réponse à M. de Lally-Tollendal,* Paris, 1797, pp. 104–5.

2. *Journal d'économie politique, de morale, et de politique; rédigé par Roederer de l'Institut national de France,* Paris, 1797, II. 370. It is curious to note that Montesquieu's conservatism, although it was often attacked during the Revolution, was also very often "explained away" as representing nothing more than the exoteric principles of a basically radical but prudent political thinker who was obliged to use the subterfuge of a double doctrine under the oppression of the *ancien régime.* See, for example, Destutt de Tracy, *M. de Tracy à M. Burke,* p. 9; *La Décade,* 1795, V. 468; Brissot, *Le Patriote Français,* No. 915, 11 February 1792, pp. 167–68; Thomas Paine, *The Rights of Man,* 1791, Part I, p. 75.

Confidence in the future of the new Republic and the reasoned hope that it would consolidate its forces now that the days of anarchy were over thus seem to have been the prevailing attitude on the Left at this time. Some republicans, however, despite such assurances, did in fact worry about the Stuart parallels. Typically concerned was Antoine Boulay de la Meurthe, a member of the Conseil des Cinq-Cents, who in December 1797 became president of the Assembly. Although Boulay had himself narrowly escaped the Terror, he became in this post-Terror period a strong advocate of harsher measures against refractory priests and against members of the nobility who had not emigrated. Such measures are best described as indicative of his own pronounced fears of a counter-revolution. At his suggestion even, a special promise not to aid in attempts to restore the monarchy was added to the oath of civil officers at this time.

It can safely be said, I think, that much of Boulay's preoccupation with the dangers of a counter-revolution came to him from his study of Stuart history.

The English republic had not survived because, obviously, the English had made mistakes. But what were those English mistakes? As an answer to this question, Boulay published in 1798 his popular essay showing the causes of failure in the English revolution.[3]

The basic implication of Boulay's work is that the art of revolution is a difficult one—more difficult certainly than was admitted by those who had nursed France's great social experiment through its earliest years. The English had faced the same original problem. They too had overthrown the monarchy in hopes of destroying despotism: "One of the more immediate causes of this revolution was monarchical despotism, elevated to a great height by the princes of the House of Tudor and imprudently sustained by the House of Stuart that followed."[4] They had failed to maintain their republic, however, because of rigorous extremism. The English re-

3. *Essai sur les causes qui, en 1649, amenèrent en Angleterre l'établissement de la République; sur celles qui devaient l'y consolider; sur celles qui l'y firent périr.* Par Boulay (de la Meurthe), Représentant du Peuple, Paris, An VII.

4. Ibid., p. 4.

public would have survived if patriots had steered a middle course between the servile policies of the royalists—which Hume, Boulay asserts, despite all his airs of impartiality, obviously supports—and the fanatical conduct of the extreme Left wing. Boulay admits, of course, that some harsh measures were necessary at the time:

> However much one might wish to take pride in moderation, it would be difficult to deny that, once the revolution was accomplished, the people's leaders had every right to repress the royalist party by reducing it to a situation where it could do no harm. When a political change has been carried out in the interests of the people and with their approval, it is obvious that all necessary measures to consolidate it are not only authorized but required by justice, not that distributive justice which operates among individuals, but general justice that sees to the preservation and the happiness of societies, whose acts, though always advantageous to the majority, may at times not seem favorable to the minority.[5]

But having gone this far, Boulay warns, leaders of revolutions must be careful to go no farther. Harsh measures must be restricted to what is absolutely necessary: "The fine art of revolution is to attain your goal while doing the least possible harm."[6] The delicate trick of survival entails giving only a half-turn to the political wheel, which must come to rest at precisely the right point, that is, before the necessity of reaction sets in. There are implications in the following passage which make it possible for us to understand how republicans were soon able to reconcile in their minds both the Revolution and the arrival of Bonaparte—however much they were to murmur eventually at the title of Emperor:

> One of man's greatest needs, and, especially, one of the greatest needs of any society, is the need for tranquillity....One of the first duties of government is thus to secure the public peace, not the kind of peace sometimes provided by despotism and which resembles too closely the peace of the graveyard, but rather, the peace that combines with dynamic action in proportions that are most salutary for both the body politic and its individual members, such

5. Ibid., p. 121.
6. Ibid., p. 122.

peace being always the fruit of liberty wisely and firmly regulated by the constitution and by laws.[7]

Disagreeing with Boulay de la Meurthe's position on several points but supporting basically his view that extremism could only harm the Revolution, the young republican Benjamin Constant in an earlier work had also invoked Stuart history to warn France of the dangers of counter-revolution.

First of all, Constant maintained, it was a mistake to say that the English revolution had failed. Confusion had arisen on this question because it was assumed that the French and English revolutions had had similar goals:

> When we attempt to measure the success of revolutions—the product of ideas—we sometimes confuse their secondary and primary goals. We assume, for example, that the revolution of 1648 in England failed because the monarchy was later restored. But it was not the idea of a republic that sparked the revolution, it was the idea of religious freedom. The notion of a republic was no more than an accessory goal, and in this respect the revolution fell short.[8]

Even though an ideological identity did not exist, there were important lessons to be learned from Stuart history by those who wished to maintain the Republic in France:

> The English revolution, which was essentially an attack on popery, having gone beyond its goal by abolishing royalty, provoked a violent reaction: twenty-eight years later a second revolution was required to forestall the restoration of popery. The French Revolution, which was essentially an attack on privilege, having likewise gone beyond its goal by attacking property, has now provoked a terrible reaction and there will be need for, not another revolution, I hope, but for much precaution and extreme care to ensure that privilege is not reinstated.[9]

---

7. Ibid., pp. 126–27.

8. *De la force du gouvernement actuel de la France et de la nécessité de s'y rallier*, 1796, p. 95, note f.

9. *Des réactions politiques*, An V, pp. 2–3.

Stuart history shows, according to Constant, that the greatest difficulties are encountered when one attempts to restore to its just and moderate limits a revolution that has gone too far. The political pendulum swings an equal distance in both directions. Repressive reaction equal to former excess is a constant threat. It was to warn against the dangers of such a reaction that Benjamin Constant added his own remarks to Boulay's treatment of the English revolution. Boulay had described the oppressive extremes of the English revolutionaries; he had not, however, sufficiently emphasized the greater horrors perpetrated by those who subsequently restored the monarchy. This was, Constant urged, the lesson of Stuart history that called for France's immediate attention:

> The present state of the republic has been an additional reason for me to undertake this work. Men of every party, in their books and in their speeches, seem to be saying that a transition would be desirable, that coming to terms would be possible. I would like to demonstrate that contractual agreements between the republic and royalty are never more than deceitful arrangements intended to disarm those targeted for punishment; that compromises with kings are always without guarantee; that the same impulses that argue for a restoration of the monarchy lead invariably to overturning the barriers with which one hopes to limit monarchical power; finally, that the nation that does not know how to live without a master knows even less how to keep him in check.[10]

To prove these points, Constant proposed to quote authorities who could not be suspected of republican bias. He deftly agrees to leave aside Mrs. Macaulay's account and promises to use the royalists Clarendon and Hume. Even these historians, he implies, had found it impossible to veil the atrocities of the bloody Jefferies and Kirkes. What is more, the force of this English lesson had to be multiplied several times over for proper application to circumstances in France, since conditions in England had been of such a nature as to soften the violence of counter-revolution.

10. *Des suites de la contre-révolution de 1660 en Angleterre*, Paris, An VII, pp. viii–ix.

...what attentive reader will not be struck by the differences that distinguish our current situation from what prevailed in England at the time, differences that would make the restoration of the monarchy a thousand times more dangerous here?...

To forestall the counter-revolution, to maintain the republic, is thus in the common interests of all Frenchmen of every class. Why then is there this universal indifference, this pervasive lethargy, in which the people, despite the dangers that surround them, seem to be submerged?[11]

As we have already noted, not all republicans were as worried about the Stuart parallels as Constant and Boulay seem to have been. Commenting in the same year on Boulay's work, J.-B. Salaville objected that such a show of uneasiness was bad for the morale of republicans generally, and politically most unwise. Boulay had no doubt been well intentioned in his desire to warn the French by citing the failures of the English revolution. But however laudable his motives were, he was guilty in effect of telling his compatriots that much of what they had already accomplished was somehow invalid and that the course of the revolution would have to be changed. Was this not, Salaville asked, the very line preached by French royalists who also liked to talk about the revolutionary failures of the English? Had not Boulay unwittingly played into the hands of the counter-revolutionaries? "I am assured," Salaville asserted, "that your work has had an effect quite different from what you expected; that it has discouraged republicans, the sincere friends of liberty; that, conversely, it has singularly revived the hopes of royalists because of the resemblance they think they can see between the English revolution and what has just taken place here, a conformity that sufficiently guarantees in their eyes the counter-revolution they yearn for."[12]

11. Ibid., pp. 77–80.

12. J.-B. Salaville, *De la Révolution Française comparée à celle de l'Angleterre ou Lettre au Représentant du peuple Boulay (de la Meurthe), sur la différence de ces deux révolutions; pour servir de suite à l'ouvrage publié par ce Représentant sur celle de l'Angleterre*, Paris, An VII, p. 2.

France's republicans had to be encouraged, not told that their efforts had been wasted. Royalists, on the other hand, had to be stripped of any comforting and politically dangerous illusions. The best way to effect both of these salutary measures was, in Salaville's opinion, to prove that the English and French revolutions, which even republicans now seemed to see as "perfectly similar," were in fact quite dissimilar and that nothing at all could be concluded from the one to the other except perhaps that re-establishment of the monarchy in France, in any form whatever, was henceforth an impossibility.

To begin with, the English would not have had a revolution had it not been for the disagreement over religion. This in itself, Salaville maintained, was enough to show that the French and English revolutions were quite different. England's quarrel over religion could have been resolved without a political revolution. France's revolution, on the other hand, had grown out of the vicious socio-political structure of the *ancien régime;* a political revolution had been absolutely necessary to change that structure.

Salaville also repeated—only a few months before the 18th Brumaire—the arguments so popular with those members of the Convention who during Louis's trial had rejected the Stuart parallel:

> I think one could successfully argue that there has never been a republic in England. Cromwell was already king when Charles mounted the scaffold; there is nothing more to be seen in that event than the elimination of one despot by his competitor. The same thing has occurred in countless monarchies.... Hiding under the Protectorate label, royalty became all the more absolute, and in the end, when Cromwell was allowed to name his successor, it was even made hereditary.
>
> In France royalty was abolished both in law and in fact; no individual took it upon himself to assume under any title whatever the former occupant's place; the generals stayed with their armies.... No revolution had ever before provided such an example....[13]

13. Ibid., p. 26.

The 18th Brumaire was, of course, and very soon, to spoil even this splendid example. Once again we are forced to think, with all our advantages of hindsight, of Roederer and the warm sense of security he felt as he contemplated the two million copies of Voltaire, Helvétius, et cetera, that existed in France, providing an "insurmountable" barrier to the religious revival! The makers of parallels frequently showed, it must be admitted, less innocence at least in their empirical prophecies. Innocence too is perhaps the word that best characterizes Salaville's apparent inability to equate more meaningfully the factor of religion in the seventeenth century with that of politics one hundred and fifty years later. He illustrates the deficiency well in the following criticism of Boulay:

> Moreover, *Citoyen représentant,* these factions or these parties that, especially in your work, seem to bear such a striking resemblance to those created by our Revolution, might very well, after fairly rigorous analysis, turn out to be quite different in both their principles and procedures; everyone has seen in your Presbyterians the equivalent of our *Fédéralistes* or *Modérés,* and in your Independents those we have specifically labeled *Jacobins;* but the fact is that the Presbyterians and the Independents, in conformity with the spirit of the English revolution, were bigots and fanatics, concerned mainly with religion; politics had only a subsidiary rôle as a means to achieve the changes they wished to see made in their forms of worship; there is not much there that resembles the motivating forces which inspired in turn our own various parties.[14]

With the concluding thought that Salaville, even for his day, was perhaps too exclusive in his application of the terms *bigot* and *fanatic,* let us turn now to those whom he described as sighing for the counter-revolution and as excessively comforted by the belief that what had happened in England was happening even then in France.

---

14. Ibid., pp. 29–30. Salaville rather than Mirabeau is sometimes credited with the publication in 1789 of *Théorie de la royauté, d'après la doctrine de Milton,* par le comte de M******* (see *supra,* p. 140, n. 89).

2

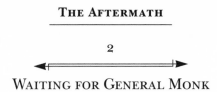

Waiting for General Monk

The Abbé Duvoisin in his *Défense de l'ordre social contre les principes de la Révolution Française* (1798) gives, along with the usual history-inspired theocratic account of the origin of society, perhaps the most precise expression to the royalists' counter-revolutionary hopes at this time. God is the author of society in the sense that he made man a social creature. Hereditary monarchy gives the best demonstration of this natural form of government; the "force of things" as evidenced in the reassuring example of Stuart history must inevitably return the French to their old *régime:*

> Similar to the English republic in its origins, the French Republic will likewise end in the same manner. After the death of Cromwell, England, tired of both parliamentary anarchy and protectoral tyranny, saw in the restoration of the slain king's son its only hope for peace. The Directoire, which subjugated the legislative body, which destroyed all national representation, which stripped the people of all their constitutional rights, the Directoire is the Cromwell of the French Republic. It will fall, and with it will disappear all that remains of the republic, its nomenclatures and its forms. . . .
>
> Monarchical government is a restorative for nations that are exhausted by civil discord.[15]

Duvoisin then provides hints, drawn from his knowledge of Stuart history, as to how France's government would become legal once more:

> Zealous or ambitious generals, armies that have been enticed away, have lent their support to the Directoire against the nation. In the midst of these same armies, a more noble and enlightened ambition may raise up a Monk who, as he unfurls the royal standard, will see himself as the leader and liberator of the nation. . . .
>
> If the past can provide us with conjectures for the future, history

---

15. *Oeuvres complètes de Duvoisin*, p. 1302.

abounds with actions that seem to justify the hopes of the friends of religion and royalty....[16]

That the counter-revolution would be the work of a few men was also the opinion of Joseph de Maistre in his famous *Considérations sur la France*, published in 1796, two years before Duvoisin's work.

> When we advance hypotheses regarding the counter-revolution, we too often commit the error of thinking that the counter-revolution will be, and can only be, the result of a popular decision.... How pitiful! The people play no rôle in revolutions, or at least they are involved only as passive instruments. Perhaps four or five persons will be responsible for giving France a king.... If the monarchy is restored, the people will not be involved in its reinstatement any more than they were involved in its destruction or in the establishment of a revolutionary government.[17]

Benjamin Constant had warned republicans that a counter-revolution would be bloody and vengeful, and he had cited Hume's *History* to prove this. De Maistre, also writing with the pages of Hume's *Stuarts* open before him, sees the exact opposite to be the case. He soothingly reassured his republican enemies that the restoration would be forgiving:

> It is a very common piece of sophistry these days to insist on the dangers of a counter-revolution in order to show that we must never go back to the monarchy....
>
> Are people perhaps convinced that ... because the monarchy was overturned by monsters it must be reinstated by men who are their counterparts? Oh! may those who employ this sophism do it full justice by looking closely into their own hearts! They know that the friends of religion and of the monarchy are incapable of committing any of the excesses that stained the hands of their enemies....[18]

16. Ibid., pp. 1307–8.

17. *Oeuvres complètes de J. de Maistre*, I. 113.

18. Ibid., I. 121–22.

A return to the monarchy, far from producing such evils, would put an end to the maladies afflicting France. Only the forces of destruction, de Maistre blithely asserts, would be destroyed. Were there foolish sceptics among his readers who still remained unconvinced? For these he marshals his weightiest arguments, the evidence of history:

> . . . let us at least believe in history, history which is experimental politics. In the last century, England presented more or less the same spectacle that we see in France today. The fanaticism of liberty, fired up by religious fanaticism, penetrated men's souls there much more deeply than it has in France where the cult of liberty is based on nothingness. What a difference, moreover, in the character of the two nations and in the actors who played a rôle on the two stages! Where are, I will not say the Hampdens, but the Cromwells of France? And yet, in spite of the blazing fanaticism of the English republicans, in spite of the austere determination of the national character, in spite of the well-deserved fears of many guilty persons, and especially of the army, did the restoration of the monarchy in England cause the kind of divisions that were generated by the regicide revolution? Show us the atrocities, the vengeful reprisals of the English royalists. A few regicides perished by authority of the law, but no battles took place, no individual scores were settled. The king's return was marked only by a great cry of joy that was heard throughout England. Enemies embraced, and the king, surprised at what he saw, exclaimed with great emotion: *It must surely have been my own fault that I have been absent so long from such a good people!* . . .[19]

After citing that impartial historian David Hume as his source, de Maistre in aphoristic style defines the one great truth he wished the French to make theirs: "The restoration of the monarchy, which is called a counter-revolution, will not be a contrary revolution, but the contrary of the revolution."[20]

De Maistre saw Stuart history, properly interpreted, as a marvellous specific against the unfounded fears of even the guiltiest republicans. They had no need to be anxious about a future

19. Ibid., I. 153–56.
20. Ibid., I. 157.

restoration of the monarchy. That Stuart history could also give unique hope and assurance to long-suffering royalists is made equally clear by the last chapter in de Maistre's book, the title of which is self-explanatory and needs no further comment. It is called, quite simply, "Extract from a History of the French Revolution, by David Hume."[21]

21. See *supra*, p. 90, n. 16. Royalists were immensely pleased with this clever bit of editing. (See, for example, the *Spectateur du Nord*, July–September 1797, pp. 93–94.)

The influence of Hume on de Maistre is undeniably profound but defies simple analysis. He quotes the "orthodox" Hume often, as, for example, in the following attack on *a priori* constitutions: "The principle that the people are the origin of all just power is noble and specious in itself, but it is belied by all history and experience." (*Oeuvres complètes de J. de Maistre*, I. 286–87.) He also quotes (or misquotes) Hume's authority on the origins of European government (I. 440–41); against the alleged superiority of English eloquence (I. 194, 527); on the Council of Trent (II. 28–29); against the Reformation: "Hume who held back nothing since he believed in nothing, openly admits that the true foundation of the Reformation was the desire to 'make spoil of the plate and all the rich ornaments which belonged to the altars.'" (II. 413, 521); against so-called English tolerance in religion: "How much patience did England—which is always haranguing other nations on the subject of tolerance—itself show when it thought its own religion was under attack? Hume has reproached it for its Inquisition against Catholics, *worse*, he states, than that of Spain, since it exercised its whole tyranny *though without its order.*" (III. 359); against the Enlightenment heroes Bacon and Locke (IV. 272, 375; VI. 44–45, 56–57); and on the worthy rôle of the Church in preserving civilization during the Dark Ages (VI. 473–74), et cetera.

On the other hand, it is also clear that David Hume represented for de Maistre perhaps the most frightening example possible of human wickedness: "Who has not heard of David Hume, *cui non notus Hylas?* I think, everything considered, that the eighteenth century, so fertile in the genre, produced no enemy of religion equal to him. His icy venom is far more dangerous than Voltaire's rabid frothings.... If ever among men who have heard the Gospel preached there has existed a true atheist (a question I shall not take it upon myself to decide), it is he. I have never been able to read any of his anti-religious works without experiencing a kind of terror, without asking myself how was it possible for a man who possessed every capacity for discovering the truth to fall to such depths of degradation. I have always felt that Hume's hardness of heart, his insolent calmness of mind, must be the ultimate form of punishment, beyond mercy, for a certain rebellion of the intellect that God punishes only by withdrawing." (III. 386–87.) The long letter against Hume from which this quotation is taken, along with several other passages in de Maistre's works, indicates a quite extraordinarily ambivalent attitude to the Scottish historian whose political conservatism attracted traditionalists with much the same force as his religious scepticism repelled them. De Maistre nevertheless insisted that the David Hume *Fragment* remain in later editions of his noted counter-revolutionary work.

There was little doubt in the minds of most royalists that the French revolution was going exactly the way of its English predecessor. The only question that remained involved the length of time the whole inevitable process would take. Was it necessary, for example, for the French Republic to pass through the Cromwell phase? Was it not possible that the Cromwell era had already occurred? We remember that Duvoisin had seen the Directoire in 1798 as the equivalent of Cromwell although, earlier still, others had maintained that Robespierre was Cromwell and that counter-revolutionary France had to make itself ready to welcome its General Monk.

Charles de Villers expressed the belief in 1798 that this last

---

Also influenced by Hume but in a more straightforward manner is Joseph de Maistre's fellow theoretician of the counter-revolution, Louis de Bonald. De Bonald and de Maistre shared similar views concerning the prophetic significance of English history and on many other subjects as well: "Is it possible, Monsieur," de Maistre wrote to his friend in 1818, "that nature has been pleased to tighten two strings in such perfect harmony as your mind is with mine! They are in perfect unison, a truly unique phenomenon...." (From Turin, 18 July 1818, ibid., XIV. 137.) De Bonald too attacks *a priori* politics and maintains that constitutions are as natural as gravity and can never be "pocketable." History is the sole validating principle of all political speculation. Like de Maistre, de Bonald also attacks Hume for his irreligion but cites his authority against Calvinism, English republicanism, et cetera. (See, for example, *Oeuvres complètes de M. de Bonald*, Paris, 1859, II. 224: "Hume rightly remarks that in England since the last revolution, public freedom and independence, from which individual security is derived, have been more uncertain and precarious.") He too applauds Hume's impartiality and fairness to France: "Monsieur Hume notes with respect to the rivalry between our two nations, that the French hate the English much less than the English hate the French" (ibid., II. 509). De Bonald even found Hume less "English" in his prejudices than the historian Lingard, who was not only a Catholic but a member of the Catholic clergy (ibid., III. 917). He also invokes Hume's authority against the physical determinism of Montesquieu (ibid., II. 28–29) and against divorce (ibid., II. 113, 121, 125).

In many ways the use of these "orthodox" themes taken from Hume by de Maistre, Duvoisin, de Bonald, and others, although it represents a fresh reading of the Scottish historian in the counter-revolutionary context, consists of little more than a routine repetition of material already exploited to the hilt by such historical conservatives and *anti-anglomanes* of the pre-revolutionary period as Gerdil, Bergier, the editors of the *Mémoires de Trévoux*, Lefebvre de Beauvray, et cetera. It would deserve a more lengthy treatment here were it not for the fact that we have already given a good deal of attention to the writings of these others in our first chapter.

opinion attributed possibly too much importance to Robespierre, who is described in a dialogue by de Villers as newly arriving in hell and greeting the English Protector as follows:

> *Robespierre:* "I have been looking for you ever since I got here. The striking resemblance of our two destinies, the conformity of our projects, of our methods and our talents, naturally draws us close to each other and prompts us to reminisce together about the great events that we set in motion."

Much offended, Cromwell disagrees and scornfully points out that Robespierre is nothing more than a "minor rabble-rouser, a market-stall schemer":

> *Robespierre:* "All the same, people back on earth openly compare me to you."
> *Cromwell:* "That is because people back on earth are obsessed with making comparisons; and most of those who put you on the same footing with me know me only by name. . . . If France ever has a Cromwell, he will be an army general, a great leader, a statesman, an orator, and above all, a man blessed with good fortune."
> *Robespierre:* "And who, pray, will this fortunate person be? Quite obviously, it must, as they say, end with a master."
> *Cromwell:* "Time will tell. . . ."[22]

Time would indeed tell. Mallet du Pan, perhaps the wisest royalist spokesman in this period, indicated in December 1798 that the answer to de Villers's question was close: "The Directoire," he stated, "is now at the stage Cromwell was in when he drove out Parliament. There is no Cromwell in France, but the similarity of situations requires a similar outcome."[23]

Not long after this, however, he began to express important doubts about the tactical wisdom of counting on such parallels: "To try to throw light on the history of the revolution by these means is to demonstrate that one is quite ignorant of its true char-

---

22. "Dialogue entre Cromwel et Robespierre," *Le Spectateur du Nord; journal politique, littéraire et moral,* Hambourg, July–September 1798, VII. 76–85.

23. *Mercure Britannique ou notices historiques et critiques sur les affaires du tems,* par J. Mallet du Pan, Londres, 25 December 1798, II. 23.

acter."[24] Not only were there bad analogies involved; politically speaking, the parallels made the counter-revolution seem just a little too easy: "It is asking much to suggest to the individual who has barely managed to save his life and his few rags from Robespierre's executioners that he should once more trust his fate to the hazard of events! It takes a rare combination of circumstances to retemper a man's spirit once it has been broken."[25] The Stuart parallel was especially harmful if, as seemed to be the case, it encouraged royalists merely to sit back and wait complacently for the English restoration to be duplicated automatically in France. Much active preparation had to be carried out:

> The elements of a huge royalist party are there but the party itself —without leaders, without concerted effort, without funding, without weapons, without power, without gathering places—the party itself is yet to be formed.
>
> Four fifths of all Frenchmen detest their government; but, as David Hume rightly points out, the English royalists living under the republic made the mistake of thinking that all those who complained about the new regime were supporters of the monarchy....
>
> The King of France has fewer enemies to vanquish than he has uncaring self-servers to convince; it is less a question for him of urging royalists on to action than it is a matter of *creating them:* reducing the number of those opposed to his authority will be his most useful victory.[26]

Mallet du Pan, himself an active agent of the counter-revolution, is probably one of the few royalists at this time who, for various reasons, felt it was necessary to abandon the fashionable parallel. Speaking of this current "abuse of similitudes," he made the following objection:

> Heaven preserve the cabinets of Europe and the councils of Louis XVIII from deluding themselves with these romantic parallels. A schoolboy could easily discern the crude similarities that seem to equate the two revolutions; but it is the tableau of their differences

24. Ibid., 25 April 1799, III. 31.
25. Ibid., 10 August 1799, III. 481.
26. Ibid., III. 482–83.

that must be examined by anyone dedicated to annihilating the French Republic.

It was not necessary to arm Europe, or to invade England with foreign troops, to bring about a restoration whose constituent parts were already in place and well matched to the task. When you compare these with the rubble to which the customs and institutions of old France have been reduced, when you see in England the nobility, the clergy, and nearly all English gentlemen continuing to occupy their homes, retaining their titles and their lands as well as the respect and admiration of the public, when you contrast the intense spirit of religion, the manners, customs, and laws of England, the judiciary powers, the national character, the character of the army, when you hear Cromwell address a member of the Upper House who appeared before him as *Milord,* when you set all that off against the catastrophic ruins under which France lies buried, you throw all of your parallels into the fire and yield to the realization that identifying the specific combination of factors that will bring France back to its original state might well be an entirely new problem under the sun.[27]

Mallet du Pan's warning about the potential dangers of such comparisons seems to have had little effect. English-French parallels, almost all foretelling the imminent appearance of a French General Monk, became the hackneyed prediction and commonplace hope of much *émigré* literature, threatening even to grow to the proportions of an elegant literary genre. Sometimes the treatment was very light indeed, as can be seen in the following passage, judged by its author Pierre-Jean-Baptiste Nougaret as a "curious and intriguing piece, worthy of being considered part of our history":

Referring to the time when the parties divided the British Isles, when its citizens were at war with one another and blood flowed everywhere, Hume writes of two citizens who presented themselves to the king, "with lean, pale, sharp, and dismal visages: faces so strange and uncouth; figures, so habited and accoutred, as at once moved [according to Lord Clarendon] the most severe countenance to mirth and the most cheerful heart to sadness. . . ."

Do we not have here a portrait of our hideous Jacobins, dirty, disgusting, wearing short jackets called carmagnoles, long breeches or

27. Ibid., III. 483–85.

trousers, their grimy, greasy hair topped with a fur cap or a red woollen bonnet like those of galley slaves, the same colour as the blood they loved to shed so abundantly, wide moustaches, gaunt and hollow cheeked from the forced abstinence of their recent state of beggarliness and poverty?[28]

Admittedly, we are not dealing here with the most ponderous examples of the genre, and Nougaret derived few great prophecies from his observation that both Round Heads and Jacobins had the bad taste to be cosmetically below standard. Other parallels pretended, however, to greater things. Chateaubriand in his *Essai sur les Révolutions* (1797) states that the Jacobins directly imitated the English execution of Charles I when they put Louis XVI to death: "I dare to go even further: if Charles had not been decapitated in London, Louis, in all probability, would not have been guillotined in Paris."[29] Supporting such claims, Rivarol complained at the turn of the century that only the leftist leaders had taken the trouble to learn from previous revolutions. He affirmed, even, that he had personally seen members of the Constituent Assembly in 1789 reading Stuart history for the first time "to see how the Long Parliament dealt with Charles I."[30]

The 18th Brumaire, immediately viewed by many royalists as a first step in the long-awaited fulfilment of the great prophecy, rallied immensely the hopes of those who had been carefully tending their parallels: "Royalists are thinking of Monk," wrote Rivarol, "and are more in favour of Bonaparte than the democrats; meanwhile, he is fawned over like Necker, Lafayette, and Pétion."[31] Even the head of the counter-revolutionary party, Louis XVIII, at first expressed the hope that Napoleon would be magnanimous enough to play the rôle of Monk. On Bonaparte's refusal to be so generous and after a later counter-proposal from the French *consul à vie* that Louis XVIII renounce his claim to the throne in exchange for

---

28. Pierre-Jean-Baptiste Nougaret, *Parallèle de la Révolution d'Angleterre en 1642, et celle de France*, Metz, p. 13 [see Hume, *History of England*, VII. 501].

29. *Oeuvres complètes*, Paris, 1834, I. 153.

30. *Pensées inédites de Rivarol*, Paris, 1836, pp. 80–81.

31. Ibid., p. 92.

certain indemnities, the latter turned to an equally common practice of the day, that of calling Bonaparte a Cromwell. As the French monarch in exile explained to Cardinal Maury in 1803: "...if Cromwell, after conquering Jamaica, had offered it to Charles II, he could not have accepted it: it would have implied recognition of the Protector's legal existence. My case is the same...."[32]

Bonaparte's own "republican" admirers felt that all the modern parallels were too confining when it came to describing the greatness of the French Consul. The younger Lacretelle, for example, made this sentiment dramatically clear in 1802:

> Because of his astonishing destiny he has been compared to every extraordinary man who has ever appeared on the world's stage. I can see no one in recent times who resembles him.
>
> I'm told that a few superficial or malicious observers have compared him to Cromwell. Some lunatics hope he is a new General Monk. France and Europe find in him a striking resemblance to Caesar.[33]

The truth is, of course, that the epithet Cromwell was still seen as highly insulting by everyone in France at this time. Jean-Baptiste Say, writing in *La Décade* in 1801, indignantly took to task Sir Francis d'Ivernois for having made the "comparison, so threadbare and so false, between our Bonaparte and Cromwell. The name Cromwell," he added, "has always been used to stigmatize the friends of every kind of reform. During the American war it was applied to Washington; even before our revolution it became the appanage of Fox, and during the Constituent Assembly, if I'm not mistaken, the label was applied to Lafayette, who deserved it even less than the others."[34]

---

32. Letter of 10 August 1803, from Warsaw, in *Correspondance diplomatique et mémoires inédits du Cardinal Maury,* annotés et publiés par Mgr Ricard, Lille, 1891, II. 271.

33. *Parallèle entre César, Cromwell, Monck et Bonaparte: Fragment traduit de l'Anglais* (published anonymously by Charles-Jean-Dominique de Lacretelle, Paris, 1802), p. 2.

34. *La Décade,* XXVIII. 281.

Decidedly the tag of Caesar was better. There would be no rest ahead for the French if Bonaparte was a Cromwell. Cromwell inspired fear; Bonaparte inspired admiration and hope. "The one destroyed," wrote Lacretelle in 1802, "the other heals."

CONCLUSION

We shall end here our considerations on the influence of Stuart history, and more particularly David Hume's *History of the Stuarts,* in France from the *ancien régime* to the counter-revolution.

Although the high point of critical French interest in the English revolutionary period had passed by the time Napoleon made his dramatic appearance on the scene, the force of Hume's enormous influence over a subject which was so remarkably suited to exploitation by pundits and prophets of the Right was by no means entirely spent. Rivarol before his death in 1801 gave a fair indication of how it would be possible, for some time yet, to continue playing the merry game of parallels. His French projection of Stuart history, well worth quoting here, provided in fact an advance outline of many similar future speculations which events of the following thirty years seemed to justify: "There is a singular parity between the English revolution and that of France; the Long Parliament and the death of Charles I; the Convention and the death of Louis XVI; Cromwell and Bonaparte. If there is a restoration will we see another Charles II dying in his bed and another James II leaving his kingdom and then a different dynasty? It's as good a prediction as any."[35]

Whatever the true merits of Hume's presentation of the English revolution, it is undeniable that the case he put to the French during the critical years from roughly 1760 to 1800 had had profound and far-ranging effects. It is no exaggeration to say that his particular interpretation of that revolution, in a sense almost written for France, had become an integral part of the French histor-

---

35. Rivarol, op. cit., p. 111.

ical consciousness and had imposed etiological categories which the vast majority of Frenchmen on the political Right and even a fair number on the moderate Left felt obliged to follow when giving explanation to what were seen as similar political processes in their own country. Admittedly, much of the detailed use made of Hume's *History* was purely polemical. That the greater part of it cannot be dismissed as such, however, seems obvious. We have only to look into a work such as *De l'usage et de l'abus de l'esprit philosophique durant le dix-huitième siècle* by Jean-Etienne-Marie Portalis to see the permanent importance of Hume's total impact at this time on the thinking of French rightists.

Portalis's book was written between 1798 and 1800. It did not exert the influence or enjoy the reputation of Chateaubriand's more frothy production, the *Génie du Christianisme,* perhaps because its message came too late. It appeared first as a posthumous publication in 1820, thirteen years after its author's death. It nevertheless represents one of the few truly important end-of-the-century French rejections of the Enlightenment and was motivated not by the cramped and brutal spirit of some of Joseph de Maistre's formulas, but rather by a certain wise science of man which Hume himself, on whose writings some of it is based, would probably not have disavowed.

Portalis approved of the eighteenth century's love of philosophical history and Hume, he felt, had surely written his history of England "as a philosopher." The French *philosophes,* on the other hand, had not produced an equivalent history of France. Voltaire, it is true, had boasted of writing philosophical history but had succeeded, like Gibbon, only in writing history that was anti-ecclesiastical.[36]

The eighteenth century had prided itself on having no religious superstitions. It had nevertheless ended up being politically superstitious. It was an eighteenth-century superstition, not shared by Hume, to imagine that any political act was good provided it was committed in favour of liberty: "In politics, all factional crimes are canonized for fear of violating the rights of peoples.... Some

36. Portalis, op. cit., seconde édition, Paris, 1827, II. 24–26.

have dared to accuse Hume of bias because he criticized the excesses committed during England's revolutions."[37]

Thinking no doubt of histories like that of Catherine Macaulay, so highly praised by the Mirabeaus, Condorcets, and Brissots, Portalis pointed out that not only had revolutionary opinion dared to question Hume's impartiality, it had attempted as well to make history over again into an arsenal of political propaganda: "Some philosophers now regard historical facts as nothing more than a basis on which to construct the most arbitrary systems." But history, wrote the man of the Concordat, could not be denied, nor could its true function, which was to present "an immense collection of moral experiments carried out on the human race,"[38] be frustrated.

Such history damns forever all *a priori* political theorists: "All of our false ideas, our exaggerated principles concerning the rights of man, his independence, all of our ranting speeches against civil and political institutions, derive initially from the notion we have fashioned for ourselves of a so-called state of nature.... Let us abandon all systems if we wish to be philosophers; let us renounce our wanderings in the land of illusion...."[39]

History never confronts us with a state of nature; society does not exist by reason of any social pact. It cannot therefore be dissolved at will like a business arrangement simply because of an alleged breach of contract. Society is not a pact but a fact:

> Society is, at the same time, a mixture and an unbroken succession of persons of all ages and genders, constantly brought together or pulled apart at every instant by interest, chance, and a thousand diverse connections.... The social order has as its object the permanent good of humanity. It is founded on the essential and indestructible relationships that exist among men. It is not dependent on any gratuitous or arbitrary institution: it is commanded by na-

37. Ibid., II. 28.
38. Ibid., II. 39.
39. Ibid., II. 299.

ture;...its source is the very structure of our being and it can end only with that structure.[40]

Men are united in society because such is the wish of nature which made them social creatures. Of course, nothing is immutable; time brings the necessity of change and adaptation, but a society, in its transformations, must be very careful that it does not put its very existence to the test: "It thus requires very great, very extreme, highly intolerable evils, before the idea of change—always devastating, always marked by the most violent turmoil—can be authorized, before a revolution that attacks the very wellspring of legitimacy can be legitimized."[41] Politics is not the art of the ideal but of the real: "Let us not feed on false notions, let us take care not to seek in human institutions a perfection that is foreign to them."[42] If man were a totally reasonable creature such perfection would be possible. The sad truth is, however, that he is not so constituted. The human cogitative aspect is probably of less importance in our practical behaviour than the sensitive parts of our nature. Man's sentiment, his irrationalism, is as basic and natural to him as his reason. Politically man is a creature of emotion, habit, opinion, and prejudice. When political reforms prove necessary, these less flexible elements must not be forgotten. Reforms must be approached with circumspection: one does not tolerate everything, nor must one destroy everything:

> Since man's nature is not altered by an alteration in customs, forms must be modified without abandoning the principles that take their origin in the very nature of man.
> Characteristically, an erroneous philosophical approach impairs our ability to distinguish principles. We imagine that institutions that may have degenerated were never useful....All religious or secular establishments in which we no longer believe are judged to be politically fraudulent.[43] We want only absolute verities and maxims,

40. Ibid., II. 301.

41. Ibid., II. 334.

42. Ibid., II. 363.

43. Portalis, though fully aware of Hume's religious scepticism, believed along with a number of other French conservatives that Hume regretfully bore his

as if such existed in politics and in legislation. We replace the lessons of experience with hollow speculations. . . . We deny that we have been shaped by those institutions and laws that, disparaged and weakened today, nevertheless survive in the habits we acquired through them. . . .

We compromise the civilization of a people when, under the pretext of giving it better government, we do away with everything that civilized it; we plunge it anew into barbarism by isolating it from everything that originally rescued it from that state.[44]

---

disbelief as an unwholesome burden. He makes some of the same distinctions we have already encountered in Trublet and opposes religious sceptics to the eighteenth-century atheists: "In truth, these sceptics do not pass censure on religious institutions. They want free access to religion for those who feel uplifted by it; they even seem to complain of their own philosophy, which prevents them from believing. We sense, they say, that unbelievers are less fortunate, that nothing can fill the void in the human heart that a lively faith in religion would otherwise satisfy. And so it was that J.-J. Rousseau would say to his friends: 'I would rather be a believer than a philosopher.' Similarly, Hume, after one of those touching and sublime scenes that only religion can present so wondrously, cried out: 'I would have been much happier had I never doubted!'" (Ibid., II. 191–92.) Portalis is not the only victim at this time of a purely fictional anecdote concerning Hume; the "Story of La Roche," contributed by Henry Mackenzie to the Scottish publication *The Mirror* in 1779 but which, perhaps not too strangely, received wide circulation in France after the Revolution. We find it reproduced in *La Décade* in 1796 (VIII. 554–62); the *Bibliothèque britannique* in 1798 (VII. 199–215); and in the *Spectateur du Nord* (VII. 297–312) also in 1798.

The long sentimental anecdote which shows the sceptic Hume weeping almost religiously at his own incredulity (so different a picture from Joseph de Maistre's icy sketch!) helped to reinforce occasional efforts to rehabilitate the whole Hume in the eyes of those orthodox thinkers who warmly appreciated his "politics" but who were dismayed by his "philosophy." Similarly his "social" ethics —often opposed to the "egotistic" moral philosophy of the materialists—had invariably seemed a redeeming feature in the eyes of such men as Gerdil, Bergier, Barruel, de Bonald, and Portalis. Hume's moral views were even adduced on one occasion as sufficient proof that he was not the guilty party in the quarrel with Rousseau! Of course, the essential feature of Hume's image in the eyes of the Right remained his political conservatism. Religious disbelief was not always seen, moreover, as incompatible with royalist sentiments. (See Jean-Joseph Mounier, *De l'influence attribuée aux Philosophes, aux Francs-Maçons et aux Illuminés sur la Révolution de France,* Tübingen, 1801, p. 70.) Hobbes versus Milton was a good case in point and, although Hume might very well be an unbeliever, he was, in the words of the *Spectateur du Nord,* "the best of the unbelievers."

44. Portalis, op. cit., II. 503–4, 512.

One can hear echoes of Hume's own science of human nature in Portalis's important manifesto of revolt against some of the more transient bursts of illumination emitted by the *siècle des Lumières*. One also notes, of course, the influence of Burke; but it should be remembered that Burke himself was probably influenced by Hume to an extent greater than his Christian Whig principles may have cared to admit. Soon, completing the image and contributing to the destruction of what were seen as Enlightenment excesses in non-political fields, a new Hume was to enter France via Kant's Germany. Hume the philosopher as opposed to Hume the *philosophe* was destined to make the world almost forget that there had ever been an "English Tacitus."

But Hume's radically empirical *History*, which some modern scholars have tended to view as quite unrelated to his radically empirical philosophy, was not yet completely dead in France. Quite to the contrary, after the Restoration, during the reign of Louis XVIII, its importance seemed still great enough to ultra-royalists for several of their number to set about editing a completely revised translation preceded by a long study of Hume's life and works by the French academician Vincent Campenon.[45] Needless to say, the foreword of this new edition begins by reverently calling Hume nothing less than "the most impartial and the most judicious historian who has ever lived."[46]

Other editions of this work were to follow but as France's political events evolved toward more liberal goals, Hume's great historical reputation and influence fell. A different, although not necessarily a more serious, conception of history was being born. Guizot in 1826 triumphantly proclaimed the new era: "Today... the history of the English Revolution has taken on a different complexion: Hume was once the arbiter of European opinion on that

---

45. *Histoire d'Angleterre depuis l'invasion de Jules-César jusqu'à la révolution de 1688 par David Hume et depuis cette époque jusqu'à 1760 par Smollett.* Traduite de l'anglais. Nouvelle édition, revue, corrigée et précédée d'un *Essai sur la vie et les écrits de D. Hume,* par M. Campenon de l'Académie Française, Paris, 1819.

46. Ibid., I. v.

---

subject; and in spite of Mirabeau's support, Mistress Macaulay's declamations never managed to shake his authority."[47]

Europe, Guizot was happy to announce, had at last recovered its independence. Two pages farther on, he voiced the judgement that seems to have endured among many historians of the "English Revolution" ever since: "Hume no longer satisfies anyone."

47. *Histoire de la Révolution d'Angleterre depuis l'avenèment de Charles Ier jusqu'à la restauration de Charles II,* Première partie, Paris, 1826, I. xvii.

INDEX OF NAMES
AND TITLES

Accord de la Révélation et de la Raison contre le divorce (Chapt de Rastignac), 108

Actes des Apôtres, 105, 112–16

Adresse à l'ordre de la noblesse de France (d'Antraigues), 120, 168

Alembert, Jean Le Rond d', 30–31, 34–35, 46–47, 54–55

Algarotti, Count Francesco, 13

l'Ami du Roi, 47

'Anagramme-Epigramme sur deux chefs de parti trés connus,' 105

Analogies de l'histoire de France et d'Angleterre (de Bonald), 89

l'An deux mille quatre cent quarante (Mercier), 70, 72

l'Angleterre instruisant la France, 8, 122

Annales patriotiques, 140

Annales politiques, civiles et littéraires (Linguet), 46, 121

Année littéraire, 12, 24, 46–47

Antraigues, Emmanuel de Launay, comte d', 111–12, 120, 168

Aristotle, 5

Artois, comte d', 2, 91, 119

Autobiography (Gibbon), 6

Avis à la Convention Nationale sur le jugement de Louis XVI (de Montjoie), 153–54

Azéma, Michel, 166

Bacon, Sir Francis, 104, 189

Bailly, E.-L.-B., 164

Balestrier de Canilhac, abbé L.-S., 81

Bancal des Issarts, Jean-Henri, 100, 138, 160

Barailon, Jean-François, 164

Barnave, Joseph, 111, 122

Barruel, abbé Augustin, 200

Basset de la Marelle, Louis, 39

Baudin, Pierre-Charles-Louis, 164

Baudot, Marc-Antoine, 169

Bayle, Moïse-Antoine-Pierre-Jean, 168

Beccaria, Cesare de, 13

Belot, Mme Octavie-Guichard Durey de Meynières, 11

Bergier, abbé Nicolas-Sylvestre, 32, 47–54, 55, 57, 78, 103, 108, 190, 200

Berkeley, George, 40

Bernardin de Saint-Pierre, Jacques-Henri, 74

Berry, duc de, 1. *See also* Louis XVI

Bertrand de Molleville, Antoine-François, 144–45

Bezard, François-Siméon, 167

Bibliothèque britannique, 200

Bibliothèque de l'homme public, 81

Bibliothèque de Madame la Dauphine (Moreau), 17

Bibliothèque des Sciences et des Beaux-Arts, 6, 20, 21, 23

Bibliothèque d'un homme de goût (Chaudon), 14

Birotteau, J.-B.-B.-H., 164, 171

Blackstone, Sir William, 83

Bodin, P.-J.-F., 164

Bolingbroke, Henry St. John, 1st Viscount, 28

Bonald, Louis de, 3–4, 42, 51, 89, 190, 200

Bonaparte, Napoléon, 120, 169, 170, 180, 194–95

Bordas, Pardoux, 164

Bossuet, Jacques-Bénigne, 44, 52, 66, 103, 106, 119, 120, 155

Boswell, James, 68

Boufflers, Marie, comtesse de, 11, 75

Boulay de la Meurthe, Antoine, 179–81, 182, 183, 185

Bourlet de Vauxcelles, abbé Simon-Jacques, 34

Bradshaw, John, 120

Brissot de Warville, Jacques-Pierre, 64, 72, 73, 78, 99, 123–32, 133, 136, 153, 162, 178, 198

Brosses, Charles de, 12

Brutus, Lucius Junius, 161, 168–69

Brutus, Marcus Junius, 167–69, 173

Brutus (Voltaire), 121

Buckingham, George Villiers, 1st Duke of, 65

Buffier, Claude, 38

Burke, Edmund, xiii–xiv, 31, 67, 81, 82, 84, 90, 111, 123, 134, 140, 151, 178, 201

Burnet, Gilbert, 12, 25

Burney, Fanny, 3

Buzot, François-Nicolas-Léonard, 160

Caesar, Julius, 174, 195–96

Calas, Jean, 70

Calonne, Charles-Alexandre de, 110

Cambacérès, Jean-Jacques de, 4

Campan, Jeanne-Louise Genest, Mme, 143

Campenon, François-Nicolas-Vincent, 201

Captivité et derniers moments de Louis XVI, 146

Carra, Jean-Louis, 100, 140

Cartouche, Louis-Dominique Bourguignon, *called,* 66

Castilhon, J.-L., 19

Catilina (Crébillon), 66

Cazalès, Jacques de, 122, 128, 153, 155

Cecilia (Burney), 3

Cerutti, Joseph-Antoine-Joachim, 17, 82

Chabroud, Jean-Baptiste-Charles, 120

Chapt de Rastignac, abbè Armand-Anne-Auguste-Antonin-Sicaire de, 108

Charlemagne, 110

Charles I, King of England, xiii, xv–xvi, xxi–xxii, 16, 17, 22, 24, 29, 60, 64, 66, 70, 71, 72, 77, 89, 91, 112, 114, 116, 118–30, 131, 141–65, 184, 194, 196, 202

Charles II, King of England, 105, 114, 122, 131, 132, 163, 195–96, 202

Charles IX, King of France, 148

Charles IX (Marie-Joseph Chénier), 121

Chasset, Charles-Antoine, 164

Chastellux, F.-J., marquis de, 5, 10, 12, 31

Chateaubriand, François-René, 92, 194, 197

Chaudon, Dom Louis-Mayeul, 14, 40

Chaumette, Pierre-Gaspard, 148

Chénier, Marie-Joseph, 133

Clarendon, Edward Hyde, 1st Earl of, xiv–xv, 142, 182

Clarissa Harlowe (Richardson), 108

Cledel, Etienne, 169

Clément, Amable-Augustin, 175

Clermont-Tonnerre, Stanislas, comte de, 123–32, 136, 162

Cléry, Jean-Baptiste-Antoine Hanet, *called,* 143, 147–48

Collection complète des oeuvres de l'Abbé de Mably, 63

Common Sense (Paine), 97

Complete History of England (Smollett), 5, 19

Comte de Strafford (Lally-Tollendal), 121

Condé, Louis-Joseph de Bourbon, prince de, 146

Condorcet, Antoine-Nicolas Caritat, marquis de, 81, 98, 99, 134, 198

Congreve, William, 28

Considérations sur la France (de Maistre), 34, 90, 187–89

Considérations sur les principaux événements de la Révolution Française (Mme de Staël), 145

Considérations sur l'esprit et les moeurs (Sénac de Meilhan), 8

Constant de Rebecque, Benjamin, 181–83, 187

Constitutions des principaux états de l'Europe et des Etats-Unis de l'Amérique (Delacroix), 111

Contrat social (Rousseau), 3, 42, 56

Corday d'Armont, Marie-Charlotte, 176

Corneille, Pierre, 35

Correspondance diplomatique du Cardinal Maury, 195

Correspondance d'un habitant de Paris (d'Escherny), 134

Correspondance entre quelques hommes honnêtes (Servan), 34, 87–88

Correspondance littéraire (Grimm), 3, 27

Correspondance politique (Mallet du Pan), 85

Correspondance universelle (Brissot), 64

Court de Gébelin, Antoine, 14

Crébillon, Prosper Jolyot de, 66

Cromwell, Oliver, xix, xxii, 23, 24, 37, 45, 65–67, 69–70, 112, 115, 117, 126, 130, 140, 142, 148, 153, 157–60, 162, 164, 167, 168–69, 170, 184, 186, 188, 190, 191, 193, 195, 196

Cromwel (Maillet-Duclairon), 66, 69

Cromwel ou le général liberticide (Tardy), 140, 169

Damiens de Gomicourt, Auguste-Pierre, 18

Danton, Georges-Jacques, 120, 170

Dauphin of France (son of Louis XV), 1

Décade philosophique, littéraire et politique, 99, 139, 168, 170, 178, 195, 200

Defence of the English People (Milton), 140, 167

Défense de l'ordre social contre les principes de la Révolution Française (Duvoisin), 186–87

Défense de Louis XVI (Cazalès), 153

Défense des émigrés français (Lally-Tollendal), 153

Defense du Siècle de Louis XIV (Voltaire), 20

De J.-J. Rousseau considéré comme l'un des premiers auteurs de la Révolution (Mercier), 99

Delacroix, J.-V., 111

De la félicité publique (Chastellux), 31

De la force du gouvernement actuel de la France (Constant), 181

De l'Allemagne (Mme de Staël), 8–9

De la manière d'écrire l'histoire (Mably), 63

De la philosophie de la nature (Delisle de Sales), 32

De la Révolution Française comparée à celle de l'Angleterre (Salaville), 183–85

De l'esprit (Helvétius), 27–28

De l'Etat de la France, présent et à venir (Calonne), 110

Deleyre, Alexandre, 169

De l'homme (Helvétius), 29, 34

De l'influence attribuée aux Philosophes, aux Francs-Maçons et aux Illuminés sur la Révolution de France (Mounier), 200

Delisle de Sales, J.-C. Izouard, *called*, 32, 69, 142

Delolme, Jean-Louis, 83

De l'origine des principes religieux (Meister), 80–81

De l'usage et de l abus de l'esprit philosophique (Portalis), 197–201

Descamps, Bernard, 172

Descartes, René, 3

Des droits et des devoirs du citoyen (Mably), 63

Des Emigrés Français ou Réponse à Lally-Tollendal (Leuliette), 153, 178

Des lettres de cachet (Mirabeau), 60–63, 133

Desmoulins, Camille, 128, 140

Des premiers principes du système social appliqués à la révolution présente (Meister), 81

Des principes et des causes de la révolution en France (Sénac de Meilhan), 86

Des prisons d'état (Mirabeau), 60

Des réactions politiques (Constant), 181

Des révolutions dans les grandes sociétés civiles (Servan), 87

Des suites de la contre-révolution de 1660 en Angleterre (Constant), 182–83

Destutt de Tracy, Antoine-Louis-Claude, comte, 178

'Dialogue entre Cromwel et Robespierre' (de Villers), 191

Dialogues concerning Natural Religion (Hume), 31

Dictionary (Sheridan), 139

Dictionnaire anti-philosophique (Chaudon), 40

Dictionnaire philosophique (Voltaire), 45

Dictionnaire philosophique de la religion (Nonnotte), 45

Dictionnaire social et patriotique (Lefebvre de Beauvray), 35–38

Diderot, Denis, 29–31, 54

Différence du patriotisme national chez les François et chez les Anglois (Basset de la Marelle), 39

Diogène moderne ou le désapprobateur (Castilhon), 19

Dionysius the Younger, 171

Discours choisis sur divers sujets de religion et de littérature (Maury), 103, 104

Discours contre la Défense de Louis Capet (Carra), 100

Discours et opinions de Cazalès, 122, 153

Discours et projet de décret de Henri Bancal, 100

Discours philosophique sur l'homme (Gerdil), 42–44

Discours sur la divinité de la religion chrétienne (Gerdil), 41–42

Discours sur la sanction royale (Maury), 105

'Discours sur la science sociale' (Cambacérès), 4

Dubois-Crancé, Edmond Louis Alexis de, 167

Du Deffand, Marie de Vichy Chamrond, marquise, 6, 27

Dugour, A.-J., 112, 156, 170

Dumouriez, Charles-François, 120

Du Pape, (de Maistre), 45

Durival, J.-B., 133

Duvoisin, abbé Jean-Baptiste, 53, 186–87, 190

Elizabeth I, Queen of England, xvi, xvii, xix, 45

Eloge de Milord Maréchal (d'Alembert), 46

Emile (Rousseau), 37, 42, 56

Encyclopédie Méthodique, 15, 31, 47

Enquiry concerning Human Understanding (Hume), 4–5, 27

Enquiry concerning the Principles of Morals (Hume), 34

Erreurs de Monsieur de Voltaire (Nonnotte), 46

Escherny, François-Louis, comte d', 133–134

Esprit de l'Histoire (Ferrand), 83

Esprit des Lois (Montesquieu), 6, 31, 60, 76, 78

Essai polémique sur la religion naturelle (Duvoisin), 53

Essais pour servir d'introduction à l'histoirie de la Révolution française (Sallier-Chaumont de la Roche), 86

Essai sur la manière d'écrire et d'étudier l'histoire (Levesque), 99

Essai sur la tragédie (Delisle de Sales), 69–70

Essai sur la vie et les écrits de D. Hume (Campenon), 201

Essai sur les causes qui amenèrent en Angleterre l'établissement de la République (Boulay de la Meurthe), 179–81, 183–85

Essai sur les Moeurs (Voltaire), 26, 31–32, 45

Essai sur les Révolutions (Chateaubriand), 92, 194

Essai sur l'histoire des comices de Rome, &c. (Gudin de la Brenellerie), 75

Etudes de la Nature (Bernardin de Saint-Pierre), 74

Etude sur la souveraineté (de Maistre), 4

Fairfax, Thomas, 3rd Baron, 120

Falkland, Lucius Cary, 2nd Viscount, 114, 122

Faure, Pierre-Joseph-Denis-Guillaume, 163

Fénelon, François de Salignac de La Mothe, 106, 108

Ferguson, Adam, 83

Ferrand, Antoine-François-Claude, comte, 42, 83–84

Formey, Reverend Samuel, 14, 50

Foucault, Etienne, 176

Fox, Charles James, 195

'Fragment d'une histoire de la révolution française par David Hume' (de Maistre), 90, 189

la France plus qu'Angloise (Linguet), 121

François de Neufchâteau, Nicolas-Louis, 66

Frederick the Great, King of Prussia, 55

Fréron, Elie-Catherine, 12, 14, 24–26, 47

Gaillard, Gabriel-Henri, 7

Galilei, Galileo, 104

Garat, D.-J., 6

Garilhe, François-Clément Privat de, 159

Gassendi, Pierre, 38

Gazette littéraire de l'Europe, 5, 13

Gazette Nationale, ou le Moniteur universel, 134, 137–38, 170

Génie du Christianisme (Chateaubriand), 178, 197

Genovesi, Antonio, 13

Gerdil, Hyacinthe-Sigismond, 41–44, 52, 55, 103, 107, 108, 190, 200

Gertoux, Brice, 169

Gibbon, Edward, 3, 6, 142, 197

Girard, Antoine-Marie-Anne, 161

Girot-Pouzol, Jean-Baptiste, 163

Graffigny, Françoise de, 28

Grégoire, abbé Henri, 120

Grimm, Friedrich Melchior, baron de, 3, 27, 29

Grosley, Pierre-Jean, 70

Gudin de La Brenellerie, Paul-Philippe, 75

Guide de l'histoire (Née de la Rochelle), 14

Guillaume Tell (Lemierre), 121

Guillermin, Claude-Nicolas, 167

Guillon, abbé Marie-Nicolas-Silvestre, 119–21, 140

Guiraudet, Charles-Philippe-Toussaint, 133

Guiter, Joseph-Antoine-Sébastien, 159

Guizot, François, 202

Gustavus III, King of Sweden, 75

Guyomar, Pierre-Marie-Augustin, 164

Guyton-Morveau, Louis-Bernard, 169

Hampden, John, xix, 114

Hébert, Jacques-René, 148

Helvétius, Claude-Adrien, 12, 15, 27–28, 33–34, 178, 185

Henri IV, King of France, 7

Henriette-Marie de France, 155

Henry VIII, King of England, xv, 24

Hentz, Nicolas-Joseph, 167

Herodotus, 74

Herring, Thomas, Archbishop of Canterbury, 16
Herschel, Sir Frederick William, 6
Hertford, Francis Seymour Conway, 1st Earl of, 1
Hippocrates, 5
Histoire abrégée de la session de 1828, 89
Histoire d'Angleterre (Bertrand de Molleville), 145
Histoire de Cromwel (Dugour), 170
Histoire de la Révolution d'Angleterre (Guizot), 202
Histoire de la Révolution de France et de l'Assemblée Nationale (Montjoie), 109
History of England (Hume), xiv–xxii, 2, 5, 10, 12, 15, 16, 21, 26, 27–28, 32–33, 35, 57, 58, 64, 75–76, 77, 109, 134–40, 154, 182, 187, 198
History of England (Macaulay-Graham), 63, 64–65, 67–69, 99–100, 126–30, 133–34
History of the Rebellion and Civil Wars in England (Clarendon), xiv–xv, 142, 182
Hobbes, Thomas, 38, 42, 200
Holbach, P.-H.-T., baron d', 34, 48, 52, 53, 54
Holland, G.-J., 34, 48
Hudibras (Butler), 113, 115

Ichon, Pierre-Louis, 172
'Idea of a Perfect Commonwealth' (Hume), 34
Index librorum prohibitorum, 41
Introduction à la Révolution Française (Barnave), 111
Ireton, Henry, 120, 130
Ivernois, Sir Francis d', 195

Jacquin, *procureur du Roi à Darney*, 52
James I, King of England, xv, xvii–xviii, 68, 133, 178
James II, King of England, 20, 24, 46, 64, 110, 132, 138, 163
Jean-Bon Saint-André, André Jean-Bon, *called*, 169

Jefferies (or Jeffreys), George, 182
Joannet, abbé Jean-Baptiste-Claude, 41
Johnson, Samuel, 28, 68
Journal Britannique (Maty), 19–20
Journal Chrétien, 40–41
Journal de ce qui s'est passé à la tour du Temple (Cléry), 143, 148
Journal d'economie politique, de morale, et de politique (Roederer), 178
Journal de l'Abbé de Véri, 60, 77
Journal de M. Suleau, 119
Journal de Paris, 170
Journal des débats et des décrets, 106, 171
'Journal des livres suspendus,' 75
Journal des Savants, 134
Journal du Licée de Londres, 65, 73
Journal Encyclopédique, 8, 12–13, 19, 65, 67, 68–69
Journal Etranger, 16–17
J.-P. Brissot à Stanislas Clermont, 124, 136
Jullien, Marc-Antoine, 171, 172–73

Kant, Immanuel, 34, 201
Keith, George, 10th Earl Marischal, 46
Kersaint, Armand-Guy-Simon de Coetnempren, comte de, 162–63
Kirkes, Colonel Percy, 182

Laclos, Pierre Choderlos de, 3
Lacretelle, Charles-Jean-Dominique de, 145–46, 195, 196
Lafayette, Marie-Joseph Motier, marquis de, 120, 176, 194, 195
La Harpe, Jean-François de, 120
Lally-Tollendal, Trophime-Gérard, comte de, 110, 111, 114, 121, 122, 132, 152–53, 155, 178
Lambert, Charles, 164
Laud, William, Archbishop of Canterbury, xviii, 65, 127
La Vauguyon, Antoine de Quélen, duc de, 141
Le Blanc, abbé Jean-Bernard, 6, 10, 18, 28–29

Le Chapelier, Isaac-René–Guy, 81

Lefebvre de Beauvray, Claude-Rigobert, 35–36, 55, 190

Le Long Parlement et ses crimes (Comtesse de Montrond), 116–18

Le Mercier de La Riviére, Pierre-Paul-François-Joachim-Henri, 3

Letter to the Earl of Stanhope (Macaulay-Graham), 134

Lettre à Monsieur Rabaut de Saint-Etienne (Servan), 87

Lettre de Charles Ier (François de Neufchâteau), 66

Lettre de M. Cerutti adressée au café de Foix, 83

Lettres à Sophie Volland (Diderot), 54

Lettres de Madame Roland (1788–1793), 139

Lettres philosophiques (Voltaire), 3, 7, 28, 35, 40, 103, 122–23

Lettres sur l'imagination (Meister), 81

Leuliette, Jean-Jacques, 153, 177–78

Levesque, J.-J.-G., 99

Life of Johnson (Boswell), 68

Lingard, John, 190

Linguet, S.-N.-H., 46, 121

Livy, 8, 86

Locke, John, xv, 3, 27, 40, 42, 69, 93, 130, 189

Londres (Grosley), 70–71

Louchet, Louis, 168

Louis XIV, 7, 14, 20, 24

Louis XV, 91

Louis XVI, 60, 71, 91, 92, 100, 111, 114, 118–19, 120, 121, 141–65

Louis XVII, 148

Louis XVIII, 83, 192, 194, 201

Louvet, Pierre-Florent, 161

Louvet de Couvrai, Jean-Baptiste, 160, 170

Ludlow, Edmond, 130

Lycée ou cours de littérature (La Harpe), 120

Mably, abbé Gabriel Bonnot de, 63–64, 75

Macaulay-Graham, Catherine, 63, 64–65, 67, 68, 69, 72, 99–100, 126–30, 132–40, 153, 182, 198, 202

Mackenzie, Henry, 200

Mailhe, Jean-Baptiste, 153, 156, 157, 161, 175

Maillet-Duclairon, Antoine, 66

Maistre, Joseph de, 4, 34, 42, 44, 90, 104, 108, 187–90, 197

Malesherbes, Chrétien-Guillaume de Lamoignon de, 10, 76, 77, 147

Malesherbes (Delisle de Sales), 142

Mallet du Pan, Jacques, 85, 191–93

Malouet, Pierre-Victor, 57

Manon Lescaut (Prévost), 152

Manuel des autorités constituées (Balestrier de Canilhac), 81

Marat, Jean-Paul, 163

Marec, Pierre, 159

Marey, Nicolas-Joseph, 164

Marie-Antoinette, 17, 143, 146, 148

Martin, Jean-Marie, 148

Mary Stuart, 17, 71

Mary Tudor, 45

Maty, Dr. Matthew, 19–20

Maury, abbé Jean-Siffrein, 42, 43, 103–8, 195

Mazade-Percin, J.-B.-D. de, 159

Mazarin, Jules, 104

M. de Tracy à M. Burke (Destutt de Tracy), 178

Meister, J.-H., 80–81

Mélanges de littérature (Suard), 57

Mélanges de philosophie, de morale et de littérature (Meister), 81

Mémoire de Lally-Tollendal, ou Seconde Lettre à ses Commettans, 110, 122

Mémoire justificatif pour Louis XVI (Dugour), 112, 156

Mémoires de Brissot, 68, 72, 133

Mémoires de l' Abbé Morellet, 10

Mémoires de l'Institut National des Sciences et Arts, 4

Mémoires de Madame Roland, 138–40

Mémoires de M. Cléry, 148

Mémoires de Montlosier sur la Révolution française, 106

Mémoires de Trévoux, 21–24, 28, 31, 190

Mémoires historiques et politiques du régne de Louis XVI (Soulavie), 60, 91, 92

Mémoires historiques sur le 18e siècle (Garat), 6

Mémoires secrets pour servir à l'histoire de la derniére année du régne de Louis XVI (Bertrand de Molleville), 144

Mémoires sur la librairie et sur la liberté de la presse (Malesherbes), 76

Mémoires sur la vie privée de Marie-Antoinette (Mme Campan), 143

Mennesson, J.-B.-A.-P., 161

Mercier, Louis-Sébastien, 70, 99, 135, 140

Mercure Britannique (Mallet du Pan), 191

Mercure de France, 3, 5, 148

Mes Souvenirs (Moreau), 146

Meynard, François, 164

Millar, Andrew, 16

Milton, John, 28, 63, 128, 129, 140, 166–67, 200

Mirabeau, Honoré–Gabriel Riquetti, comte de, 17, 43, 60–63, 72, 99, 103, 105–8, 120, 133–35, 198, 202

Mirabeau's letters during his residence in England, 133

Mirror, The, 200

Mohammed, 37

Monk, General George, 66, 93, 163, 193, 194

Montague, George, 16

Montaigne, Michel de, 38

Montesquieu, Charles de Secondat, baron de La Bréde et de, 6, 60, 78, 82, 83, 84, 86, 87, 178, 190

Mont-Gilbert, François-Agnès, 171–72

Montjoie, Félix-Louis-Christophe de, 109–10, 135, 153–55

Montlosier, François-Dominique de Reynaud, comte de, 106

Montrond, Angélique-Marie Darlus du Taillis, comtesse de, 116–18, 120

Montrose, James Graham, 1st Marquis of, 120

More, Sir Thomas, 42

Moreau, Jacob-Nicolas, 17, 146

Morellet, abbé André, 10

Morisson, C.-F.-G., 164

Mort de César (Voltaire), 121

Mounier, Jean-Joseph, 111, 122, 200

My Own Life (Hume), 15–16, 21, 58

Naigeon, J.-A., 31, 53

Natural History of Religion (Hume), 27, 42, 49

Nebuchadnezzar II, 178

Necker, Jacques, 91, 105, 120, 142, 149–50, 152, 155, 162, 194

Necker, Mme Suzanne Curchod, 76

Née de la Rochelle, Jean-François, 14

Newton, Sir Isaac, 79, 80

Nonnotte, Claude-François, 45–46, 55, 108

Nougaret, Pierre-Jean-Baptiste, 193–94

Nouveaux mélanges de Mme Necker, 76

Nouveaux Mémoires de l'Académie de Berlin, 15

Nouvelles Observations sur les comités des recherches (Clermont-Tonnerre), 125

Nyon, Jean-Luc, 143

Observateur Français à Londres (Damiens de Gomicourt), 18

Oeuvres complètes de Stanislas de Clermont-Tonnerre, 123–28

Oeuvres complettes de M. Helvétius, 34

Oeuvres de Louis XVI, 71, 141, 146–47

Oeuvres de M. Linguet, 46

Oeuvres diverses de M. Cerutti, 17

'Of Miracles' (Hume), 27

'Of Suicide' (Hume), 54, 73

'Of the Balance of Power' (Hume), 39–40

'Of the Immortality of the Soul'
(Hume), 54, 73
'Of the Original Contract' (Hume),
43, 58, 107–8
Opinion de L.-M. Revellière-Lépeaux, 85
Opinion sur la souveraineté du peuple
(Maury), 106–8
*Oraison funèbre de Henriette-Marie de
France* (Bossuet), 155
Orléans, le Père-Joseph d', 12, 14, 73

Paine, Thomas, 81, 97, 108, 163, 178
Paradise Lost (Milton), 167
*Parallèle de la Révolution d'Angleterre et
celle de France* (Nougaret), 193–94
Parallèle des Révolutions (Guillon),
119–21, 140
*Parallèle entre César, Cromwell, Monck et
Bonaparte* (Charles-Jean-Dominique
de Lacretelle), 195
*Paris pendant la révolution ou le nouveau
Paris* (Mercier), 137
Patriote Français, Le (Brissot), 124,
125, 128–29, 130, 132, 178
Pensées inédites de Rivarol, 194
Pétion de Villeneuve, Jérôme, 195
*Peuple anglais bouffi d'orgueil, de biére et
de thé,* 40
Peyssonnel, Claude de, 81
Philippeaux, Pierre-Nicolas, 166
Philosophical Essays (Hume), 2, 14, 26,
32, 40, 74
Pinet, Jacques, 162
Pitt, William, 134
Plaidoyer pour Louis XVI (Lally-
Tollendal), 152–53
Plantagenets (Hume), 11, 21, 26–29,
30, 31, 32
Plutarch, 139
Political Discourses (Hume), 2, 10, 26,
74, 105
Politicon ou choix des meilleurs discours
(Balestrier de Canilhac), 81
Politique tirée de l'Ecriture Sainte
(Boussuet), 44

Polybius, 4
Portalis, Jean-Etienne-Marie, 197–200
*Précis historique de la Révolution
Française* (Charles-Jean-Dominique
de Lacretelle), 146
Prévost, abbé Antoine-François, 10,
28, 133, 152
Prost, Claude-Charles, 169
Provence, comte de, 1. *See also* Louis
XVIII
Prunelle-Lière, Léonard-Joseph, 164
Pym, John, 68

*Quelle est la situation de l'Assemblée
Nationale?* (d'Antraigues), 112
Quotidienne, La, 9

Rabaut Saint-Etienne, Jean-Paul
Rabaut, *called,* 87, 160, 172
Racine, Jean, 35
Rapin-Thoyras, Paul de, xv, 12, 14, 19,
63, 121
Rapport et Projet de Décret (Mailhe), 91,
153, 156–58, 175
*Rapport sur les trente-deux membres de la
Convention* (Saint-Just), 101
Raynal, abbé Guillaume-Thomas, 76
*Recherches sur les causes qui ont empêché
les Français de devenir libres*
(Mounier), 111
Recueil philosophique, 53–54
Reflections on the Revolution in France
(Burke), 90, 151
*Réflexions philosophiques sur le Système de
la Nature* (Holland), 34
Réflexions politiques sur la Révolution
(Barnave), 122
*Réflexions posthumes sur le grand procès
de Jean-Jacques avec David,* 33
*Réflexions présentées à la nation française
sur le procès de Louis XVI* (Necker),
142, 149–52
*Réflexions sur mes entretiens avec M. le
Duc de La Vauguyon* (Louis XVI),
141

Règne de Richard III (Walpole), 142

Répertoire général des sources manuscrites de l'histoire de Paris (Tuetey), 170, 176

Réplique de J.-P. Brissot à Stanislas Clermont, 126–30

Réponse de J.-J. Rousseau au Roi de Pologne, 66

Rétablissement de la Monarchie Françoise (Ferrand), 83–84

Revellière-Lépeaux, L.-M., 85

Révolutions de France et de Brabant (Desmoulins), 128, 140

Richard III, King of England, 143

Richardson, Samuel, 16

Riffard St. Martin. *See* Saint-Martin

Rights of Man (Paine), 81, 97, 108, 178

Rivarol, Antoine, 194, 196

Robertson, Reverend William, 8, 11, 28, 83

Robespierre, Maximilien de, 74, 97–98, 113, 120, 136, 169, 173–74, 191

Rochester, John Wilmot, 2nd Earl of, 28

Roederer, Pierre-Louis, 178, 185

Roland, Marie-Jeanne (Manon) Phlipon, Mme, 99, 138–40

Rosanbo, Louis Le Peletier de, 142

Rousseau, Jean-Jacques, 3, 7, 11, 13, 33, 37, 42, 52, 55–56, 62, 63, 66, 78, 98, 99, 131, 139, 168, 178, 200

Royou, abbé T.-M., 46, 55

Rühl, Philippe-Jacques, 167

Saint-John, Oliver, 130

Saint-Just, Louis-Antoine-Léon de, 100–101, 169, 174

Saint Louis, King of France, 7, 104

Saint-Martin, François-Jérôme-Riffard, 164

Salaville, J.-B., 183–85

Sallier-Chaumont de la Roche, G.-M., 86

Sallust, 8, 86

Saumaise, Claude de, 140

Say, Jean-Baptiste, 195

Scaevola, Gaius Mucius, 173

Séances des écoles normales, 4

Seconde Lettre de M. de Lally-Tollendal à M. Burke, 111

Semaine-Sainte, 139

Sénac de Meilhan, Gabriel, 8, 86

Sergent, Antoine-François, 165

Servan, Joseph-Michel-Antoine, 34, 87

Shaftesbury, Anthony Ashley Cooper, 3rd Earl of, 28, 38

Shakespeare, William, 28, 35

Sheridan, Thomas, 139

Sidney, Algernon, xv, 129, 168

Sieyès, abbé Emmanuel-Joseph, 94–97, 132

Smith, Adam, 150–51

Smollett, Tobias G., 5, 19

Société des Jacobins: recueil de documents, 130

Soulavie, Jean-Louis Giraud, 7–8, 60, 91, 92

Spectateur du Nord, 189, 191, 200

Staël-Holstein, Anne-Louise-Germaine Necker, baronne de, 8–9, 142

Stanhope, Charles, 3rd Earl, 134

Stanislas I, King of Poland, 66

Stone, George, Primate of All Ireland, 16

'Story of La Roche' (Mackenzie), 200

Strafford, Thomas Wentworth, 1st Earl of, xviii, xx, 16, 65, 120, 121–22, 127, 128

Stuarts (Hume), xiii–xxii, 1, 10–14, 15–24, 26, 29, 31, 32, 36–37, 46–47, 58, 75, 77, 83, 89–90, 108, 112–26, 132, 133, 142–43, 146–48, 151–54, 157, 177, 180, 187–89, 196–98

Suard, Jean-Baptiste-Antoine, 6, 57

Suleau, François-Louis, 118–19

Supplément à la manière d'écrire l'histoire (Gudin de La Brenellerie), 75

Sur la dernière réplique de J.-P. Brissot (Clermont-Tonnerre), 131

Sur la destruction des Jésuites en France (d'Alembert), 30

Sur l'admission des femmes au droit de cité (Condorcet), 134

'Sur les rapports de idées religieuses et morales avec les principes républicains' (Robespierre), 98

Sur l'instruction publique (Condorcet), 99

Système de la Nature (d'Holbach), 34

Tableau historique de la littérature française (Marie-Joseph Chénier), 133

Tacitus, 1, 3, 5, 8, 10, 12, 32, 86, 140, 201

Tardy, M.-L., 140, 169

Tarquins, 161, 163

Théorie du pouvoir politique (de Bonald), 4

Theory of Moral Sentiments (Smith), 150–51

Thomas, Jean-Jacques, 163

Thou, Jacques-Auguste de, 86

Thucydides, 8

Tom Jones (Fielding), 108

Traité de la composition et de l'étude de l'histoire (Soulavie), 7–8

Tressan, Louis-Elisabeth de La Vergne, comte de, 14

Trublet, abbé Nicolas-Charles-Joseph, 40, 55

Tudors (Hume), 11, 20, 24–26, 32, 50–51

Tuetey, Alexandre, 170, 176

Turgot, Anne-Robert-Jacques, baron de L'Aulne, 10, 33, 54–60, 62

Vauxcelles. *See* Bourlet de Vauxcelles

Velly, abbé Paul-François, 7, 86

Vergniaud, Pierre-Victurnien, 160, 167

Véri, abbé Joseph-Alphonse de, 77

Vertot, abbé René Aubert de, 86

Vies des hommes illustres (Plutarch), 139

Villers, Charles-François-Dominique de, 191

Volland, Sophie, 54

Volney, Constantin François de Chasseboeuf, comte de, 4

Voltaire, François-Marie Arouet de, 3, 6, 7, 12, 13, 18, 20, 24, 25, 26, 27, 28, 29, 32, 35–40, 45, 99, 103–4, 122–23, 178, 185, 197

'Vues sur les moyens dont les Représentans pourront disposer' (Sieyès), 94

Walpole, Horace, 16, 28, 142

Washington, George, 195

Wedderburn, Alexander, 2

Wilkes, John, 35, 58

William of Orange, 12

Wolsey, Thomas, 24

Xenophon, 8

Zaïre (Voltaire), 39

The typeface used for this book is New Baskerville, which is based on the types of English type founder and printer John Baskerville (1706–75). Baskerville is the quintessential "transitional" face: it retains the bracketed and obliqued serifs of "old style" faces such as Caslon and Garamond, but in its increased lowercase height, lighter color, and enhanced contrast between its thick and thin strokes, it presages "modern" faces.

This book is printed on paper that is acid-free and meets the requirements of the American National Standard for Permanence of Paper for Printed Library Materials, Z39.48-1992. ∞

Book design by Martin Lubin Graphic Design, Jackson Heights, New York
Typography by Brad Walrod/High Text Graphics, Inc., Brooklyn, New York
Printed and bound by Edwards Brothers, Inc., Ann Arbor, Michigan